EX LIBRIS

merry Helen Hedges

A Hillspeak Bookplate ● Printed in Eureka Springs, Arkansas

The CRAFTING of LITURGY

The CRAFTING of LITURGY

•A Guide for Preparers•

Daniel B. Stevick

THE CHURCH HYMNAL CORPORATION • NEW YORK

The Church Hymnal Corporation
800 Second Avenue
New York, NY 10017

10 9 8 7 6 5 4 3 2 1

Liturgy is a complicated balance of elements. What is the relationship of horizontal to vertical? What is the balance of spontaneity and rule? Where shall the line be drawn between the communal participation and individual private space, or between group consciousness and personal conscience? How far is liturgy personal and meditative, how far political and activist? To what extent is it a treasure-house of past being and ancient resource, or an ideal mirror of our present state, or an anticipation of a transformed future? How is the **theologia crucis** combined with the **theologia gloriae,** the signs of suffering with the hope of glory?

David Martin
The Breaking of the Image

Contents

Introduction

The present Prayer Book and today's liturgical situation require that worship in congregations of the Episcopal Church be more conscious and intentional than it usually has been. Most Episcopalians seem to be trying to use the 1979 Prayer Book honestly and intelligently. They affirm it and enjoy it. Even after more than a decade of use, the book still seems, in many ways, a challenge.

The Prayer Book, by its flexibility, in effect asks that there be persons in each congregation who will actively cooperate with the requirements it sets and make wise use of the permissions it grants. Even though preparing liturgy is a task to be done, it is more. Week-by-week liturgical preparation opens intellectual and spiritual questions—questions in many cases new to the persons who undertake this ministry. Preparing for worship is fully as much a reflective task as it is a practical task. The task leads thoughtful people to ask "why?"

Persons who remember older Prayer Books know that mental habits suitable for putting them into practice may now mislead, but it is not clear what mental habits suit the present book. And how does one develop appropriate mental habits when one must? The books that explained the content of former Prayer Books and guided congregations in their use are now obsolete. In the years since the full authorization of this Prayer Book, a supportive literature has begun to appear, but little of it is written specifically for those who must use their judgment in shaping worship week by week.

This book means to introduce this ministry of liturgical preparation;

to suggest some of the historical, liturgical and theological understandings that support it; and to provide some nonprescriptive counsel on procedures and skills that it may require. My aim is to help liturgy committees, celebrants, lectors, musicians, the persons who lead intercessions, and other liturgical ministers to understand their own work and to collaborate more fully in carrying out a common task.

Many denominations are commending the careful preparation of each worship event, and good books on the subject can be gotten from several publishers. (Section 4 of the reading list at the end of this volume suggests some of them.) Most groups that work at the task in the Episcopal Church could find value in any of these guides. Yet the resources and opportunities for the Episcopal Church are specific, and the literature written for it is, so far, not abundant. This book is intended particularly for persons and groups that are using *The Book of Common Prayer 1979,* the *Hymnal 1982,* and the supplemental books that have been published in support of these basic liturgical texts.

An early draft of this book was subtitled "A Handbook on Liturgical Planning." There is something unsatisfactory about the term "planning." Common though it is in the literature, it suggests an event contrived rather deliberately and virtually from scratch by a quite conscious group of experts. However modest a working group may be in its approach to its task, terms such as "planning" or "planning group" can sound like a task force of engineers designing a new rocket! One of the best writers on the subject, Austin Fleming, in his *Preparing for Liturgy: A Theology and Spirituality,* 1985, prefers the more self-deferential term "preparing." He argues that a liturgy *cannot be planned,* but that a liturgy *must be prepared.* He has persuaded me—and I gather persuaded some other authors and publishers as well, for the term "preparing" has begun to replace the term "planning." So, despite the continuing use of "planning" in many books that are eminently useful, I have chosen to speak of "preparing."

In working at this book over a period of years, I have gathered some indebtedness that should be acknowledged. Early drafts of portions of this book were read by my friends and colleagues Owen Thomas, Lloyd Patterson, John Snow, David Siegenthaler, Katharine Black, and James Dunkly. From each of them I received the sort of comments that clarified my own thinking. Lloyd Patterson prepared the prayer that is the final Note appended to Chapter Seven, giving him the last word. Professor

Frederick Erickson, who is now at the Graduate School of Education of the University of Pennsylvania, carried out, a number of years ago (when he was at Harvard), the analysis that is cited in the section of Chapter Three on "rhythm." He has not published his findings, but he approves my general summary of them. A version of one of the prayers in Chapter Six appeared in *Intercessions for the Christian People* (Pueblo Publishing Company, New York, 1988), edited by Gail Ramshaw. The publisher has given permission for me to use it here in another form. The readers and editors of The Church Hymnal Corporation have been more than ordinarily helpful. From many parish clergy, congregations, students, and from the worship at St. Andrew's Chapel at the Philadelphia Divinity School and at St. John's Chapel at the Episcopal Divinity School, I have learned some of the pitfalls to be avoided in liturgy, but more importantly I have learned to appreciate both the value of careful liturgical workmanship and the wide distribution in the Church of the gifts that good liturgy requires.

Daniel B. Stevick
Episcopal Divinity School
Cambridge, Massachusetts

CHAPTER ONE

●

Why Preparation?

● **The Need for Intentional Order** ●

Good liturgy does not come about by accident.

Even a simple liturgical event has some complexity. Many things happen in a brief time. Several persons in succession take (or should take) vocal, leading parts. The congregation and the leaders are arranged (sometimes, but not always) expressively and intelligibly; arranged in a space. They are very likely wearing garb unlike their ordinary street dress; they use unaccustomed gestures; and they use unaccustomed speech forms to speak of things, many of which are far removed from the everyday. Together these persons carry out, through words and bodily movement, a corporate action in which music assists, or else distracts.

The parts should contribute to a convincing, satisfying whole. But there is a great deal that can go wrong. Elements can compete with or subvert one another. The strength of the spoken texts can be weakened by hymns that are too subjective, if they are not mawkishly sentimental. Strong, colorful ingredients can follow one another so closely that none of them shows up to advantage. Runaway virtuosity can heighten some nonessential action, while important acts are allowed to pass unnoticed. Or the liturgical event can be experienced as a series of parts that follow one another without shape, consecutiveness or flow.

If the parts of an act of worship are to contribute to one another, and if together they are to fashion a whole, there is need for care, for criteria, for thought, discrimination, and priorities. Shaping good liturgy is a craft. Rather than being a science, it is an art, calling for taste, judgment and design. It requires practical sense of the possibilities and limitations of one's spatial and musical resources. It, like good and spontaneous-seeming dance or drama, may require timing and practice. And those who make the advance preparations for a liturgical act must learn to be self-critical. Not every idea that comes to mind—not even every good idea—can be used. The blue pencil is a valuable tool of those who prepare liturgy. Good intentions are not enough.

• "What about the Prayer Book?" •

When one speaks along these lines in the Episcopal Church one some-times hears it said (indeed, I can almost hear myself saying), "But don't we have *The Book of Common Prayer?*" The comment assumes that al-though intentional preparation of liturgy may well be necessary in churches that lack an authorized liturgy, in the Episcopal Church—apart from such simple tasks as hymn selection and seasonal decoration of the church—the Prayer Book automatically "plans" each act of worship and the succession of such acts over the year.

Surely the Prayer Book is a great asset. Preparing worship in a church with an authorized liturgical text and preparing in a church without such a text are markedly different tasks. To adapt something that Robert Frost said about poetic meter and free verse: One is like playing tennis with a net and a marked court; the other is like playing tennis on an open field. But the Prayer Book is not in itself so much an end to the process of liturgical preparation as it is a starting point.

The Prayer Book is a fabric of words, with a few directions for their use. Its careful editing provides the church with rites that have structure and focus—beginning, middle and end. Its language gives texts with clarity and power, restrained drama and movement. It is important that all the persons who prepare liturgy in the Episcopal Church understand this book—that they acquire interior sympathy with it. The preparers of each act of worship should cooperate with and bring to actualization the church's intentions, as represented by the Prayer Book. The business of preparing for worship should never, whether intentionally or not, sub-vert this normative text.

But the 1979 *Book of Common Prayer* leaves many things up to the officiants. It is more full of material and less prescriptive about its use than any previous American or English Prayer Book. It seems at times like a rich repository of elements whose intelligent use invites—indeed requires—choices, discrimination, and care exercised in advance.

Moreover, as in previous Prayer Books, few ceremonial acts of ministers or of the congregation are expressly required or forbidden. When one sets out to enact the Prayer Book's words, one must determine many things, with only minimal guidance from its rubrics.

• Words and Actions •

The function of the Prayer Book might be explained this way: Liturgy is an act or event that exists in time, like drama or music. Although it is a complex act, it is, to a marked extent carried by words. Much of the time of Christian worship is spent in speaking, or singing, and listening. In the print era (that is, since the sixteenth century) all churches use books in worship—at least the Bible and a hymn book. Some churches, the Episcopal Church conspicuous among them, commit their central prayers and canticles to a book as well. But the written or printed text is for the sake of the action it facilitates. The fundamental medium of liturgy is that most elemental of all forms of the word: the oral/aural. A liturgical text is rather like a printed play or a musical score. The volume of Thornton Wilder's *Our Town* or of Franz Schubert's songs makes the drama or the music possible. But the printed form is not the play nor the songs. These only come into being when they are performed; they come into being fully when they are performed very well.

Thus the Prayer Book, central though it is, does not stand alone. Worship is carried forward by many media. Through these media (to indulge in a momentary McLuhanism) we signal many "messages"— perhaps partially conflicting. We use *words*—many of them traditional and biblically derived, most of them the language of image, narrative, presentation, confession, or doxology, rather than the language of definition or explanation. Since much of worship is organized by speech, it is valuable to create space for reflection by the alternative to speech: the eloquent language of *silence*. We use the language of *arrangement in space* and of *people in space* so as to express community, order, differentiation and function. Liturgy makes use of *movement* of people in space and of bodily *gesture,* restrained or exuberant. It speaks through the language of *visual and spatial environment*—the room, its light, color, dimension and adornment. And most powerfully of all in unifying and conveying the emotional tone of the worship act, liturgy speaks through *music,* some of it with words, some of it wordless.

Some of these languages or media are extremely powerful—so powerful that they can dominate or distort an action of which they are part. Some traditions, fearing this power, have removed certain of these expressions from worship altogether. One thinks, for example, of unadorned Cistercian chapels or Quaker meeting houses, or of the absence of instrumental music in some Eastern and some Reformed traditions. How can one be attentive to God when one's eyes and ears are distracted? Anglican worship has not taken this "negative way," but it has incorporated (sometimes cautiously, sometimes with rich affirmation) much of human art, culture and embodiedness. Yet the prohibitions that are observed by certain traditions can warn those who prepare liturgy of the tendency of some of the "languages," verbal and nonverbal, to take over the worship event.

• The Loss of Traditional External Authority •

These non-Prayer Book and nonverbal factors are changing today. They, as much as revision in *The Book of Common Prayer* itself, require that liturgists raise to consciousness the determinations of what is to be done. One can no longer fall back on doing "the going thing." With regard to liturgical space, visual environment, vestments, musical style, gesture, and the like, no one practice is now "going" with such authority that it can be followed without question. Moreover, now that choices must be made, even if it is decided that an old practice will be continued, it must be rethought and repossessed in a situation different from that in which it was commended by authorities of even the recent past. Unless the question is asked "Why are we doing this?" any part of worship risks being perceived by sensitive worshipers as careless perpetuation of tired habit. In a changed situation, the unthinking continuance of customs that may once have had integrity may be a sign of decadence.

Perhaps the point should be itemized:

Architecture, Liturgical Space: Much of the movement of ministers and the ordering of the worshiping community in Episcopal churches has assumed neo-Gothic buildings—axial structures, with clearly defined nave, choir and sanctuary.

During the colonial period, American congregations built, on the Eastern seaboard, many churches of the sort being erected in late seventeenth and early eighteenth century England perhaps thought of as "Wren" churches, although architects other than Christopher Wren built well in this style. Such churches generally centered on a wide, well-lit eucharistic room, with the pulpit, reading desk, and holy table clearly visible throughout it; the communion rail was often on three sides of the table; musicians were in a gallery at the west end of the building to assist the congregation.

Despite this inheritance, the churches of the Episcopalians' great building era—mid 1800s to early 1900s—came to be dominated by the authority of the Cambridge ecclesiologists and their dogmatic idea of architectural correctness. Very often the Episcopal church in a town was expressing its identity by erecting a building that stood in marked contrast to the "auditorium churches" of much of Protestantism and the more baroque-inspired structures of the Roman communion. The Gothic churches of England, which served as model, had been developed to suit the worship of the late Middle Ages—a worship whose character was radically altered by the Reformation and the Prayer Book. When these nineteenth-century neo-Gothic buildings became all but normative in the Episcopal Church (the confirmation manuals implied that if you did not have such a building, you *ought* to!), the space had to be used. The very important east-west seating between the rood screen and the steps to the sanctuary was filled by a vested choir that had to process in and out. To a marked extent, liturgy and a general Episcopalian sense of the church came to be dictated by a style of architecture.

In recent decades, however, church designers have thought more functionally and less imitatively. The architecture that has been influenced by the liturgical movement asks about the worshiping community and its actions and its differentiated functionaries before it turns to the arrangement of space or the face the building turns to the community. As new churches are built and old ones are refashioned, new spatial arrangements, expressing new conceptions of the community of faith gathered for worship are commending themselves. The possibilities for the people in relation to one another and to the visible and vocal leaders of words and music, and to the focal centers for Eucharist, preaching, reading, prayer and baptism are indefinitely open.

This topic will return in later chapters. Here it is enough to note that when one thinks of liturgical space one no longer supposes that the gathered community must be ordered so as to fit a neo-Gothic floor plan.

Gesture: As to ceremonial at the Holy Communion, not so many years ago parishes, even quite plain evangelical parishes, used a modified version of (what some of them would have been shocked to realize was, in fact) Roman low mass. The communion vessels were either on the altar at the start of the liturgy or else were brought in by the celebrant as he (they were all "he's" at the time) entered. The corporal was laid, and the chalice and paten were left at the center of the altar under a brocaded veil, with a matching burse on top. The Epistle was read from its side of the altar; the book and its stand (often a cumbersome object of brass) were moved so that the Gospel could be read from the other side. At the offertory, the bread and wine were brought to the altar from a nearby credence shelf by a vested server. The elements began in the sanctuary and were administered from the sanctuary. During the consecration and communion, many clergy used bowings and crossings, and they quietly said prayers of an essentially private character, but since all of it was done in the eastward position, it did not necessarily seem fussy or a violation of the public, representative role of the priest.

Now, however, when celebrants commonly face the people who have unobstructed sight lines to the holy table, new criteria must be applied to what celebrants do with body, face, hands and voice. And it is no longer taken for granted that the area of the eucharistic room remotest from the people is the best place from which to read the Scriptures nor that the people's intercessions should come from a distant leader whose back is to the congregation.

One could go on, but these instances from a simple communion service will suggest that the new Prayer Book and the new liturgical understandings it expresses have called into question a fabric of ceremonial actions that had—more by custom than by rubric—become very common. New possibilities are being explored along functional, expressive lines.

Music: For forty-five years, the congregation's part in the church's music was directed by *Hymnal 1940*. This book was often judged the best of the denominational hymnals; it was a work of discrimination and fine musical editing. It contained some plainsong hymn settings and service music—an idiom that had been making its way into the church's musical consciousness in the 1920s and 1930s—and contained some new music by contemporary composers such as Ralph Vaughan Williams and Martin Shaw. Some of this work, which may have been thought daring when it was proposed, has become widely known and deeply loved. But *The Hymnal 1940* as a whole was overwhelmed with nineteenth-century hymns, some of which are so sentimental as to have become widely unacceptable in the experience of four tumultuous decades.

Not all of the material that was newly introduced in 1940 has won its way since. Of the four settings of the Holy Communion, Merbecke was simple, and the *Kyrie* and *Sanctus* became widely known; but it was hard to make this austere music very expressive. Healy Willan's setting won a genuine place for itself; the honest music stood up well under much use. The third setting, by Holroyd, never had much of a following, and it seems strangely dated. The plainsong setting (IV) was very beautiful and expressive, but its florid melodic line set it beyond the ability of all but a few congregations. In short, time has limited and relativized the contents of this splendid book.

Meanwhile other musical idioms, old and new, were commending themselves in the ecumenical Christian community. There were, to name a few: the Gelineau psalm style for nonmetric texts; folk (some older and genuine folk music, some freshly written in folk style); black hymns and spirituals; early American music (William Billings and *Southern Harmony,* for examples); contemporary (including synthesizer music and some eloquent twelve-tone material). The whole "early music" movement—a stir that has opened to modern listeners some of the finest music of the Christian tradition—has made its impact since 1940. These are not individual compositions, but new kinds of church music—or at least kinds new to the Episcopal Church. There is good and bad, suitable and unsuitable music in all of these idioms. But it is clear now that good church music does not mean one sort of thing. There are many ways of being good.

In recognition of some of these changes since 1940, the Joint Committee on Church Music issued *Songs for Liturgy,* (1971) containing new service music and hymns. In time other supplements were published. A revision of the authorized hymnal could not be undertaken without approval by the General Convention, but meanwhile, through these supplements, the church could explore new directions in music for liturgy.

Of course, at the Convention of 1982 the Episcopal Church issued a new hymnal—many years in the making. However, only the *words* of the hymnal were authorized in 1982. It was three more years before a usable book was produced, with words and music. But even while the varied and exciting content of *Hymnal 1982*—six hundred hymns and a large body of service music, most of it new in this book—is becoming familiar and being sorted out, the music that had become familiar through the various supplements is still in hand. Moreover, as new liturgical texts were authorized for trial use, starting at least as early as 1967, composers were challenged as they had not been for several generations. Hundreds of eucharistic settings came into use. They are of unequal merit, but the best of them are very good. Some of them may be so well established locally that the settings in the *Hymnal* will not entirely displace them. In sum, this is a time of enormous musical creativity in the churches. If congregations are not to be unfairly limited, those persons who prepare liturgy must acquire familiarity with an extensive and varied resource. If congregations are not to be given second-rate new material in exchange for first-rate old material, planners of liturgy must seek discrimination.

• A New Situation •

Episcopalians will experience and describe this new turn in liturgical practice in their own way of course, but the turn itself is ecumenical. It belongs to the whole people of Christ (or at least large units of the Western portion of it) meeting a fresh challenge as the common culture turns a corner. All churches are moving, each in its own way, into a new rhetoric, a new sound, a new look, a new decorum. Such a time of newness breaking in upon oldness is certain to produce pain and waste, as well as discovery and exhilaration. Great continuities need to hold, even as new things are given a fair trial. Not the wisest and most informed of liturgists will move with total confidence in such a time.

We have simply observed in this chapter that old guidelines have weakened or disappeared while new guidelines have not yet taken their place. Indeed, it is unlikely that new guidelines of the old sort would suit the contemporary situation. There are now few external rules in the worship of the Episcopal Church, and little in the way of an imposed style. Yet the alternative to external direction need not be stylelessness. Norms for good liturgy remain important. They are discussable and discoverable. Style is essential; A.N. Whitehead once spoke of style as "the ultimate morality of mind." However, acquiring style in the absence of outside authority may require the demanding task of discovering and applying interiorized criteria. Acquiring style may well mean finding a style appropriate to this person, in this configuration of persons, in this place, with this resource, for this occasion.

That is not to say that since there is no liturgical king in liturgical Israel, every celebrant, reader, musician, or congregation may do what is right in his, her, or its own eyes. Nor is it to encourage unsettling novelty or caprice. There is the Prayer Book and its inner spirit; there are bonds among churches so that discoveries in one place may be widely usable; and there is the ritual tradition, whose wisdom often becomes apparent after one has struggled on one's own for a time. Liturgy is responsible to profound inner judgment. In the present situation in the Episcopal Church, what the faithful worship of the God of the Christian revelation, as that revelation has been received in the Anglican tradition, all comes down to will be determined, to an unprecedented degree, by the local worshiping unit. This is a liberating opportunity and a terrifying demand.

•

CHAPTER TWO

Three Interacting Factors

In churches that have a prescribed liturgical text the preparation of worship involves three sets of factors. They can be named and described separately, but in any well-prepared act of worship they combine so that only the most informed and analytic worshipers are likely to distinguish them:

1. Persons who prepare liturgy must reckon with some important *givens.* They encounter a design and intent in the liturgical events—a design and intent that are not of their own making. Their first task is to listen and observe. They must discover and cooperate with the deep structure of the authorized liturgy. It is not something they determine. Rather, it is the thing through which their own identity as Christians and their own participation in the continuing liturgy of the Great Church are given to them. In the real but limited ways that are granted, they are shaping the thing that shapes them. The task is approached with reverence.

But there is something important to be done. The latent printed forms are there, waiting to be filled by the energy of a community of faith gathered to do its characteristic work. To put the point negatively, no cleverness or good ideas on the part of preparers should subvert or displace the liturgical structures through which they derive their real, but not unrestricted, standing as preparers of liturgy.

2. Liturgical preparers must also reckon with a number of relatively *fixed* things that are neither given by the Prayer Book nor chosen by them—things which, while they can be changed, cannot be changed

quickly. Some favored congregations seem to have just about everything that one might seek to make good liturgy possible. In most places, those who are responsible for liturgy will be grateful for some of these fixed things, but they will think of others of them as obstacles or limitations: a conspicuous reredos that looks abandoned if a table for the communion is thrust toward the congregation; a long, east-west building housing a congregation that tries to think of worship as people around a table; the chronic absence of tenors for the choir . . . , and the list could go on.

Persons involved in preparing liturgy will often have standards that are informed by experience in other places that have more advantages. We all need good models, but the integrity of worship is flawed if a congregation seems, to itself or to others, to be a poor copy of some other envied community of worship. Some changes can be made in space, color, furnishings and the like, but for the most part these fixed things must be accepted or incorporated as they are. Where these things impose limits, worship can work with those limits. Continued dissatisfaction with the conditions under which worship must be carried out can create a mind-set in which God-given possibilities in the community may go unobserved. Persons who prepare worship must be open to the joyful discovery and use in liturgy of unusual gifts and assets that may make the worship in any place very good worship *of its own sort.*

3. The persons who prepare liturgy must work creatively in the wide area of *choices.* To any liturgical event, the preparers can bring a range of resources, old and new. In exercising the discretion that the liturgical texts themselves invite, the preparers can be sensitive to the particularities of community and occasion. Where the liturgical texts step aside (as the modern texts often do), the preparers can enter with creative work from the local community of prayer. Liturgical texts are seldom prescriptive about how their words are to be enacted. If that absence of regulation makes it possible to do things that are careless and slovenly, it also makes openings for doing things that are imaginative and tasteful.

Clearly more may be said about all three of these factors.

• The Given Things •

The Episcopal Church is a liturgical church within a great liturgical tradition. *The Book of Common Prayer* is authorized by a churchwide representative process. Most generations of the church receive and use with gratitude the liturgical work of previous generations. But, as Episcopalians of the 1960s and 1970s know, when revision is undertaken it is a lengthy, participatory business. The General Convention, through the Standing Liturgical Commission, appoints informed persons who receive and make proposals; they shape and test them throughout the church; and finally the Convention, as the synod of the entire church, accepts and authorizes them. The resulting liturgy is not the triumph of any person or party or idea. It is a large, complex document that, as a fabric of prayer, praise and sacramental act, represents the largeness, wholeness and balance of the church from which it emerges. It does so, not by accumulating ideas from every quarter so that all may think they have won and deserve prizes. An eclectic liturgy would not wear well. The Prayer Book that is finally presented and authorized is a coherent whole that holds the church's faith before each congregation, with economy and centeredness.

Thus *The Book of Common Prayer* is not used because it is required by canon. Rather, it is freely chosen and deeply loved; it commends itself by its intrinsic qualities. When it is tested in a varied community, worshiping in a variety of situations, it proves its adequacy as a guide in corporate Christian prayer.

The qualities of the Prayer Book do not, at their deepest, arise from the wisdom of the General Convention or the Standing Liturgical Commission. Rather, the Prayer Book derives its character from its participation in enduring forms older than itself. It is a contemporary fashioning of elemental liturgical structures that are as old as the Christian impulse itself. Utilizing Jewish models, the church in its first two centuries developed several basic forms: (1) the synagogue-like service of the word, (2) the communal meal with bread and wine, (3) initiatory ritual and catechesis, (4) observance of ritual time through the year, centering in Passover-Easter, and through the weekly Lord's Day, and (5) the setting apart of persons for special ministerial and liturgical functions. It created such components as hymns, doxologies, confessional acclamations, and catechetical forms. They all had deeply Christological content and expressed the new time, the new life, the new people.

These structures, roughed-out very early, were coherent and catholic. They were not separable actions or moments, but together they formed and supported the common life and the faith of the individual Christian.

They bodied forth the human engagement with God opened by the incarnation, cross and ultimate lordship of Christ.

As heirs of that creative, faithful body of work, we are entitled to claim for ourselves what might be claimed for the early Christian generations: The liturgy is so bound up with the Gospel itself that *the structures of liturgical life are the structures of redemptive life.* Participation in these shared liturgical forms is participation in the living Christ—which is the interiority of the church.

So integrally are these liturgical forms the enactment of the Christian message that churches which drop some of them, but which seek to hold to that central message (as many Protestant groups have done), eventually must painfully and joyfully rediscover them. Similarly, churches which have allowed these forms to fall into a non-system of isolated actions (the problem of the modern Roman and Anglican communions) must recover their intrinsic relatedness.

When preparers of worship struggle to come to terms with these great liturgical "givens," it is not just that they are deferring to the past nor that they seek a contrived dramatic unity among liturgical actions. Rather, it is through engagement with these elemental forms that the redemptive note is sounded in our worship. Liturgy is not an occasion to air our interests, our current ideas, our hobbies—or even our profound concerns—except as these are judged, enlarged and reordered through engagement with the great realities of faith. When we take a liturgical occasion in hand and seek to turn it in a direction of our choosing, the Prayer Book is there to resist us and to invite second thoughts. As persons of faith, we grow by recognizing and coming to terms with the "otherness" of Scripture and liturgy.

The great elemental structures of liturgy—undoubtedly the most important of the "given" things—are conveyed in *The Book of Common Prayer.* Earlier paragraphs listed some of them, but only to speak of their early emergence. More needs to be said of them in the form in which they are encountered now.

> **The Christian Year:** Christ is indivisible, and in a sense the Church is continuously engaged with the whole Christ. But Christ is made known in story—the determinative story of Jesus, embedded in the stories of Israel and of the church. The form of the Christian revelation is linear, sequential, dramatis-

tic. We too are story; we live in time—the repetitive times of days, weeks and years; and the unique critical moments in our biographies and our shared collective histories. As faith sees it, the story of Christ is the story of stories. Our stories are understood, judged and opened to new possibility in relation to that story. The liturgy orders the individual occasions of worship into a coherent, sustained yearly presentation of the redemptive saga.

The church's seasonal pattern is governed by two major festivals of Christ. One, Christmas, is on a fixed day, as birthdays fall on a specific date. The other, Easter, is movable, as Passover was and is movable. Thus two seasons, Epiphany and Pentecost, must be of variable length to accommodate earlier or later dates of Easter. These central days are both festivals; the message of Christ is essentially good news. But the seasonal structure that is governed by these festivals is built of contrasting blocks of time. We are carried from anticipation to fulfillment, from austerity and penance to celebration. The Christ-story that is retold each year in these seasons and days has its origin in the Bible, Old Testament and New. Over this seasonal structure, biblical readings are distributed—a three-year cycle for the Eucharist, and a two-year cycle for the Daily Offices. Prayer, canticles, colors, music, ceremonial and visual environment all interpret the season. By such devices the church gives variety and drama to its ritual shaping of time. The central Christian message is not simply something told or talked about, but through the use of ritual time it is something in which Christians participate.

The Service of the Word: One of the characteristic actions of the liturgical assembly is to rehearse in its own hearing the primal, indispensable, prophetic sources from which its faith stems and by which it continues to live. We meet as the Christian synagogue for a service of the reading of Scripture, of reflection, of proclamation, and of wide-ranging prayer. We not only listen to the Scriptures, we reply in psalms or biblical (or biblically-derived) canticles. A writer some years ago, speaking of the constitutive role of the Scriptures in liturgy, said, "The church responds to God by the Word of God." The church is a community of shared meaning—meaning whose ultimate source is the believing perception of redemptive event, of which the Bible is our testimony literature, written from faith, and speaking to faith. In hearing the Word of God, the church is renewed in its own memory and hope. It learns freshly whose it is, what it is here for, and whither it is bound.

The principal extended forms of the service of the Word are the opening portion of the Eucharist and the offices of Morning and Evening Prayer. A substantial liturgical event, in each case, centers on the presentation of the Scriptures. But it is worth observing how extensively other liturgical actions in the Prayer Book also take their rise from the Bible. Because they are set in the context of the Eucharist (either necessarily or as a norm), there are biblical readings at baptisms, confirmations, marriages, burials and ordinations. Indeed, all of the Pastoral Offices in the 1979 Prayer Book contain some ministry of the Word. This ministry is thus not only a separable liturgical action, it is a pervasive factor throughout the fabric of the church's worship.

The Liturgy of the Holy Table: Another characteristic action of the Christian assembly—one as old as the records of the Christian movement itself—is the gathering for a corporate ritual meal. Bread and wine, signs of our life, are presented. A presiding person says, in the name of all, a full prayer of thanksgiving for creation and redemption in Christ. It is a performative fabric of words as, for Jews, the prayers of blessing were a consecration of life. The bread and wine are distributed. In the eating and drinking, what began as sign of our life is returned to us as sign and bearer of the life of God. The meal is a seal of the union with one another and with God.

It is sobering to reflect that the eucharistic actions that we shape and plan and carry out, sometimes to our satisfaction, sometimes not, are ultimately to serve this profound divine-human sharing. We carry out a meal at which Christ himself is host, provider and food.

Since the Eucharist is so central in Christian liturgical life, several later chapters of this book will discuss preparing for worship in terms of Eucharist. It is noted here among the given factors with which the preparers of liturgy work.

Christian initiation: The church is a recognizable bounded society, tracing to a specific historical origin. As such, it necessarily has a rite of entry: One does not join the people of faith by being born, but by Christ's death and resurrection. Baptism (and its associated ritual, pastoral and catechetical acts) is the outward sign of the ever-renewed coming-into-being of the church.

One could identify at least two other groups of liturgical acts as belonging to the very identity of the church. The **Pastoral Offices** relate the forgiveness and blessing of the Gospel to unrepeated individual life events, such as repentance, marriage, childbirth, sickness and bereavement. **Ordinations** continue the supply of called, gifted and tested persons, maintaining for the community the ministries of word and sacrament, of pastoral support, and of corporate leadership.

These *given* things, identified briefly here, belong essentially or necessarily to the life of the church and to its fabric of worship. The forms are not decorative or optional. Although they have been and continue to be variously adapted, no generation, no church, and surely no congregation is free to make of them what it will. They are profoundly bound up with the church and its divine charter. As such, although any of them can be misused, obscured and treated perfunctorily, they have a power of recovering and reasserting themselves in their authenticity. For the individual believer, these are forms that stand in such vital relation to the Gospel itself that one only tires of them when one tires of it.

Moreover, just at a practical level, the presence and authority of these great liturgical *givens* can be benign. Perhaps one should not speak critically of a tradition of worship that may be imperfectly understood and that one knows can, at its best, be very good. But it is not my impression that churches which work without these classic structures—that is, churches of the "free" worship tradition—carry out their liturgy with imagination and variety. Rather, guided only by custom (an inflexible guide), they fall too easily into a prosy, dull monotony. When the problem is recognized, they often attempt to rise out of it by gimmicks or theatricality.

Persons who are familiar with the Prayer Book, and hence familiar with the problems of using it, should not restlessly look elsewhere, following the lure of "spontaneity" or "freedom." It is not that freedom or spontaneity in worship are in themselves unworthy aims. It is just that, as aims, they offer more than they in themselves can deliver. After exposure to freedom, creativity and spontaneity, serious Christians often seem to begin to search for structure, order and discipline. Their intense experience looks for adequate, sharable, sustaining forms. The problem arises when freedom and form are set in opposition to one another. (That is the tired antithesis which has bedeviled Christian worship since at least the seventeenth century.) It seems possible to argue that in liturgy, as in art or social order, freedom and form need one another. Or to be less abstract, as persons internalize deep structures of Christian response to God, such as those carried by *The Book of Common Prayer,* they become competent to be free in Christ. Or to put the point the other way around, it is persons who most intelligently claim their freedom in Christ who best appreciate and most confidently enter the structures opened by the great liturgical heritage.

Faith has created the forms of liturgy. Faith has often refashioned them. As a sign of its authenticity, faith will continue to do so. Yet at the same time, faith is taught, prompted, informed and carried by liturgical structures. Good liturgical forms can awaken conscious faith when it seems dormant. They can shape and develop it when it seems directionless. At times we can be impatient with *The Book of Common Prayer.* But more often we have the experience of making some exciting spiritual discovery, only to find that the Prayer Book had known it all along and, now that we know it too, the Prayer Book will share it with us. In sum, the relation between the worshiper and the liturgy is complex and dialectical.

• The Fixed Things: •

In addition to the *givens* that are represented by the Prayer Book, there are, in any specific congregation, *fixed* things that are not in the form of printed texts authorized by churchwide authority. Yet account must be taken of them. The wordings and rubrics of *The Book of Common Prayer* are meant to be usable in the varied life of the church. Hence they are general. But they are put to use in particular congregations in specific settings, and this particularity opens some possibilities and imposes some restraints. These nontextual fixed things will differ from congregation to congregation. A few general groupings may suggest where these factors will be encountered by persons who are preparing liturgy.

Perhaps the first factor to identify is *the liturgical president* who customarily leads a congregation's worship. His or her voice will usually not be the only voice that will be heard. But often it will be the first spoken voice; it will take central parts; and it will, to a great extent, organize the parts taken by others. The president's style will set the tone (formal or conversational, festive or sombre) of the event. It will establish the bonding between the gathered people and the visible and vocal leaders. It will impart pace, flow and rhythm to the action as a whole.

Some persons ordained for this liturgical role seem, by such signals as voice, enunciation, bodily movement, gesture, or facial expression, to lead a worshiping group easily, modestly and convincingly. (Whether their competence came easily or whether it was won by practice, self-criticism, prayer and fasting, they usually do not say.) But others, who may have wonderfully compensating gifts in other parts of the varied pastoral task, find that liturgical leadership is a role in which they never feel fully confident.

Some persons are (or in their public *personae* seem to be) relaxed, free and resourceful, while others are constrained and uncomfortable outside the most routinized words and actions. Such characteristics are no doubt rooted quite deeply in individual personality. Bad habits can, of course, be identified and corrected, and individuals are full of surprises—a quite undramatic officiant can tap unexpected inner resource and carry off a grand liturgical occasion with flair and poise. Generally speaking, persons who prepare liturgical events need to take account, from the beginning, of the particular abilities and limitations of a celebrant. It subverts the effectiveness of liturgy if a planning group, by its initiative, creates a liturgical setting in which the presider feels ill at ease, or if it makes demands unsuited to the abilities of the central executant. Those who prepare liturgy should do so with the principal celebrant, not in spite of her or him.

The *other ministers* who will be taking part in a liturgical event similarly represent a factor that cannot be changed at will. What of the readers? Are they informed and competent so that they do their task with only a minimum of suggestion? Or are they new at the job and quite hesitant? Similar competences must be known in servers and other assisting ministers. Sometimes they are resourceful and can respond well to unexpected demands; or they may have so much experience that they can bring in an old parish practice alongside a new one just by hearing it mentioned. Of course others are inexperienced, timid, or easily confused. They can be helped by training and encouragement. Those who prepare liturgy may have to ask, "Who will do the necessary coaching? And is there time?" It is better to set aside a good liturgical proposal than to go ahead and carry it out badly. When a cherished idea must be abandoned, the planners need to think about programs of training, about scheduling walk-throughs, and about getting their own plans underway longer in advance.

The *musical resource* of a congregation represents an important fixed factor. The person generally in charge of the music may be a conservatory graduate, or a well-meaning player of quite limited ability. In either case, this musical leader may have or may lack a sense for liturgy. A parish may have a superb pipe organ and an extensive music library, but, needless to say, many have neither. Unfortunately, many small parishes (and most parishes in the Episcopal Church are small) try to do something like the better-equipped parishes do, and only do it badly. Choirs try anthems beyond their ability, or they sing (almost parody) great choral numbers in reduced soprano–alto–bass arrangements. It is possible for a small parish—even one with an asthmatic pipe organ or none at all; or no choir—to do quite good music of its own sort, and on its own scale.

Liturgical preparation needs to accept the musical resource (much or little) of a congregation and integrate it satisfyingly into liturgical events as a whole. In many places, coming to terms with things as they are might require an altered mind-set. Instead of trying to be like churches that have professional-level choirs, large pipe organs, and generous budgets—and feeling third-rate because one cannot measure up—a parish might look for the intimate sound of a couple of recorders accompanying the singing voices, or it might find the musical satisfaction there is in singing unaccompanied.

A further conspicuous fixed factor is the *liturgical space* with which planners must reckon. Usually the space in which we worship was made as it is by an earlier generation, and often there is little that can be done to change it. To put spatial considerations in a series of questions: Is the eucharistic room open and unobstructed? Or is it tight and narrow? (Indeed, is it one room, or is it separate units of space so arranged that people in one are quite distanced from people in the others?) Is the room large—allowing, or perhaps requiring, voice and gesture on something like the grand scale? Or is it small and intimate, a space in which large gesture would be pretentious, and a conversational manner more appropriate? Is the room dimly lighted or bright? Plain or busy? Is the space flexible, or is it filled with large, immovable furnishings?

Sometimes a few small changes are possible and can make a great deal of difference. While the removal of a front row of pews loses some seating, it can open some space. Light and color can be introduced into a drab chancel, or objects can be removed from a chancel that is hopelessly cluttered. But if a building is of basically good design, and its furnishings represent fine workmanship, large changes must be made sensitively, and they may require an architect and substantial funds. Meanwhile, the existing space with the opportunities it offers and the limitations it imposes, is the most obvious of the fixed factors with which the strategists of liturgy must reckon.

The liturgical event cannot seem to *fight* these stable, audible, visible factors. A powerful building will fight back! A celebrant who has been put in a position in which she or he feels awkward will send out signals of that discomfort—by body language at least. Rather, the planners should seek to shape a liturgical event that is *good* on terms set by such bits of reality. Few congregations work in conditions that would be thought ideal. Rather like restaurant reviews that give ratings for decor, menu choice, service, food, and the like and then sometimes confer a surprisingly high rating for the "total experience," the liturgy can bring together a whole that is better than a look at the separate parts would lead one to expect. Many generations ago, Richard Hooker, writing about guidelines for worship, said, "When the best things are not possible, the best may be made of those that are"—a text to be placed in every sacristy and choir room, to reassure every celebrant, choir and altar guild!

In the previous section of this chapter, the point was made that the *given* things of liturgy have a theological significance. This section needs to say that the *fixed* things too are theologically significant. They speak of the continuity of worship in the Christian community. What we take from those who have gone before us is a mixed inheritance. When we are annoyed that they should have left us something so bad and so permanent, we can simply reflect that had we been in their place, we might well have thought it was quite splendid. And when they have left us something for which we are truly grateful, we can hope that we shall do as well by our heirs as they did by us. Our predecessors were not more nor less intelligent than we; their taste was quite convincing to them.

Ideas of liturgy change, and the artistic climate is in flux. The continuity of liturgy must be perceived within wide changes in culture and custom. We know that we do not look at things as people of a generation ago, or more, did; and we can be quite sure that some people who reap where we have sown will ask, "Since they were so intelligent about some things, how can they have been so stupid about others?" We may hope they ask kindly. Yet we do not build, nor should our predecessors have built, temporarily or flimsily. We incorporate the best materials and workmanship we have into the best designs we can create. But our achievements and our folly will simply be built into the achievement and folly of those who were in Christ before us. And we are quite bad judges as to which will be seen as which. The *fixed* things we inherit speak to us of the past whose heirs we are, and the *fixed* things we bequeath to others will require them to deal with the greatness and the limitation that we cannot readily recognize in the work of our own generation.

• The Chosen Things: •

Having written of the given things and the fixed things at some length, the chosen things can be touched on to complete the ideas of this chapter. They are the principal subject of the later portions of this book.

Rather than preempting our choices, the present Prayer Book requires them. Former editions, from 1549 to 1928, were relatively prescriptive about the form of words. There was a single consecration prayer in the Holy Communion and a single general intercession. Except at the Communion of the Sick, the Nicene Creed and the General Confession could not be omitted. The supposition might well arise that the sacrament was intrinsically bound up with this one text. The church officially provided no alternatives whereby essential and nonessential features could be sorted out, and certainly the book gave no encouragement to wordings made on one's own. The model of the Prayer Book produced among Anglicans some superb writers of prayers, for private or public use. One thinks of Lancelot Andrewes and Jeremy Taylor in the seventeenth century, of Samuel Johnson in the eighteenth, and, in our own time, of E. Milner White. But apart from the tradition of freely chosen prayers "after the third collect" at the Office, and the long-standing largely Evangelical practice of extempore prayer before (or before and after) sermons, that creative work did not get back into the public prayers.

But the Prayer Book of 1979 (in use in many congregations since it was the Proposed Book authorized in 1976) *requires* choices and *invites* discrimination and creativity. The one-to-one union between act and text which had seemed implied in previous Prayer Books is qualified. The Eucharist is obviously an action with an inherent meaning. Thus it must be conveyed by words, and its meaning can be distorted or lost by inept or mishandled words. But its richness is not captured by any single, definitive, or "incomparable" form of words.

Just to identify the Eucharist (an act so central that what is true of it will carry over into other liturgical events as well), one cannot, on a moment's notice, step into a chancel and celebrate. The Prayer Book requires that a choice be made among three acceptable rites: Rite I (pp. 323–40), Rite II (pp. 355–66), or "An Order for Celebrating the Holy Eucharist" (pp. 400–01). What are the differences? Which would one prefer? Why? There are six eucharistic prayers (two for Rite I and four for Rite II) and quite a lot of flexibility in the "Order for. . . ." There are eight printed general intercessions (One for Rite I, six for Rite II, and "The Litany for Ordinations," pp. 548–51), but the rubric does not require that the prayers follow these texts (see Chapter Six). The penitential material need not always be used, and when it is used it may fall in one of two locations, neither of which is the location it occupied in previous American Prayer Books. How would one decide whether and where to use it?

The foregoing list, which could be greatly extended, indicates that the Prayer Book requires congregations to become, to a significant extent, responsible for their own liturgy. A previous chapter spoke of choices that must be made in matters beyond the Prayer Book itself: determinations of liturgical space, movement or gesture, music, and visual environment. There are many ways, many good ways, of ordering a liturgical event. The Prayer Book will not itself tell us how it should be done. It will give us outlines and structures and a rich variety of usable, but not definitive material. And then the Prayer Book will, in effect, ask us "Now, what do you think?"

Having proposed earlier in this chapter that the *given* and the *fixed* factors in liturgy have theological significance, it may be useful to note that the *chosen* factors too are theologically significant. The Prayer Book text, rooted in the great liturgical tradition that long antedates it, brings to each worshiping congregation the enlarging, corrective, redemptive sense of universality. The local community is interpreted through the faith and prayer of the Great Church and through the Gospel which gives rise to that Church. But paradoxically the universal church only becomes real and apprehensible in the time-and-space-specific communities of believers gathered in the Name. Paul wrote to "the church of God which is at Corinth" (1 Cor. 1:2). That existence in time and place is one of the characteristics of the time-embracing, place-transcending people of God. The liturgy needs to give voice to this actualization of the church in the assembly of faith. If we, in our "Corinths," need to hear the name of Christ in our midst, a name that Scripture and liturgy provide, we also need to hear our many names alongside that Name. The liturgy (as we receive it in an authorized book) does not know our names—nor our pain, our joy, our here-and-now situation. Only we know them. So we take the liturgical event in hand (always we do so under authority) and bring into its fabric the touch of earth and human circumstance. The liturgy trusts us to be the authorities on this matter essential to prayer.

•

CHAPTER THREE

Some Words about the Nonverbal

Three books are in conspicuous use in Episcopalian worship. Two are in the pews and in the hands of each worshiper: the Prayer Book is the community's essential prompt-board for prayer; and the frequent congregational hymns, and the music for such texts of the Prayer Book as are sung, are found in the Hymnal, also in the pews. The Bible, prominently located (usually on a lectern and occasionally in the pews as well), is the source for the readings that figure in the eucharistic Service of the Word, in the Daily Offices, and elsewhere. (In practice, other books or printed sheets, such as gradual psalms, may also be in use.) Public worship in Anglicanism has, to a marked extent, been wedded to print; it requires lots of paper.

Perhaps this dependence on print is limiting. It might be good if Episcopalians could do more without books. One notes, however, that two of these three books, the Bible and a hymn book, are also in use in virtually all other churches. It is the four centuries of popular use of one of these books, a vernacular *Book of Common Prayer,* that makes Anglican worship distinctive. One may note further that, as liturgical change has been sought ecumenically, churches of many traditions have put printed texts in the hands of the congregation. Generally speaking, such agreed wordings are more participatory and more open to deliberate change than are the purportedly "free" or extempore styles. If there are drawbacks in being liturgically a people of the book, this same loving commitment of the principal texts of their rites to a Prayer Book—a single book for officiants and congregations alike—is also a source of the characteristic strengths of the worship of Anglican Christians.

These printed forms emphasize the extent to which Christian liturgy is a fabric of language. During much of the time that they engage in worship, Christians are either speaking or singing words, or else hearing words spoken or sung. It is easy for anyone who stands in a tradition with a relatively fixed text or "script" to think, or half-think: "Here, between the covers of these books—these words are our worship."

Much of this present guide for preparers of worship (and much of the time that such preparers spend at their task) is properly concerned with the *words* that are used by leaders and congregations. Although many of the words of worship are provided in the three liturgical books of the Episcopal Church, the liturgical texts themselves expect that at times ministers will step outside their prescribed roles. A strange impression is created when persons whose words have been careful and measured when they were the church's words from the authorized liturgy, abruptly become slapdash and slangy when these persons speak on their own, as at the parish notices or the sermon. Such a shift of styles suggests that while one has been the church's person, one has not been oneself. Is it evidence of some unresolved discomfort in one's role as a leader of liturgy? "Your speech betrays you."

Leaders, whether they are using prescribed words or speaking freely, should be unaffectedly themselves. One does not want to become over-scrupulous and constrained. Liturgical language should be a people's language, which should flow and breathe. But the flow of language requires care; preparers of liturgical events must listen for nuance. What is the social "placement" of various possible expressions? What emotional tone do they carry? Liturgists need to cultivate an awareness of words such as one associates with poets or dramatists.

Yet worship is a complex psychosensory action in which words are not the constitutive or exclusive medium. Liturgical speech should not be separated from the whole of which it is part. We act through our words, and we speak through our acts, some of which may be carried out silently. Attention to the mixture of the verbal and the nonverbal is important, for most liturgy in the Western churches has suffered—and when left to its own still suffers—from wordiness, prosiness, and static talkativeness.

Counsel in the nonverbal components of liturgy can sound like: Do nothing to excess. Earlier in this book it was remarked that liturgy is an art, not a science. In matters of art, teachers and coaches can often give useful warning about pitfalls that experience has shown to lie on this side and on that. But such cautionary counsel is likely to produce bland, inoffensive work—hardly the highest aim of art. If they are wise, teachers stand in awe of the mystery of creativity. If they can impart a sense for excellence, they cannot reduce it to rules. At a certain point, a teacher of writing, painting, sculpture, composition, or architecture—or worship—stops warning and explaining and begins to trust the imagination of the student. Creative things are done, not by cautious following of prescriptive rules, but by unforced vision and by willingness to imagine and to venture.

In making suggestions on matters of art, it is easier to describe what is bad and to tell why it is taken to be bad than it is to identify, at least in other than the most general (and hence trite) terms, the qualities of excellence. Especially in our time, when liturgy takes on the pluralism of culture and society, one learns that there are different ways of being good. In a liturgical situation which is in many respects new, some ministers seem to be floundering. Guidance and modeling would be useful. But to describe, with conviction and in detail, one way of doing liturgy, even if it is a generally quite good way, could seem to absolutize one's own idiom or one's cultural preferences. Carried too far, it would apply elitist criteria to an action that belongs not to academic or artistic experts, but to the diversified people of God.

Yet some comments may be ventured on the nonverbal matters that deeply affect the art of public worship.

• Community and Its Ministers •

The intent of the redemptive divine initiatives, as they are witnessed to in the scriptures of Israel and the Church, is to bring into being a people—a collective body, the firstfruits of a universal saving purpose. When one person is summoned by God individually and dealt with in the depth of his or her unshared personhood—an Abraham, a Moses, a Jeremiah, a Mary, a Jesus of Nazareth, a Saul of Tarsus—it is for the sake of a collective whole. When one nation is dealt with, it is so that it may be a light to the nations. The ultimate human unit as the Gospel sees it, is the member in the body, not the member alone.

The church, which is called into being by God, represents deeply bonded persons who share a common life, who live in and through one another, who need and are needed, who support one another and allow themselves to be supported. In worship this community turns its life toward God in thanksgiving, renewed forgiveness, praise, petition, and rededication to witness and service. In the interpersonal relation that persists between God and the church, the church must, for the continued reality of the relation, devote special time to the listening and speaking, the giving and receiving, the mutual exchange of liturgy. Thus, in worship as in redemption, the unit is the body and the member in the body. We offer the shared life, we confess the collective sin, and we join in united praise. The liturgical pronoun is "we." Liturgy is intrinsically, fundamentally corporate. We are worshiping persons in the midst of a worshiping people. We find our own voice through the collective voice; and the voice of the church speaks for the voiceless world.

This catholic sense of the redeemed and redemption-bearing community is brought to focus in specific congregations—people who know one another face-to-face, who care about one another, who have a history together, who share one another's joys and sorrows. The community that is united in life shares also in prayer and praise.

Although the worshiping unit is the whole people, it is not an undifferentiated community. There are liturgical leaders, who act according to gift, training and appointment. But they act for all and in relation to all. A constant exchange takes place between the leaders and the led; the devotion of the community depends significantly on those leaders. Yet it is not uncommon to find seminarians and younger clergy who do not feel comfortable in a presiding role. They think that such roles are necessarily overbearing. But the ordered, somewhat complex actions of worship usually require a presiding person, even if such a central person acts in collaboration with other ministers. And the persons who are called and set apart to fill this central role in and for the liturgical assembly must come to terms with the special prerogatives and restraints it carries. Liturgical presidency in the Christian community is marked by a fundamental modesty. It is not a performance in which one's gifts or one's personality are put on display. Affectation and self-importance are out of place. It is a representative, pastoral role whose bonds with a people are created and sustained by love and care. Presidential leadership is made effective by a strange reciprocity; if the worship of the people depends on trusted leaders, the effectiveness of liturgical leaders depends, to a great extent, on the trust that is extended to them.

In some liturgical functions, leadership may be taken by any competent person; but the church reserves presidency in its central sacramental rites to those who are set apart as bishops and priests. (Whether these central roles are always, and necessarily to be so reserved is under some discussion today, and the issues are not simple.) Anglicans would contend theologically that the ordained ministries are, in some sense, God-given. They do not represent just functional arrangements arrived at pragmatically. Even though the ministry is God-given, it was originally, and continues to be, given through social and historical means. Some historians have developed the thesis that the orders of the ordained ministry grew out of roles required by liturgy. Whether that is so can best be seen in the liturgical assembly: the variousness of function; the complementarity and mutual necessity; the representative significance of the clerical orders and of those lay persons who act in related leadership roles; and the relation of such leaders to the baptized assembly are manifest.

The 1979 Prayer Book gives explicit guidance as to what roles properly fall to whom (the bishop, if the bishop is present; a priest in the absence of a bishop; a deacon; readers, sponsors, others), and these directions are carefully worded. Some persons fill certain roles by reason of order; others *may* be used; the use of others is commended as "appropriate." Certain Prayer Book rites do not require clergy at all. The page of the Prayer Book at the start of each major office is something like a *"dramatis personae"* for the rite that follows. The liturgical assembly is not just a community at prayer, it is an ordered, functionally diversified community, visible to itself and acting in its ordered–ness.

• Participation •

It is almost commonplace now to hear active participation in liturgy commended as a right, privilege and joy of every baptized Christian. For some years, in some Roman Catholic publications, when the phrase "active participation" was used, it was set in quotation marks. In the opening section of his encyclical *Motu Proprio,* issued in 1903, Pope

Pius X said that the true Christian spirit is acquired from "the active participation in the holy mysteries and in the public and solemn prayers of the church." The expression, coming with papal authority, so strengthened the hand of the early leaders of the liturgical movement that for half a century Roman writers continued to write "active participation" with inverted commas as a gesture of recollection and gratitude.

The proposal that the faithful participate actively is not just an ideal; it is also an act of repentance. Both Roman and Protestant congregations had in fact, for many generations, been quite passive and nonparticipatory.

The *Roman* liturgy had been said in Latin for centuries, and the people were left with little more than private, rather individualistic devotions to occupy them while they watched and listened. Although large numbers attended Mass, only a few received communion. They had learned nonparticipatory ways, and hardly thought to complain of them. *Protestant* worship, for its part, was, with the important exception of the congregational hymns, a monologue by the clergyman before an interested, but silent congregation. Protestants had less to watch than Catholics did, but they became very good listeners—and supposed that listening was what Christian worshipers were expected to do. *Anglican* worship had, through the Prayer Book, engaged the congregation in psalms and creeds and in many important prayers, such as litanies, confession, and thanksgiving. Through ritual movement—kneeling together, standing, at certain times walking in procession—the congregations acted unitedly. But the people who spoke and acted together interacted only minimally with one another. Moreover, in some parishes choral settings usurped the vocal role of the people; and in most places the voice of the congregation was a little stiff. (In a few congregations, anyone who actually sang the hymns audibly risked being stared at, discreetly of course.) Habits of congregational passivity had become deeply set in Western churches.

Thus, once it was recognized that worship is not a speech or a performance before an audience, but a shared action, and that the worshiping unit is the believing community, all churches (each coming at the matter from its own historic experience) have sought to bring congregations into more "active participation." The expressions of praise, the confession of sin, the pledges of faith, the public intercession, the thanksgivings, the hymns and psalms, the offering and receiving—the constitutive actions of the liturgy—belong to the people. No clericalism, catholic or evangelical, should assign the roles that belong to the congregation to a single person who does all the reading and praying, as well as all the preaching. No professionalism should give to the choir the hymns of the liturgy that belong by right to the Christian folk (nor deprive the congregation of its "Amen"). With varying degrees of regret over past failure, congregations (through new liturgical texts and new customs by which such texts are now enacted) have been introduced to larger and more active roles, which they have entered with varying degrees of acceptance and understanding.

This change is, of course, all for the good. It arises from a theological sense of the constitutive role of the people of God in liturgy and from a fresh sense that the officiating clergy, the assisting ministers, and the musicians are to support a collective action, not to take it over. But worship is complex, and "participation" is not a simple matter. We misunderstand liturgy if we suppose that any part of the community has a passive role. It is also a misunderstanding to suppose that all persons must have the same role.

Of course, with respect to each person's ultimate worth or the care due to each from the community, equality (based in the deeply egalitarian rite of baptism) is a godly democratic social postulate, but, in gifts or abilities, people are manifestly not equal. A falsely applied ideal of equality can lead to a leveling-down of common effort. It can suggest that no one should do (or get recognition for doing) what everyone cannot do—a sure route to drab liturgy. But the New Testament requires the Church to look for varied gifts among its members, gifts that are the self-investment of the Creator in the human community. (The principal New Testament discussion of gifts of the Spirit and responsibility in their exercise comes in a long passage, 1 Corinthians, chapters 11 through 14, which St. Paul devotes to issues that arose in the worship assembly at Corinth.) Common worship should bring such gifts to expression in ways that are not for virtuosic display, but for the enrichment of the shared life in Christ.

Churchgoers participate in a complex act in which they take a succession of roles. Leadership passes among a number of persons, each contributing to the shared whole. Since much of this versatility goes unnoticed, a brief account of a short sequence of actions in the Service of the Word in the Eucharist may illustrate:

- At one moment the celebrant reads or sings the collect of the day. All others, who are standing (or perhaps kneeling), are silent, until, at the end, they identify with the prayer by their said or sung "Amen."
- Then leadership passes to a lector (either vested and seated as one of the designated ministers, or preferably in street dress and sitting in the congregation) who goes alone to an appointed place to read. The lector stands, facing the congregation, announces and reads a passage from the Scriptures, while all others sit and listen.
- When he or she is finished, there is a period of silence during which there is, for a time, no visible or vocal leader, yet the congregation is active and united in inward, unspoken meditation and prayer.
- The silence is brought to an end when the leader of the music begins a gradual psalm or hymn. This musician does not take a vote on when the silence should end, nor on the key or tempo of the music. All accept this leadership and take their part in the singing.

In these few moments, liturgical leadership has passed among three people, and for a time no one was leading or speaking. Each of these persons has a special role to play: voicing a prayer, reading a lesson, playing the organ. The quality of the united action depends on each part being done responsibly.

During all of this time, the congregation has been *participating.* At one time it joined silently in a prayer spoken in its name by someone else, and ratified the prayer by its *Amen.* Its role at another time was that of listener to a portion of the foundational witness literature of the great community of Christian faith. Although it was listening silently, the reading was for the sake of the listening. The congregation's participation may have been signified by the little dialogue between the reader and the congregation that often follows the reading: "The Word of the Lord/*Thanks be to God.*" The silence that followed the reading was an opening created to make room for further participation—but in a changed mode: silent thought or prayer. Then participation continued through congregational singing, in which a cantor may have taken the principal verses and the congregation the refrain, but the psalm was nonetheless a united act.

This simple instance, covering only a few minutes of the Eucharist, indicates the complexity of liturgical worship. Leadership passes in an almost kaleidoscopic way among appointed persons, each of which does her or his own part and then steps aside so that another may take a role as leader. The congregation indicates its versatility by slipping easily into several different ways of accepting leadership and of taking its part. For persons who are accustomed to this series of actions, it all seems simple and natural. But someone who was unfamiliar with it might watch and comment, "How complicated! How do they all know just what to do?"

A little later in the eucharistic rite, the varied, interactive character of the liturgy will be further demonstrated when one person preaches, and then all join in the creed. Someone else may lead the Prayers of the Faithful, during which the congregation will make responses, and perhaps enter freely voiced prayers of its own. Bearers and ushers gather and present the offering of alms and of bread and wine, in which all are represented. One person prays The Great Thanksgiving in the name of all. (A priest is by definition a representative person.) Within most of the Prayer Book prayers of consecration the congregation makes acclamations, and it says an important "Amen" at the end of them all. Throughout this Thanksgiving, all have been praying through the voice of one. The congregation prays the Lord's Prayer unitedly. Then the bread and wine are prepared for distribution and are received by all. The persons who consecrate and administer do their work for the sake of the persons who receive; those who receive are active in the Thanksgiving. In the profound mutuality of liturgy, each acts for the sake of all. None is made perfect without the others.

If the contemporary emphasis on active participation makes it seem that one is not participating when one is not speaking or singing, the misunderstanding needs correction. Persons take public, vocal and active roles in worship by reason of their gifts and training, or they may be chosen (as offertory-bearers frequently are) in some sort of rotation to represent groups that might be taken to comprise the congregation. The designated persons take their tasks seriously—preparing intercessions, practicing a difficult biblical reading, working for weeks on a demanding choir anthem. The whole is made as good as it is by the quality of its many parts. Often these leaders will carry out their tasks better than most members of the congregation could. They are the best readers and singers the community has; they are the best people for greeting and seating persons who arrive at the door. The task of the worshiper is to take joy in saying and doing what she or he is to say and do. The worshiper's task is also to take joy in that which others do expertly, but in behalf of all. While the choir, with its skilled voices and its diligent preparation, is singing an anthem that would be quite difficult for me, I am nonetheless participating—not in the singing of a piece of music that the addition of my inexpert voice would only flaw, but in the worship of God, in which that choir is, for the moment, the leader. It supplies me with a voice I would not have on my own.

While thinking of participation and the desirability of united actions and words, perhaps two cautionary remarks are in order.

> **Room for Individual Differences:** Persons differ as to how demonstrative or how reticent they are. Prayer Book worship has, since the sixteenth century, sought to provide structures within which those persons who give bodily enactment to their feelings and those who are more restrained can coexist. The "freer" forms of worship (which are in use in some churches and which are sought by some Episcopalians) can be perceived, not as freeing, but as tyrannical. Such styles often compel persons to adopt attitudes they do not, in fact, feel, or to perform actions they do not find natural. The "active partic-ipation" that is expected of the congregation needs restraint and objectivity so that persons can act and speak within the liturgical forms with varying degrees of interior engagement and varying modes of external demonstrativeness. The close-ness and intimacy that still seem to be desired by some shapers of worship may work well enough in a group that has agreed to agree on such a style. But unless a person is committed to using and enjoying a great deal of togetherness, a forced intimacy can seem like an intrusion on his or her private space. It is not an admirable characteristic for an individual (or for a committee) to say that what appeals to that person (or that committee) must forthwith appeal to others. Such thinking can seem sectarian—often driven by a doctrine of what is healthy and free, as contrasted with what is pathologically constrained. Someone who has been given control of the liturgical event uses the occasion to tell other people what is good for them,

and by implication good for all. One of the strengths of Anglican worship has been its ability to hold within common objective structures individuals of different temperaments. That comprehensiveness should not be jeopardized.

Moreover, most of us have times when we enjoy company and other times when we are happier to be alone. Needless to say, the fact that we are present willingly in a group can summon from us the minimum actions required of a participant. We can actually enjoy the company of others once we have arrived at church, when previously we had thought it would be pleasant not to have to meet anyone today. For reasons that may not be fully clear to oneself, and need not be inquired into by others, this may be a day when one feels rather reserved.

Thus respect must be shown, not only for the differences there are between persons, but also for the differences within the same person at different times.

Room for the Stranger: The church, in its prayer and praise, brings to expression much of its relation with God. The believing community gives voice to the secrets of its own heart. Christian liturgy is characteristically an act of and for persons of faith. Yet the actions and tone of Christian worship can be found attractive by strangers who are curious about faith.

The relatively nonparticipatory styles of worship that prevailed in the still-remembered past (a past that persists in many places), made it easy for persons to come into the edge of the congregation and observe. Other people were courteous to them, and often helpful when the newcomer seemed to want to take part, but was fumbling for the right Prayer Book page. But if such a person wanted to be quite disengaged, it was understood that he or she was entitled to be left alone. If, in time, she or he wanted to draw closer to this community of belief, service and worship, it would be done at the pace that person wished.

However, as congregations have come to take more vocal and active parts in liturgy, there have come to be more unwritten rules of conduct, rules that everyone takes for granted. An in-group cultivates its somewhat monastic style. This move in the direction of "we happy few," to the extent that it grows uncritically, can create a body language, a relational language, as well as a verbal language that excludes the outsider, particularly when the liturgical space is small. A stranger has difficulty finding a place in such a gathering. To take a nonparticipatory role makes one feel conspicuous.

Of course liturgies are not designed with observers or casual droppers-in primarily in mind. Any impression that worship may make on an observer will be made because a congregation of believing/doubting Christians is engaged honestly with God, and is largely unaware of the way it looks and sounds to others. But those charged with preparing liturgy should remember the persons who slip in unobtrusively at the edges and who may be seeking something whose name they do not yet know. Such persons should be given genuine, if a somewhat restrained, welcome and some help with the mechanics of the liturgy, if they seem to want it. They should not be made to feel awkward or uninformed or excluded, or asked to say or do things they are not ready to say or do. A liturgical style should not seem to signal that unless one is ready to join fully in the words and actions of this group, there is no place for that one.

• Structuredness •

With respect to the perennial tension that has been felt in art and culture between the free creative impulse on the one hand and the controlled form on the other (between Dionysius and Apollo), we live in complex times. In some quarters a residual romanticism decrees that the free impulse is self-authenticating, while form is intrinsically alien and alienating. And yet, at the same time, modern culture is fascinated by the deep structures that seem to underly language, the ways we think, the stories we tell, the social configurations we create, and nature itself.

A fully human expression seems to consist in some satisfying combination of the free impulse, wedded to adequate form. The impulse alone suggests much, but develops little; its potential is forever latent. Formal perfection, for its part, is sterile without an adequate creative drive behind it. We look for impulse and control in a combination so unitary that germinal idea and articulated form cannot be separated.

Liturgy is, among other things, a product of culture. As such it has and must have form. The form should not call attention to itself, yet a structured liturgy is something the worshiper can appreciate. The liturgy meets us, often gently, where we are, and it carries us, by means of an intelligible progress to a different place. Sometimes, however, the liturgy confronts us more dramatically and shocks us out of life's ordinariness.

The formed nature of liturgy is not just of value through these somewhat psychological factors, which in themselves can seem rather manipulative. Liturgy is an enactment of the Christian message, as that message has, over the centuries, created appropriate modes of response in the community of faith. Worship holds before us an order of reality that is not of our making, but is that order by which we are constituted, judged, and redeemed. The form of liturgy is, in ways appropriate to itself, the form of the Gospel. For liturgy, art, or for life, form is not an optional extra, reserved for those who have a taste for this sort of thing. It is inevitable. It can be benign. The only real question is not whether there will be form—there will be. The question is whether it will be good form or bad. "Either it will be good liturgy, theologically sound, biblically faithful, practically expressive, or it will be bad liturgy, maimed, defective, and impoverished." (Neville Clark, *Call to Worship*, 1960, p. 10.)

In preparing liturgy, we must become aware of design and shape—of centeredness, of parts in relation to the whole. Where does this liturgical act begin? Having begun, how does it progress? At its turning points, is breathing time desirable? What is its natural climax? Our conscious preparation of liturgy will not set strong elements so close to one another that none of them shows up to advantage. Neither will anticlimactic actions extend the conclusion of liturgy over meaningless minutes. We may include a fling of celebrational excess at some points, but practice economy at others.

• Liturgical Space •

This "structuredness" of liturgy has its implications for liturgical space. Color, yes; but not competing or conflicting colorful elements. Centeredness, but not stasis.

Worship, as an ordered action of an ordered community, suggests ordered space. A room that lacks a center and an intelligible relation of its foci to one another will subvert the liturgical action. The liturgical room does at least two *functional* things: It brings the people into some coherent interrelation for united worship, and it facilitates the movement of leaders and of congregation among the designated centers of liturgical action. Bound up with these functions is the room's *expressive* power. Through light (bright or dim) and shape (expansive or confined) the eucharistic room itself speaks of worship and the God with which worship is engaged.

The rooms in which Christians worship have two possible organizing principles:

Some liturgical space (the traditional Western basilican church) has been "axial": long space, suggesting movement. The internal focus of the room lies towards one end, remote from many persons in the room. But the expressive alignment of axial space often does not seem confined to a room and its interior. The room or the building seems to point indefinitely beyond itself. The persons in the room seldom see each other's faces, but for the most part they look at the backs of other worshipers' heads. Thus the space is inevitably somewhat separating and distancing. Yet space thus arranged has great liturgical power; it is well suited to suggest transcendence. God is not so much within and among us as beyond us all.

Other liturgical space (early baptisteries, many Eastern churches, some buildings of every period) is radial: square, octagonal, or circular; forms that suggest centeredness and poise; space that turns in upon itself. Such space seems to have its focus within, expressing immanence. People, in looking toward the center of the space also look toward one another.

These two modes of spatial organization are spoken of as "cosmic" and "parochial" by the art critic Rudolf Arnheim. In either mode the room itself will have a focus. The spatial center should have a relation to the liturgical and sacramental center—the holy table and the furnishings immediately associated with it. Sight lines should run to it; movement toward it and from it should be open. But the liturgical action is complex, including such functions as baptism, singing and playing music, and reading and preaching the Word of God. There will be epicenters intelligibly related to the principal focus of the space and to one another.

After many centuries, during which the churches of the West have developed axial spatial forms, there has been a notable shift in our time, so that many modern churches are either essentially radial in floor plan (or at least the community is arranged in a broad, spreading shape), or else they attempt some combination of the two organizing principles. The neo-Gothic division of liturgical space into several rooms, aligned with one another but visually and functionally distinct, and representing differing stages of ritual exclusion, has given way in favor of a single room—usually a fairly wide room, with unobstructed sight lines and suitable for preaching, music, baptism and Eucharist. Such liturgical space represents not a contemporary fad, but a rediscovery of the principles of the churches that were designed for Prayer Book worship in England and in the American colonies from the sixteenth through the eighteenth centuries.

Few groups charged with preparing liturgy today can do much to change the essential character of the space with which they must work. It is one of the more "fixed things" spoken of in Chapter Two. The challenge that arises when new building is possible or when major renovation is undertaken is, of course, a theological, pastoral and liturgical, as well as an architectural, challenge. At times effective changes can be made in existing buildings, but such changes may be a more difficult challenge than building new. A deep narrow chancel can be retained for the choir, while the altar is brought forward on a raised floor toward the congregation—but that may seem to remove the choir from the people's room.

At times committees, with expert advice, have been able to do something as drastic as turning the liturgical use of a room end-for-end, or setting the altar in the middle of what had been a long side wall rather than against a narrow end wall, and adjusting the seating and the other features of the room accordingly. Windows and wall shapes must lend themselves to such shifting of the visual center of the interior, and they do not always cooperate. As a rule, drastic changes need to be made carefully and with the counsel of a liturgically informed architect. The requirements of space for musical leadership are important, and there are no formulas for determining them. Acoustics seems to be, if that is possible, a less exact discipline than theology! Most modern congregations will inherit buildings of the axial sort—often well designed for a sort of worship that makes most present-day interpreters of liturgy restless. Without seeming ungrateful to the past, changes will be sought.

When thinking of space, one must remember that in worship the motifs of transcendence and immanence mingle. A "thesis building," organized exclusively around one spatial motif, is a building of which a congregation may well tire. God is not "out there," but is where two or three are gathered in Christ's name. At the same time God is not the property of this congregation and of its agenda for life and prayer, but is God of nations and of eternal purposes that are not ours. God is both beyond and within, Other and yet near, always a Mystery even though self-disclosed. Our designs for liturgical space should seek to say as much; and it is a tall order.

• Visual Environment •

The eucharistic room usually contains some pieces of art, at least to accentuate its principal focal points. Sometimes these were planned by the original architect, are well made, and are essential to the room. Other times they are items of no distinction (such as brass memorial plaques) that have been given over the years, add nothing and detract much.

Art that is in the service of liturgy—processional crosses, altars, candlesticks, liturgical books, windows, vestments, embroidery, furniture and carvings—all need, in ways appropriate to themselves, to share the integrity of the liturgy itself. That is to say, the liturgy expresses a Gospel that touches the depth of experience. The God of the biblical revelation does not deal with human contradiction by an indulgent wave of the hand, but by a cross and resurrection.

Religious art frequently settles for cheap grace. Piety in the maker or the user excuses the tawdry or pretentious: Paintings that seek to make a quick effect on a pious observer are rendered without competence or vision; designs treat their materials and techniques dishonestly; derivative sculpture adopts conventional religious postures that seem unearned; acres of Victorian windows are aflutter with padded angels;

churches and parish houses are full of pictures of Jesus and sheep. In short, religious kitsch.

Bad art in church can be subversive. As a nonpropositional medium, it meets observers through images, giving immediate and powerful suggestion of realities which by nature cannot be grasped empirically. An honest sermon set in a solid liturgy can, in some measure at least, be undone by a sentimental religious picture that a worshipper cannot help but see. Theological truth is compromised by deceptive art.

Yet the matter is not dealt with easily. The bad art has often come into the church through well-intentioned gifts made in the past, and removing it can be divisive or give offense. Persons can become selectively blind and excuse in church the sort of art they would not tolerate elsewhere—they just have stopped seeing it. The process of choosing new pieces brings to the surface the very different standards of judgment and awareness that prevail in a congregation. The unfortunate fact is that many churchgoers have never seen good church art. One suspects that were they to see it, they might prefer it to familiar cliches. Art selection is, in great measure, a matter of education and of broadening the artistic sensibilities of the persons who must make decisions, decisions with whose results many persons will have to live for a long time.

When congregations or individuals are considering purchasing, they often turn to the catalogs of suppliers of church goods. With few exceptions, such catalogs show lines of items that are generally characterless and inoffensive, and made to be sold in quantity. (Some suppliers do have staff artists who can work with a local church and, when the desire for quality work is expressed, turn out fine pieces. The supply suits the unimaginative demand.)

A parish can think about what it wants, and at an early stage commission an artist whose work, ecclesiastical or not, is liked. Or it can approach local potters, woodworkers, or painters who, using local materials and approaching the creative task freshly, can produce something of passion and distinction.

• Ceremonial Actions •

Bodily movements and gestures are among the most powerful of liturgy's nonverbal languages. Actions—such as standing, sitting, or kneeling; raising one's hands; extending one's hands towards another person, or laying hands on another; persons embracing one another; moving from place to place, particularly in file; or bowing—are important, expressive means of punctuating, emphasizing, and hence of interpreting, certain moments in worship.

Because the ceremonial actions of the vested ministers are quite public and visible, they need to be thought through with some guiding principles in mind, for they can easily underline the wrong things and *mis* interpret the liturgy. Such appointed actions should, in the first instance, be *functional.* The person who is to read must get to the place from which reading can best take place; the baptismal party must get to the font and be suitably arranged there for its convenience and so that the congregation can see; the bread and wine must be gotten to the altar from a place of origination in the congregation. Still thinking in functional terms, one seeks *economy.* Persons move from place to place by the most direct route; they make only such gestures as are required by their tasks. Departures from such economy seem fussy. Naturalness of movement is sought, and affectedness is to be avoided.

At the same time, the movement of persons in liturgy does take on some special *formalization,* restraint and uniformity. They do not swing their arms while walking across the area of the altar; they keep their hands together at the waist—and all other ministers (unless, of course, they are carrying something) do the same. The ministers are filling special roles, and they should do so unobtrusively. Moreover, little exchanges of courtesies are commonly built into liturgy. The celebrant can acknowledge the bearers of the bread and wine. Persons who are acting together wait for one another and move at the same pace. Then ritual movements can serve an *interpretive* function. Perhaps the Service of the Word is led from seats and stations thrust toward the congregation, while the eucharistic meal is prepared and eaten at and around the Holy Table in another part of the room. The movement of the president and other ministers from one of these locations to the other at the presentation of the bread and wine (perhaps followed by the people) can demonstrate the structure of the rite and emphasize the distinct character of each part.

Interpretive actions can be heightened by appropriate touches of the *dramatic.* In a large room, gestures on something like a grand scale may be fully appropriate. In such space, small close-to-the-body actions have little visibility and hence little representative power. In a large space, small gestures may be annoying; while in a small church with a more intimate congregation, large gestures might be pretentious. The initial breaking of the bread at the fraction might be done in an open and public way, even though such further breakings as may be required should surely be straightforward and businesslike. To carry off ceremonial with a certain flair is part of good liturgy.

Gestures which the members of the congregation use are, for the most part, matters of private choice. Some persons are exuberant and kinetic, others are more restrained. Some persons cannot think and feel unless they act out their ideas and emotions, while other persons are distracted from thinking and feeling by the expectation that they will do something. United actions of the congregations engage each person's embodiedness, and hence are powerful. Yet bringing about change in such actions can be a daunting educational and pastoral challenge.

The Episcopal Church has, for peculiar historical reasons, done an exceptional amount of kneeling. (Other churches have sometimes adopted more kneeling because they thought the Episcopalians had things about right!) But when the liturgy says "Let us pray," does it imply "Let us kneel?" And should the congregation respond to "Lift up your hearts" by kneeling? Affectively, receiving communion while kneeling at a rail is quite different from receiving communion while standing at a station. Can the two practices be compared fairly? Or is this moment so sacralized that any change is painful?

With respect to ceremonial actions, the rubrics of Anglican Prayer Books have given only minimal directions—requiring, or by implication forbidding, only a few things. It has been remarked that if the ways of Anglican worship were to perish, an archivist of the future, finding a Prayer Book, could gather from it very little of the sound, color or drama of Anglican liturgy. The churches of Anglicanism have authorized forms of words, but they have expected that the ceremonies by which these words would be enacted might vary from church to church. Although the present Prayer Book often specifies the way ministers stand in relation to the people, it has no rubrics whose wordings imply a neo-Gothic floor plan. Directions concerning required actions are mixed with suggestions as to what other actions are "appropriate" or "desirable."

The Episcopal Church's liturgy provides this indefiniteness and suggestion just at a time when past unofficial guides in ceremonial no longer give much help. Certain features of ceremony trace to the early church, and such antiquity gives them authority. But the ceremonial tradition is loose and varied, and it must be adapted for new conditions. Since the 1840s, ceremonial practice in Anglicanism had been informed by: (1) rather uncritical use of Roman ceremonial, building it around a core of *The Book of Common Prayer;* (2) attempts to discover and popularize an independent "English Use," historically rooted, compatible with the Prayer Book but at the same time catholic, rich and pleasing; and (3) efforts to select from the more elaborate norms while keeping to a rather plain standard. Books representing these ceremonial traditions—"high," or "advanced," or "low," and somewhat ecclectic—were in use until the middle of this century.

Insofar as such guides drew (sometimes without realizing it) on Roman practice, the Post-Council collapse of Roman "rubricism" has left them without a detailed, rigid standard that might be followed or adapted. Insofar as these guides were keyed to the rubrics and texts of older Prayer Books, they have become all but unusable. The Prayer Book rubrics now open room for judgment. Lacking the external guides of the past, groups that think through liturgy for a congregation may be well advised to draw and duplicate a scale sketch of the floor plan of their own building. For each important event, they might plot the movement of persons, try things, walk through events ahead of time, and change whatever does not seem to work as expected. Some reliable printed guides, suited to the present liturgies, are beginning to appear (see Section 10 of the reading list). Good parish models are becoming more common; advice can be sought and found. But the creation of a local "customary" is a task for which local talent remains best.

• Intelligibility •

The contemporary emphasis on popular participation in liturgy has led also to an insistence that liturgy be clear. People must know what they are hearing, saying and doing. They must be treated as the intelligent adult persons they are.

Such a concern is undeniably important. Christians share a fundamental account of meaning. The church should, in a secular age, be a catechetical community, learning and rehearsing its own gospel and exploring its implications. Liturgy is a fabric of signs, signs that express and instruct. They should be capable of explanation, and they should be explained according to the capacity of the learners.

There is, to be sure, a strangeness or otherness about the church's language and symbol system. Terms and images that present-day worshipers use familiarly have origins remote from twentieth-century American life. In liturgy we make free allusions to a biblical past, and we place ourselves in the ancient Near East. We are Israel, and Abraham is our father. We name Semitic tribes and note with satisfaction the overthrow of Og, King of Bashan. We know about wandering shepherds, the barren wilderness, and the importance of reliable wells. At every Easter, we are brought out of Egypt. Yes, I was (tremblingly) there when they crucified my Lord. Such exotic terms and the peculiar hermeneutical process by which Christians make them their own must be learned. So intelligibility in liturgy does not mean that everything must be immediately clear to everyone who listens in. These terms and symbols are part of the complex presentation of the divine self-revelation (a revelation whose matrix is the time-space specificities of history) which bears the whole weight of Christians' living and dying. Such symbols are not learned quickly, but are appropriated in the doubting, the believing, and the personal struggle of a lifetime.

Because these terms and symbols are bound up with deep levels of the understanding of ourselves and of God, their intelligibility is of a special sort. Symbols suggest, picture, present, or intimate. They do not define, explain, or tell all. We understand them, but our understanding tells us that there is still more to be understood. Symbols are known from within, by participation; we come to understand them as through them we come to understand ourselves. Christian consciousness is so filled with this symbolic material that hymns, the liturgical texts, and popular preaching frequently move from one symbolic term to another with little worry about mixed metaphors. There is a tendency (in liturgy, and to some extent even in formal theology) to explain one symbol by others, to compound symbolic terms. Most Christians come to find this imaginative matrix of faith and worship as near to them and as life-imparting as the air they breathe. Familiar though they may be, there is always, in the symbols that impart our own meaning to ourselves, a depth of mystery.

Something always lies unexplained below our present level of understanding. When we take our symbol system in hand and seek to explain it exhaustively, or to control it, we tell it what it means. We reduce it to illustration of some discursive meaning to which we have access. When that happens, the symbol cannot tell us anything more. We have told it what we will permit it to tell us.

Thus the quest for intelligibility in liturgy must be appropriate to the character of the material. It does not consist in explanation of the sort that a geometry proof might give. It is rather the opening of inquiry from inexhaustible sources. Our intellectual quest begins with symbolic, life-interpreting material; it returns to it; and it never finishes with it. The sources of ultimate meaning are never perfectly clear. They are our mode of access to God and ourselves, and they will be somewhat opaque as long as we and God are only known in part. Liturgy will not deliberately seek confusion or obfuscation. But liturgical rationalism would be as bad as liturgical mumbo-jumbo. Liturgy holds before the believing community its basic sources of shared meaning, sources that will cease to be authoritative or effective when we think we have them all reduced to explanation.

So persons engaged in the preparation of liturgy seek clarity rather than confusion. But that does not mean linear tidiness. Visible images, poetic or mythic terms, and the like, are not left behind as one becomes more informed. Rational explanation creates an elite of those who understand and know. Before symbols, we all are learners all our lives. The preparers of any liturgical event need to acquire some appreciation for this stuff of the imagination and some skill in handling it sympathetically.

• Tradition •

The common notion that structure, tradition and model are opposed to freedom, innovation and creativity needs to be questioned. Liturgy is a continuous activity of a community that persists in time—an activity constitutive of that community's very life. As such, worship takes much of its meaning from first-century moments of formation, from rapid developments in the second, third and fourth centuries, and from later generations of testing under many conditions in many cultures. It is a mistake to think that only those things are "creative" that are original with ourselves or have been brought forth within living memory. The worship of the great tradition, far from being uncreative, is a repository of the creative work of many centuries. When one draws on that tradition, one does not deny creativity but rather one accepts the extraordinary range of creativity to which one is heir.

In liturgy we interact with the past. To fail to do so leads to faddy, trendy worship, worship that soon grows thin and unsatisfying. It can neither judge nor redeem, for it tells us what we already know. When we use, and repossess as our own, elements that have come to us from previous generations, believers of the past join our prayer and praise. They bring what we would not find from our own resources. Our faith grows by their participation in it. Edmund Burke once spoke of society as a compact between "the dead, the living, and the yet unborn." The church and its worship are something like that. It is through the inheritance we receive that we learn who we are and are given a base from which to address the problems of our day. We are supplied with a deep memory. But indebtedness to the past does not mean that all that needs to be said has been said. History, as it moves, does produce real newness; many features of our contemporary experience are without precedent. We are entitled to replicate the past—not by doing in our time only what was done in past times, but by being as resourceful and innovative in our time as the best creators in the past have been in other times.

Moreover, in a heritage as long and as rich as is the liturgical tradition, we often move best into the future by rediscovering some forgotten or repressed part of the past. Any specific tradition in which we stand is partial, a narrowing of the inheritance, and left to itself it can become decadent. Renewal often comes not from repudiating the past, but from moving from a small confining past to a more spacious, more open past. The mystery of history is the mystery of ourselves. It is never exhausted. We turn to it as a fresh resource. It is corrective for our own temporal provincialism.

These general reflections are all by way of saying that persons who take responsibility for shaping worship today should not be self-important about their task. They are present-day fashioners of a centuries-long, richly varied action of the believing community. They will misunderstand their own modern-day task if they disregard those who have forged the place from which they address the liturgical situation of the late twentieth century. In addition to looking for the latest prayer texts or music, or instead of turning too quickly to their own work, those who prepare today's liturgies should familiarize themselves with the liturgical heritage. All present-day Christian worshipers are debtors. No one should acknowledge that debt more gratefully than those charged with the preparation of worship for congregations of today.

• Routinization •

Actions that are performed repeatedly tend to be done in much the same way each time. The tendency to habit shows up in such ordinary things as where students sit at a seminar (there are few changes after the first session), or the way in which one disposes of one's raincoat and boots when coming into the house on a rainy day. This tendency to habit is not only inevitable, it can be benign; such repetition makes life simpler. It eliminates the anxiety that might otherwise arise as to where one would like to sit today and why, or what one's philosophy of hanging up one's coat really is. With habituated actions out of the way, one can get on with what is important—what today's seminar is about, or what one is going to do now that one is in out of the rain.

Such routinization seems especially to be associated with actions that lie close to the sources of personal meaning—with dealings with the sacred. In such actions, some predictability and ritual, even if not particularly graceful ritual, seem required by the character of the action.

Our liturgical actions are a fabric of words and gestures to put us in touch with God. These words and gestures are not God. Yet it is probably impossible for us to draw close to God (to use a spatial term in describing that which is not spatial) without some mode of words and gestures. We are conscious, embodied persons. We do not become more fully ourselves through shutting off our expressive words and acts. But the words and gestures fail their purpose when they intrude. They cease to be a place of vantage from which we can attend to God, and instead, they must be attended to. It is rather like a sound amplification system in an auditorium. It is meant to assist unobtrusively our immediate awareness of music or speech. But what happens when a microphone goes dead? Or when a loudspeaker begins to howl? Our attention is drawn to the thing that we should be using while remaining largely unaware of it. Many of the actions, verbal responses, visual associations of worship become routinized. In a rich liturgical system that does not mean that they never change. But it means that even the changes are within certain familiar predictabilities. There are rapid rhythms that pass within broader, slower rhythms. This constancy can be freeing. We are not made anxious about unexpected demands or unwanted surprise. We are free to concentrate on God, rather than to worry over what is likely to be sprung on us this time.

Shapers of worship will, of course, be alert to new components of liturgy, and they will care about variety. But for those features of their creative work to show up well, the designers must also respect the background of constant, stable features and actions that provide worshipers a place to stand.

• Rhythm •

A liturgical event that is satisfying seems to be held together by an inner pulse or rhythm. It is not just a matter of the rate at which persons speak—although the clustering of emphatic sounds in English makes our speech come in a series of impulses. It is the rhythm of speech, but it is also the way in which one action flows into another, the ease with which persons work together, the sense that the principal musician has for pacing the liturgical event as a whole.

I am indebted for this awareness to a group at the Graduate School of Education at Harvard University which a few years ago recorded on videotape an All Saints' Day liturgy at an Episcopal Church and later analyzed the tape as an act of communication. They found that a remarkable sense of pace ran through the liturgy as a whole. One could at some points almost conduct the action as it appeared on the recording. These analysts (led by the Reverend Frederick Erickson) were convinced that this inner pulse is felt by persons in the congregation, although most of them would be unaware of it. When the liturgy seems satisfying, the rhythm is one of the factors that make it so. And when a reliable sense of pace is missing or is broken into rather badly, the liturgy seems less satisfying and the worshipers cannot quite say why.

This analysis, as demonstrated by the example on the tape, seemed new and surprising. Yet at the same time it seemed right. One knew that one had experienced liturgies that had this unifying pacing, and liturgies that lacked it. A nonverbal factor of considerable importance, although of some subtlety, had been identified.

At the parish that was used for this test (a fairly high-church congregation), the clergy had worked together for some time and the organist had also been at the parish for a number of years. Thus the principal persons who set the rhythm for the liturgy as a whole knew one another's ways. In addition to their internalization of the liturgy itself, they had long practice in adjusting to one another and to the eucharistic room. No one was, by conscious effort, making the pulse of the liturgy what it was. Yet it was demonstrably present and important. There was no rule, and everyone was obeying it.

The matter of liturgical rhythm (like the matter of routinization just spoken of) no doubt carries some complexity. To put in a good word for rhythm (and routinization) could commend something incantatory and almost hypnotic. Such counsel seems to imply that it is acceptable if attentiveness lapses while worshipers are under the power of a pervasive beat. A liturgical rationalist might charge that although the business of liturgical rhythm, as described here, may be more refined than tom-toms or foot-stamping, it is similarly subversive of true worship. To venture a reply, is it not more a different mode of attentiveness? One does not, while at worship, want to let one's mind go to sleep. Much that is going on is important and invites thought; it should not be missed. However, in a fixed liturgy, a great deal is packed into a limited span of time. To expect worshipers to follow each word or idea with focused attention would place an unbearable burden on them. Liturgy should not be felt as a rapid succession of demands. Nor should it appeal exclusively to our cerebral side—whichever part of the brain that is taken to be. Rather, it should carry us in a large, spacious movement—letting our attention be drawn at times while letting it relax at others. While we are at worship we are not just informed by ideas, but we are carried, in our psychosomatic wholeness, by a unified act with which we engage in different ways at different times. The rhythm is a factor in establishing this unified act in which we may find ourselves as we will.

It will not help much to labor this idea of rhythm as a unifying factor in liturgy, as though ministers were under an obligation to establish such a deep inner pulse—which members of the congregation should discover and follow carefully. Probably in most places where this sort of thing is present it is present quite unconsciously. To seek to impart it by a liturgical metronome or a ballet master's baton might do more harm than good. Yet the matter is important and seldom recognized. No doubt some clergy, servers, choir members, ushers and others do this sort of thing very well without ever thinking about it. Others who do it badly will not be helped by calling attention to an awkwardness that may be beyond their conscious control. Gracefulness in such a matter probably derives from the presence of a deep inner kinetic sense.

But it may be useful to call attention to this factor as something to notice. When persons in a chancel and at an organ console are doing things well, an awareness that a somewhat impersonal rhythm has taken charge may help them know what is happening. When liturgy seems jerky and lacking in flow, the idea that a fundamental rhythm is being violated may help identify what has gone wrong. Mainly, however, this would seem to be an underlying factor in liturgy—important, but subject to conscious control in only a limited way.

• Music •

Music is undoubtedly the most powerful of the nonverbal components of worship. It gives an emotional tonality to the parts and the whole. As the seasons pass from fast to festival, and as moments within the liturgy are interpreted by hymns, we are made aware of affective meanings through the power of music. A musician and former colleague makes the point by asking, "How many people leave church humming the sermon?"

Thus the choice of hymns and the use that is made of music are among the most important decisions preparers of liturgy make. Perhaps the most useful general counsel that can be given at this point is that the music is always to be subordinate to the liturgical whole in which it takes its place. It is meant to emphasize and underline directions that are given by the liturgical event—never to take it over and lead it in uncongenial ways. It is a part, an important, interpretive part, of the liturgical whole. Many persons who are trained as musicians do not have a great deal of knowledge about liturgy. And, of course, some clergy who have a measure of liturgical knowledge may be musically illiterate. Some collaboration is called for between persons who professionally may not understand one another.

It is also the case that church musicians often think primarily in terms of the organ and the choir. Their training and their interests point in those directions. They are accomplished performers, and as a rule the only pipe organs in a community are in churches. The congregations seek good players, and the players seek challenging and satisfying instruments. But beyond the interest in organs and choirs, attention needs to be given to that central, constant feature of church music: the congregation's singing.

Congregational singing is a remarkable social phenomenon. Where else does a group of persons, who are not gathering primarily as musicians, assemble to sing? Where else is collective singing so important to a communal event? The church might be described in many ways by a student of behavior, but it would have to be described, among the other ways, as a people who sing. The frequent New Testament references to the church as a singing community (1 Cor. 14:15,26; Eph.5:18–20; Col.3:16; Jas.5:13; and [implied] Rev.4&5) suggest that sung congregational praise is as old as the Christian tradition itself.

This fundamental, constitutive role of congregational singing (that is to say, nonmonastic singing of vernacular texts) was a great rediscovery of the Reformation, and hymns were a principal carrier of the spirituality of the churches that followed the Reformation lead. The opening created by the Reformation has been entered by hymn writers from the German pietists, the English Methodists, the eighteenth-century giant Isaac Watts, and scores of nineteenth- and twentieth-century writers. Now, however, attractive styles of congregational singing are common in Roman congregations, and composers who write for the Roman church may, as a group, be producing more fresh usable material than are those who work in other traditions. Many of the texts for this newer music consist of tags from Psalms or of easily grasped congregational refrains, which in many instances alternate with verses that make greater musical demands and are sung by a choir or soloist.

The basic carrier of the music of worship should be the singing congregation. Instruments are to assist and support it. Any trained choir will have its own moments to do music that is sung for the glory of God and whose complexity puts it beyond the ability of the congregation. But it is not to do the congregation's singing for it. The people should be a singing people, and they should be heard.

This may be one of the places at which the smaller congregations—which far outnumber the larger congregations—can engage in some genuine discovery. Whatever small churches may lack in the way of an organ or a good choir, they still have that most basic component of church music—human voices. Small groups, with the singers brought fairly close together, can learn to enjoy singing and to hearing themselves sing. It is possible to investigate the resources of one's town (perhaps enlisting the help of persons in the school system) and find instrumentalists who can support the congregation with some of the gentler instruments, such as recorders, woodwinds, or strings. Guitars can be gentle and supportive, and they have come into frequent use as accompanying instruments. But it is also possible to play the guitar somewhat aggressively—to play it *at* a congregation, rather than in, with, and under a congregation.

When such resources are secured, the instrumentalists can learn to take joy in their work, to vary their playing for the hymn or the season, to be discriminating accompanists. Meanwhile, the sound of the congregation is heard.

Some of the hymns of *The Hymnal 1982* (and others in other modern collections) have musical qualities that can be heard best in a small congregation. For instance, hymns that can be sung in canon are unlikely to be sung in that way in the larger, more formal congregations. But in a smaller group, in which, in effect, everyone is choir, such a hymn can be tried until it is well in hand and sung in the liturgy with a sense of accomplishment. Small can be beautiful.

• Practice •

It is common for the value of "spontaneity" in worship to be so emphasized that the proper professionalism and care in executing worship somehow comes into question. "If an act is programmed and rehearsed, it cannot be deeply felt."

But if liturgy is a somewhat complex corporate action, in which a number of persons take complementary leading roles, and into which a considerable amount of variety is deliberately planned, it will not be done well by happenstance. The persons who prepare worship are like the choreographers of dance or the directors of drama. They are to plan the best use of people in available space that they can; they are to consider the roles of individuals in relation to the design of the whole; they are to consider words, movement, gesture, color and drama. They must judge where the central emphasis should fall. A clear customary for a parish or for an important service need not be intricate, but it does need to be the result of deliberate determinations. Then, having a clear, workable design, it must be given the necessary preparation so that it will deliver what it promises.

Such preparation may require a walk-through by the participants some time prior to the liturgy. It may require lectors to read their assigned texts aloud in the church for others to comment on. A good flow of participants to the right locations, or catching the signals on when to move, or projecting one's voice adequately in a large room are usually acquired skills, and participants should not inflict their fumbling first efforts on the congregation.

Somehow we take for granted that such preparation is required in the performing arts—the hours that a violinist spends practicing, a cast's weeks of rehearsal for a play, or even the many rehearsals that a choir uses to familiarize itself with a new anthem. At a play we can often note an actor's gesture or an exchange of lines between two characters. But when we think about it, we realize that that gesture had been planned and learned. The spontaneous exchange had been rehearsed and its pace so internalized that the actors can do it well day after day. We see the free action; we cannot but think it arose from the actor's actual feelings at the time; we see the fitting response from another actor; but we do not see the hours in front a mirror that lie behind its good execution.

Worship is not entertainment and the vested and speaking leaders are not performers before an audience. The whole congregation is a body of active participants. Whatever leading parts are taken by a few are for enabling the worship of the many, and the worship is for the building up of the church and for the glory of God. There are enough parallels, however, between the public acting and speaking roles of those who lead worship and those who perform in music or in the theatre so that some basic lessons may be learned. The point is not that ministers in liturgy should feign feelings or convictions they do not have; the point is rather that in public roles the expressive conveying of what one does feel or does want to convey is a skill that few persons acquire without effort and attention. Should those whose task is to enable the community of faith to perform its central business give less care to their work than performing artists give to theirs?

Behind every well-conceived and well-executed liturgical event, there is quite a lot of hidden disciplined work. Of course one does not want to create an atmosphere of tenseness in the participants. If someone forgets, or if an accident happens, it should be within a community of supporting persons who know that they too have at times forgotten obvious things and have been victims of embarrassing mishaps. The persons who lead in worship should be able to relax in the job and be worshipers too. But an atmosphere of relaxation in the job and of joy in work well carried through is best brought about by the sort of advance preparing and rehearsing that lets each participant internalize her or his role. Inadequate preparation heightens anxiety, while adequate preparation is freeing. There will inevitably be some tension when one has a public role to carry out—many experienced and accomplished musicians or actors or preachers say that even after many years they still get "the jitters." Such tension need not be harmful even if it is a nuisance. It can pull from leaders of worship the extra effort that leads to excellence. But there need not be the destructive tension that comes from not knowing what is expected of one.

• Offering •

The drive for quality in the preparation and carrying out of liturgy comes from within liturgy itself. One does not want to do good liturgy well just to display the personal gifts of the ministers or the good taste of the parish. Liturgy is a fabric of words and actions which, in its whole and in its parts, is an offering to God. It begins in the believing awareness of God. It catches up in it the sin and redeemed–ness of our humanity, and in Christ, it bears it all to God. The church is renewed in its own deepest life through the worship that is not primarily directed to its own instruction or inspiration but *ad maiorem gloriam dei.*

Thus, in preparing worship and in carrying it through, it is worthwhile to ask, "What does this music, or this mode of performance of it, or this ritual action, or this use of color say about God? What sort of God does this modest prayer and pageantry suggest?''

Clearly, there is worship which, without the worshipers being aware of it, suggests an indulgently sentimental God—not the God of the prophets. Or worship that projects a God who is plain, unattractive, even ugly, or a God who is austere and unapproachable. Or worship that can suggest a God who is reached primarily through intellectual processes, a God remote from our embodied wholeness. The opposite extreme, of course, suggests a God who is easily manipulated by our formulas and charms. The God of Christian worship is the God of the biblical revelation that centers finally in the cross and resurrection of Jesus, the place where God has met and overcome our human fallenness. This God reaches us by gift, an initiative from the other side. And before this God and the wonder of divine acceptance, all persons are equally debtors to grace. The biblical story realistically touches the depth of human tragedy, and it discloses, beyond the tragedy, a glory at the heart of things. Worship is asked to hold some of the richness of this redemptive whole before us week by week.

This standard, interior to the very principle of worship, requires that nothing cheap, tawdry, or self-important pass into worship. Such things are not worthy to be laid on the altar.

It is easy to say such a thing, but harder to know what one has meant by it. Perhaps such a comment implies an understood body of criteria by which it is clear what is and what is not cheap, tawdry, or self-important. But some persons are genuinely touched by something that other persons find superficial and banal. Who sets the standards? Such questions go to the heart of the complex issues of liturgy and culture. The answer is not to accept for liturgy some mode of elitism—what is accepted by "the best people." Liturgy is, in the right sense of the term, "vulgar," an expression of the people. One remembers of Jesus that "the common people heard him gladly." But neither is the answer to accept ingredients into worship uncritically because they happen to be popular. True worship arises out of a specially called people, a people delivered and renewed by a great Gospel, not out of a people who have let the Gospel become captive to bourgeois sentiment.

So persons who prepare liturgy must frequently make discriminations—and there is no objective criterion for knowing that all of their choices are wise. Some hymns that will never get into anthologies of masterpieces of the language are yet good poetry *of their own sort.* Many outstanding works of Christian art, rhetoric and music are devout and deeply moving, but they are not suitable for specifically liturgical use. The credentials of those who prepare liturgies are established, not by their always knowing what is worthy of God and permitting nothing less, but by the fact that they are endlessly working with this question.

•

CHAPTER FOUR

Background of the Eucharistic Rites

Episcopalians who take part in the preparation of liturgical events are engaged with a powerful text, *The Book of Common Prayer.* The parts of this book comprise an organic whole in which the here-and-now experience of worshipers is enlarged by the classic structure of Christian confession, proclamation, doxology, initiation, Eucharist, festival and the like—all of them expressing the given faith. The Prayer Book rites have unity, design and sequence. Their words are chosen with care; their rubrics give adequate direction without prescribing in oppressive detail. Despite the choices that it allows, *The Book of Common Prayer* is more than a resource book on which planners may draw for purposes of their own determining. Its services convey meaning; they embody centuries of devotion and the intention of the Great Church. The task of those who prepare liturgies (like that of a theatrical producer with a good play, or of an orchestral conductor with a well-crafted score) is to understand and cooperate with their text. They ask: What does it give to us and require of us if we are to enact it responsibly and joyfully?

To some extent, an interior sympathy with the Prayer Book is accessible to every grateful user of it. No other qualification can substitute for intelligent regular participation in Prayer Book worship. Other sources can teach us about the Prayer Book best if the Prayer Book itself has been our primary teacher.

Now those who take part in preparing liturgical events will want their sympathy with this basic text for corporate prayer to be an informed sympathy. In part, the desirable information is historical. The Prayer

Book is a contemporary form of the long heritage of Christian worship. It carries much of that prior history (early, Medieval, English and American) within itself. How did these present-day rites come to be? What forms have they taken at other times among the divergent Anglican churches, and among the equally loyal Christians in other traditions? From such historical information come questions of judgment. Is there any definable norm or authority as to what a rite is when it is most fully and truly itself? But another part of the understanding that persons who prepare worship events might seek is functional. Each rite in the Prayer Book is a fabric of words to be said or sung and of directions for actions. What is the purpose of this rite? Where is the dramatic center? How is it to be carried out? How do these parts contribute to the intended whole? Why is this said where it is rather than elsewhere? What persons are to speak these words that appear on the printed page? Where do these persons stand or sit, and how do they move? What use is made of music, gesture, or color to interpret the event as a dramatic whole?

Needless to say, such questions, historical and functional, could be pursued through a substantial and growing literature. (A note at the end of this chapter directs a reader to some reliable sources written particularly for the Episcopal Church, and a lengthy reading list concludes this book.)

Persons who care about worship and take responsibility for it become lifelong students. Even though the informational and conceptual background for an understanding of liturgy is large, for many acts of worship the heart of the matter is fairly accessible. This chapter, which concerns the Holy Communion, can be only an introduction, but we need not wait until we are fully informed before we take a role in liturgical preparation. The basic wisdom required for understanding the rites of the church is not terribly recondite. It is as much a matter of sensitive attention to what we (together with thousands of other worshipers) half-know already as it is a matter of new learning.

The Prayer Book, in its opening words, identifies the Holy Eucharist as "the principal act of Christian worship on the Lord's Day," (BCP, p. 13). Those who engage in preparing for worship will be occupied with this service of word and sacrament on Sundays and other feast days. Any principles put forward for this central act can be adapted by resourceful planners so as to apply in appropriate ways to noneucharistic occasions. This chapter will provide some background in the history of the Eucharist and will describe elemental factors that have shaped the structure and sequence of the Prayer Book text and given us our present understanding of eucharistic celebration. Chapter Five will discuss the process of preparing for a Sunday Eucharist using Rite I (BCP, pp. 316–49) or Rite II (BCP, pp. 350–95). The prayer of general intercession, which is a part of all of the eucharistic orders of the Prayer Book, is the subject of Chapter Six. Chapter Eight will consider the opportunities and problems in using, on appropriate occasions, "An Order for Celebrating the Holy Eucharist," (BCP, pp. 400–05).

• Major Structural Units of the Eucharist •

The Christian Eucharist has developed in a bipartite form. The two principal units are indicated by interior headings in the Prayer Book. On pages 323 (for Rite I) and 355 (for Rite II) is set the title: "The Word of God." No other heading appears in the same type face until pages 333 and 361, where the line reads: "The Holy Communion."

These divisions of the Eucharist trace to two sources in Jewish worship from which each derives its distinctive character.

1. The *synagogue* was evidently the product of the Jewish Dispersion. Although Jews in captivity might be far from their homeland and the Temple, they were not far from God, and they need not lose their corporate identity. Wherever they were, they had the Torah, the books of God's law. In exile, a form of worship grew up that was local, corporate, and nonpriestly. Persons (that is to say, male persons) functioned according to their gifts, learning, and competence.

At the beginning of the Christian era, the synagogue service, centering on the Scriptures, may have gone something like this: There were readings, usually intoned. One was from "Moses" (the first five books of the Bible), and one was from some other part of the Hebrew Bible (the "writings" or the "prophets"). Each of the readings would be followed by Psalms—the Psalter being the hymn book of the synagogue. The *shema* would be said or sung; it is a central affirmation of Israel's faith in the one God and in the unique bond between itself and God. (The text is from Deut.6:4–9;11:13–21;Num.15:37–41.) There were formal "benedictions"—intercessions for a range of concerns. If a qualified teacher were present, there would be an explanation of the Scriptures.

Jesus and his followers were Galilean villagers whose experience of worship would have been experience of the synagogue. The earliest mission of the church went to synagogue Jews of the Dispersion. The form of worship that was familiar in this setting was, over time, adapted as the first part of the Christian Eucharist. The synagogue liturgy also provided, as monasticism arose, a model for the Divine Office. The Old Testament scriptures were interpreted in a Christological way; and, as they became available, documents authoritative for Christians came to be read as well as the Greek Old Testament. Prayer was in Christ's name, but the Jewish derivation of the basic form remained clear. This form has proved remarkably durable. For the first part of the time Christians meet in the eucharistic assembly, we are, so to speak, at the Christian synagogue, hearing the Word of God and engaging in prayer and praise.

2. The *family meal* has been for Jews a sign of faith, even when Temple worship was impossible and synagogue worship difficult. The principal evening meal was an occasion for the members of a family to share with God and one another through the good things of the earth. A senior household member, usually the father, would preside. Before the meal there would be a blessing, with a brief prayer and the breaking and distributing of a loaf. After the meal a special cup of wine would be blessed and passed. The blessing over the cup would usually be a longer prayer, giving thanks for the food, recalling the covenant, and anticipating the fulfillment of God's promises.

This simple, essentially domestic ritual is the obvious source of the second major part of the Christian Eucharist. It is what Jesus and his followers did at the Last Supper, and it is what, with many modifications and adaptations, Christians have done since. By the middle of the second century the meal itself had disappeared, and the ceremonial bread which had come before it and the cup which had followed it were joined. But continuities are unmistakable. For the second part of the eucharistic meeting, we are a family at a table.

By the second century the Christians had brought these two types of assembly together for the usual Sunday gathering. Both of these ritual forms were reinterpreted in the church, so as to become Christocentric. Christ was the divine Word, and he was the Bread of Life. But it is clear that, with whatever development they may have undergone at Christian hands, both parts took their origin from Jewish forms of worship.

• The "Shape" of the Meal •

The first part of the Eucharist, the Service of the Word, is quite flexible. There can be many readings or few; much music or little; lengthy preaching or brief; full or terse intercessions. The second part, the meal, has a greater "logic" or sequence. Much is lost if this flow is interrupted or if the natural emphasis of its movement is distorted. Through a tortuous history, the sequence and emphasis of the Christian ritual meal had, by the late Middle Ages, in fact become distorted. The Reformers were unable to do much more than to react against their immediate inheritance, and the Counter-Reformation did little to address the misplaced emphases. One could argue that since the sixteenth century Anglican liturgies have been less trapped in reaction than most others, but the argument is likely to impress Anglicans more than Christians of other communions.

In our century, the Anglican liturgiologist Gregory Dix looked at the biblical and early Christian sources of the meal and identified what he called its "four-action shape." In the forty-five years since his great work *The Shape of the Liturgy* (first published, 1945), not all of his judgments have escaped criticism. Even so, Dix's analysis has been so influential that it deserves some explication. Dix found a recurrent set of verbs in the New Testament accounts of the Lord's Supper. Jesus *took, blessed, broke* and *gave* the bread. Then, after the supper, he *took, blessed* and *gave* the cup—seven named actions. Within a few decades, the meal had dropped out, and the ceremonial actions with the bread and with the wine had been joined. The seven actions of the New Testament accounts had become the four actions of the early liturgies:

Taking: A service which in its perhaps quite lengthy first part had not come to focus on bread and wine nor had the character of a meal now brings bread and wine (and on occasion other things as well) to a presiding person at a table.

Blessing: This presiding person prays words of blessing, thanks or acknowledgment for creation and redemption. These words are operative, performative words—of which more later.

Breaking: The bread and wine, which are brought and blessed in a single loaf and a single vessel, are reduced to a form suitable for the many who are to partake. In the early sources this action was interpreted as speaking of the oneness and manyness of the Church in Christ.

Giving: The climax of the action is clearly in the administration of the bread and wine to the congregation. The prior acts—placing the gifts on the table, blessing and breaking— are all for the sake of the giving.

This clear "shape" was sustained in the early liturgies, not so much because Christians carefully analyzed the language of the New Testament or other literary sources as because ritual (especially ritual of meals) is quite conservative. But in time the shape became obscured.

The action became *clericalized*. The people stopped offering, and they stopped receiving (Dix's actions 1 and 4). The story as to when they stopped and why is complicated, insofar as it is understood. It was part of a shift in sacramental piety by which the Eucharist came to be regarded as awesome and unapproachable. This reduction of the people's parts shifted the center of the action to the part most clearly reserved for the priests, the consecration. Thus this ritual moment (Dix's action 2) became virtually an end in itself; it was the moment of miraculous transformation. The fraction (Dix's third action) had, in the early centuries, been a functional transition between consecration by the priest and communion by the people. When noncommunicating attendance became usual, the fraction ceased to be functional. In the Prayer Books it came to be a mimetic action, by the celebrant, within the consecration itself.

The consecration, further, became quite *theatrical*. By the late Middle Ages, focus fell on the priest's dramatic elevation of the host and the chalice at the words "This is my body . . . my blood." This was taken to be the active, transforming moment, and the people came to watch it, rather than to eat and drink. Eucharistic participation was no longer corporate and active, but inward and passive. One watched and entertained appropriate affections. A heavy emphasis was placed on the inaccessibility of the Eucharist and the unworthiness of the worshiper. The churches were full, and Mass was every Sunday (and of course many times a day in certain churches). But communion was very infrequent, and eucharistic piety was individualistic.

To sum up these matters in terms of Dix's scheme, three of the four actions, those that most pertained to the people, had been lost; and the one that remained, the distinctively priestly act, had become all but unrecognizable.

The Reformers, Continental and English, were, of course, brought up on this strangely misshapen Mass. They sought to correct it in several ways. They wanted a balance of Word and sacrament; preaching was emphasized. They argued for the link between consecration and communion. A Mass at which the people did not receive communion was compared to a banquet that is prepared, but at which no one eats. Of course, when the people did receive, it should be the wine as well as the bread. Through the use of the vernacular (and other less successful devices, such as exhortations or little speeches in the liturgy itself) the Reformers sought to make the liturgy once again an intelligible people's expression. In these liturgical efforts, they had varying success. Preaching was given greater emphasis, but no major church of the Reformation succeeded in making a unity of Word and sacrament the regular Sunday practice. When the communion was celebrated, most of the people received; but that was on occasions once a month or once every three months. Some of the Reformers reduced the consecration prayer drastically.

Luther and his influence provided the tradition that carries his name with fine hymns from its beginning, and by the eighteenth century popular hymnody was a part of the worship of all Western churches except the Roman. Apart from this feature, worship in the reformed traditions was hardly more corporate and participatory than Medieval worship had been. New preacher simply replaced old priest. In this matter again, Anglican worship may have engaged the voice of the people more than any other from the sixteenth century to the mid-twentieth. There were important gaps in the historical knowledge accessible in the sixteenth century and much acrimonious polemic over liturgy and sacraments. The liturgical work of the sixteenth century was able to criticize late Medieval theology and practice, but it was able to transcend them only slightly. Yet the traditions of worship formed at that time have proved remarkably durable.

It is only in the twentieth century that really new forces are altering Western liturgical thought and practice. The change began first in historical scholarship, then in pastoral concern.

Since worship is a continuing function of the Christian community, it is, to a large extent, understood (and misunderstood) through its own history. In the late nineteenth and early twentieth centuries, important liturgical documents (such as *The Didache,* c.110 C.E.?, and *The Apostolic Tradition* by Hippolytus of Rome, c.215 C.E.) were discovered, correctly dated, and critically edited. A notable body of writing, largely from the 1930s and 1940s, and representing many Christian traditions, articulated a general clarity about the history, structure, and meaning of the Christian Eucharist. One thinks of scholars such as Abbe Duchesne, F.E. Brightman, R.H. Connally, Burton Scott Easton, or E.C. Ratcliff.

The inquiry that had begun as predominantly historical, enlarged to take account of theological, pastoral, and social issues. The writers in these influential years cared about the Gospel, the church, and the social order. They wrote passionately, giving expression to what Fr. Guardini called "the spirit of the liturgy." This literature too was ecumenical. Contributors included: Odo Casel, Romano Guardini, Pius Parsch, Gerald Ellard, and J.A. Jungmann, (Roman Catholics); Archbishop Brilioth, Friedrich Heiler, and Luther Reed, (Lutherans); D. H. Hislop and W.D. Maxwell, (Scottish Presbyterians); W.H. Frere, E.C. Ratcliff, Gregory Dix, A.G. Hebert, W.P. Ladd, and Evelyn Underhill, (Anglicans). All of them sought, although from their distinct histories, a Sunday service that combined proclamation of the Word with the eucharistic meal. The consensus that developed among the writers of this period seemed to promise that worship, which had been a mark of the differences among Christian traditions, might become a factor for mutual understanding and growing unity.

But through the first sixty years of this century, actual changes in liturgical rites and practices amounted to no more than infrequent small steps. Individual congregations and movements pioneered fresh ways of worship, to be sure. But in the large liturgical churches, held by institutional inertia and by official printed texts, and in the nonliturgical churches, in the grip of custom, rapid general change seemed unlikely.

Yet it is obvious that, since the 1960s, the major liturgical traditions of the West have made substantial changes. That these changes have been as responsible, as confident, and as unified in their direction as they have been traces in considerable measure to the authoritative intellectual work done by the scholars of the previous generation.

• Anglican Appropriation of a Recovered Sense of Eucharistic Order •

Each church had to respond to the call for liturgical renewal in its own way and in awareness of its own loyalties. For Anglicans, a discriminating report on the Prayer Book was issued by the bishops of the Anglican Communion at the Lambeth Conference of 1958. The heart of the report was the identification, in three lists, of: (1) features of the Prayer Book inheritance that are of the utmost value in securing the church's catholic identity and its liturgical richness; (2) other features that are of real value, even though they are not essential in the same way as those of the first list; (3) and other features that could be modified with little loss. The Lambeth Conference is not a place for original thinking, but it is a setting in which the bishops can "own" collectively original thinking that has been done by others. This 1958 report indicated that loyal criticism of the Prayer Book was acceptable. One effect of historical scholarship is to relativize forms of worship that had seemed beyond criticism and change. One learns that present forms have grown from earlier forms, and that they will, in turn, pass into different forms, all the while being true to themselves. Another effect is to discover deep unities and continuities among the varied and changing liturgical forms. The 1958 report shows such discrimination at work in the Anglican Communion.

Another representative document came from Inter-Anglican discussion in 1964. The self-governing Anglican provinces had been undertaking liturgical revision independently. Most of them had begun with the 1662 Prayer Book—the book that had been carried by colonists and missionaries from England. Many provinces had departed from it in various ways or were beginning to do so. An inevitable question for persons concerned for the Anglican Communion was: Are there, or should there be signs of liturgical unity throughout Anglicanism, especially with respect to the Eucharist? If so, what should they be?

A small committee, under the chairmanship of the Archbishop of Uganda, Leslie Brown, issued a brief, considered report. Its judgment was that no eucharistic text, 1662 or any other, should be regarded as normative for Anglicanism. Rather, it spoke of the Eucharist as an action that moves through five phases, each of which it described briefly. The report is not a complete account of the Eucharist. Nothing is discussed in detail, and some important matters go virtually unmentioned. Some of the explanatory comments of the committee correct either the general Prayer Book tradition or else parts of it. The report, dated February 1965, is as follows:

THE STRUCTURE AND CONTENTS OF THE EUCHARISTIC LITURGY

There are five phases in the celebration of the full eucharistic rite. They are:

1. The Preparation
2. The Service of the Word of God
3. The Great Intercession
4. The Service of the Lord's Supper
5. The Dismissal

1. The Preparation: This section should not be too long, but must be adequate for a congregation which may have no other opportunity of confession and explicitly and liturgically receiving God's forgiveness. This starting section ought to be, following Cranmer, subdued in tone, but ending with praise and adoration before hearing the Word of God in the next section. A suggested order is:

A prayer and psalm or hymn of approach;
Confession and Absolution;
Psalm (or portion thereof) or hymn of praise.

The first prayer might well be the so-called "Collect for Purity." An appropriate Psalm of approach might be Psalm 43, 95, or 100. The Commandments in some form or the Kyrie could be used before the Confession. The hymn of praise at the end might be Gloria in excelsis or Te Deum.

The Preparation has to be somewhat flexible depending on local needs.

2. The Service of the Word of God: This should include a prayer focusing the thoughts of the congregation on the message God is giving through His Word on that particular day, and readings from the Old Testament, or a sermon followed by the recitation of the Creed. Psalmody or canticles can well be included in this part of the service between the readings.

3. **The Great Intercession:** This should normally be in litany form and should be not only for the Church but for the world which the Church is called to serve.

4. **The Service of the Lord's Supper:** This should include the placing of the gifts on the Lord's Table and the ancient form of Sursum Corda. The consecration prayer should be in the form of a thanksgiving for creation and for God's mighty acts in Christ and in sending the Holy Spirit. There should be a recital of the words and acts of the Lord at the Last Supper and a prayer for the communicants. The Lord's Prayer makes a fitting ending to this prayer. The Breaking of the Bread follows, and the Communion of clergy and people.

5. **The Dismissal:** The Dismissal should be short. There seems a psychological need for some corporate expression of praise when all have received Communion and returned to their places and there should be a simple sending out, without a blessing.

This report had no regulative power when it was issued; and a great deal has happened since 1965; a similar committee might not conclude just these things today. The thinking it expressed is more important than the document itself. Yet this cautious, economical report, coming as it did when widespread Anglican liturgical revision was beginning, is a landmark document that can be looked at with some care.

The 1965 report does not analyze the Eucharist in the two large parts that were described earlier in this chapter, but in five. Later Anglican and ecumenical analyses identify as many as eight. The number of divisions is not important, for in each case much the same ritual sequence is being described.

To look briefly at each of the five "phases":

The Preparation: This is probably the least decisive section of the report. The Committee itself counsels "flexibility" in awareness of local conditions. The Preparation is meant to provide a readiness for the serious listening, praying, and

sacramental sharing that follow. The report suggests removing
the confession and absolution from their place within the rite,
where they had served as preparation for communion (or for
consecration and communion), and locating them as preparation for the entire rite. Prayer Book liturgies had traditionally
begun with contrition, and the report sustains that practice.
But it suggests passing rather quickly to "praise and adoration." The *Gloria in excelsis,* which Prayer Books since 1552
had set in a postcommunion location, is proposed as one alternative to end this act of preparation.

The Service of the Word of God: Here too the report
suggests changes. At the Eucharist, the readings should include the Old Testament, as the Prayer Book provision of
Epistles and Gospels had not. This problem was only about a
century old, for from the sixteenth through much of the nineteenth century Anglican practice had combined Morning
Prayer with Holy Communion, providing an Old Testament
lesson and psalmody. The report commends locating the sermon after the readings and before the creed, thereby associating the preaching with the biblical readings more closely. The
prior order of Gospel, creed, followed by parish notices,
hymn, and sermon had opened too many busy minutes between the reading and the proclamation.

The Great Intercession: This report does not cast the intercessory prayer with the Service of Word nor as part of the
liturgy of the faithful, but makes it an action in its own right.
As to form, a litany, involving the voice of the congregation,
is commended, rather than a clerical monologue. In content,
the terms of the English-derived "Prayer for the Whole State
of Christ's Church" rather assumed a Christian commonwealth. The church and the society were identical; rulers were
"Christian rulers." Such an assumption is not realistic in an era
of secular states, necessarily separated from any church. The
terms of the church's prayers needed to be recast so as to
recognize the judging and caring work of God in the world
and the summons of the Church to serve the world.

The Service of the Lord's Supper: This brief paragraph analyzes the meal using the four actions given currency by Dix. In Anglican Prayer Books, the gifts had been placed on the Lord's Table before the intercessions. The order commended here brings the "taking" to a place after the intercessions and immediately before the "blessing," an aid to clarity. The Consecration Prayer is specified as a "thanksgiving"—of which more will be said in Chapter Seven. The thanks should include creation (which, at the time of the report, was missing from most, if not all, Anglican liturgies) and the Holy Spirit (also missing in most). The Breaking of the Bread is not to be an action within the Consecration Prayer, but an action that follows it. These few sentences clarify the sequence and meal character of this central portion of the eucharistic liturgy.

The Dismissal: In the service of Holy Communion, anything that is done after the people have received the elements risks being anticlimactic. Prayer Books from 1552 through the 1928 revision required several large postcommunion actions: a fine long Thanksgiving Prayer; the *Gloria in excelsis* (or some other proper hymn); and a blessing. Custom had added ablutions, sung amens, hymn, choir and ministers' procession, prayer from the narthex, extinguishing candles, and perhaps more. Anticlimax was compounded, all with good intentions. Hence the pertinence of the counsel "The Dismissal should be short." The report commends a corporate postcommunion expression of praise and "a simple sending out, without a blessing." Liturgists had long criticized the final blessing. Persons are blessed at the Eucharist in the taking, blessing, breaking and giving. To conclude the rite with a further act of blessing certainly suggests that those who have just received the body and blood of Christ have not yet been blessed. If one is convinced that the eucharistic action is blessing, the subsequent priestly act is clearly redundant.

This report was issued while work was being done in the Episcopal Church on "The Liturgy of the Lord's Supper" (1967), the first "trial use" eucharistic text to be issued with the authorization of General

Convention. That rite reflected many recommendations of this report, and the report text was printed as an Appendix to Prayer Book Studies XVII—not as a document that had to be adhered to, but as an indication of the representative character of that pioneering liturgy. This outline, or the thinking it summarizes, stands behind later revision: the resequencing of the 1928 Eucharist in the 1979 Rite I, the fully worded Rite II of the 1979 Prayer Book, and the schematic "An Order for Celebrating the Holy Eucharist." More broadly, the structure informs in some measure most of the revised eucharistic liturgies of the Anglican Communion.

Yet nothing in this report, apart from its implied comment on past Prayer Book practice, is distinctively Anglican. This report represents an Anglican appropriation of what is often called the "ecumenical shape of the Eucharist" which has been developing as different Christian communions, each through its own historic experience, examine the common sacramental sources, and as, in interchurch conversations, groups struggle to sort out the essentials of the eucharistic rite.

The Vatican Council (1963–65) issued as its first major document the "Constitution on the Sacred Liturgy," December 1963. Within a few years the largest, most international, most centralized, and most apparently unchanging church in Western Christendom had radically altered the language, music, appearance and style of its liturgy. Since the sixteenth century, Catholic and Protestant traditions of worship had to a great extent opposed one another in fixed attitudes of reactiveness. This initiative from the Roman Communion was a challenge and a liberation to other Christian communities. Could they examine their inherited liturgical practices and understandings with comparable rigor? The actual changes in authorized rites drew on the scholarly perspectives that had been developing in the 1930s, '40s and '50s (as mentioned above) along convergent lines in many churches. The various communions found themselves consulting the same sources, describing worship and sacraments in similar conceptualities, appraising the historical inheritance along similar lines, and thinking similarly about liturgical response to contemporary pastoral and social needs. Since the revisions of the 1960's and '70s, there has come to be an observable structural similarity in the eucharistic rites of the official liturgical books of the Anglican, Roman Catholic, Lutheran, Reformed and Methodist churches. The same underlying sequence of actions can also be seen in eucharistic texts prepared by ecumenical groups, such as the liturgy for the Consultation on Church Union, the British Joint Liturgical Group, or the "Lima" Liturgy. As churches address liturgical revision, the pervasive acceptance of a common "shape" for the Eucharist is clear.

A recent book speaks of "ecumenical convergence in celebration." Old issues and divisions are being transcended. Differing texts, customs and styles prevail not only in the churches of Christendom but also within the varied life of the larger denominations. Uniformity is neither present nor desired. But beneath the differences there is, at the Holy Communion, an underlying series of moments. As we interiorize a feel for this shape or sequence, we can pass from rite to rite in the Book of Common Prayer, or from province to province in Anglicanism, and indeed from one Christian communion to another and, at the Eucharist, be caught up in a recognizable, familiar ritual movement. To be sure, in many places, there will be unexpected responses or ceremonial; there will be elaborateness here and simplicity there. But we can discount these surprises as we move with some confidence through an intelligible, expressive series of actions.

• Note: Some Sources on the Prayer Book •

By the end of its half-century in use, the 1928 Prayer Book had alongside it Everyparson's five-foot shelf of secondary helps. There were scholarly and popular books on the history and content of the Prayer Book, ceremonial guides to putting it into practice, and sensitive presentations of the spirituality of the book, or of parts of it. Moreover, the 1928 Prayer Book was so much like the English Prayer Book (still the 1662 edition) that English discussions of the liturgy and guides for its enactment were generally usable in the Episcopal Church. But the 1979 Prayer Book differs so much from previous books that the older works of explanation have become virtually unusable. When the 1979 Prayer Book was issued, it had to stand for a time without supporting comment. The last series of "Prayer Book Studies" had grown short on interpretive content. Prayer Book Studies No. 27, "Introducing the Proposed Book of Common Prayer," written by Charles Price and issued in 1976, answered many frequently asked questions about the new liturgy, but it was a brief booklet commenting on a large and complex text.

In more recent years a number of works have been produced that give valuable understandings of the content of the Prayer Book and wise counsel on its use:

Liturgy for Living, 1979, was written by Charles Price and Louis Weil for The Church's Teaching series, as an exposition of the worship system of the Episcopal Church. It is a clear, well-considered book, good for reading through or for adult discussion groups.

Soon after the 1979 Prayer Book was authorized, Marion J. Hatchett's *Commentary on the American Prayer Book,* 1981, was ready for the press. It is a large, exact reference volume, full of information, strongest on sources and background.

Leonel L. Mitchell's *Praying Shapes Believing,* 1985, considers the Prayer Book section by section, developing themes and content with clarity, learning and skill.

Byron Stuhlman's *Prayer Book Rubrics Expanded,* 1987, goes through the Prayer Book services, noting what must be done and what might be done, giving understandings of the book's requirements, and providing reasons on the basis of which one might make informed choices where the book permits them.

The same author's *Eucharistic Celebration 1789–1979,* 1988, gives a good historical review of the Eucharist in the Prayer Book literature, with emphasis on the Episcopal Church and the making of the 1979 Book.

The rites of Christian initiation figure integrally in the liturgy. Catechumens may be present and their progress towards baptism may be publicly recognized at periods during the year (*The Book of Occasional Services,* 1979, pp. 112–25). Baptism is, to the extent possible, to fall on several mandated occasions in the year—all of them major festivals (BCP p. 312, first rubric). When on those occasions there are no baptisms, the baptismal promises may be renewed by the congregation (BCP, p. 312, fourth rubric). The bishop's visit is, of course, a major occasion for the congregation, observed liturgically by a unified event, under the bishop's general presidency, that contains the preaching of the Word, and (when there are candidates) baptisms, confirmations, receptions, and reaffirmation of baptismal promises, followed by the Eucharist at which the bishop presides. For help in the liturgical, pastoral, and ritual aspects of these events, there are Theodore Eastman's valuable book *The Baptizing Community,* 1982, and Daniel B. Stevick, *Baptismal Moments; Baptis-*

mal Meanings, 1987, a broad historical and thematic study, culminating in a close commentary on the Prayer Book rites. (Section 10 of the reading list at the end of this book gives some titles on ceremonial.)

Alas, books such as those mentioned here (as well as those in the later, longer list) go out of print for reasons that have little to do with the worth of the book or its continued usefulness in the church. Liturgy, as a continuing activity of the Christian community, carries its history with it; and many books that are quite old can remain of considerable value. But even books of recent date can unexpectedly become hard to secure.

Many questions that come to the minds of persons preparing acts of worship would be answered in these books. But each has its own purpose and organization. It would be fairest to become familiar with the content of each as the author has set it forth, rather than going to the index, seeking quick and ready answers for urgent questions. They are books to be met on their own terms, to read and to live with.

CHAPTER FIVE

Corporate Preparation of Liturgy: Sunday Morning, Rite I or Rite II

Previous chapters of this book have urged that serious advance preparation now is not optional but required if liturgy is to be as good as it can be. But there is in the Episcopal Church relatively little experience of corporate shaping of worship, neither before-the-event preparation nor after-the-event evaluation. Thus questions come to mind: Who does this preparing? What are the preparatory tasks? How do the preparers go about their work? What skills are sought or developed? What problems can be expected?

To begin: regardless of the size of the congregation, the ordering of the worship life of a parish and the specific preparation of each liturgical occasion are fairly complex tasks. Lines of authority need to be clear and simple. Control of worship is by canon (III.15.1a) "vested in the Rector, subject to the Rubrics of *The Book of Common Prayer,* the Canons of the Church, and the godly counsel of the Bishop." Major decisions concerning worship and leading roles in liturgical leadership will be taken by the cleric in charge of the congregation or by persons he or she appoints. Although final responsibility is clear enough, it is self-defeating if authority in this matter is exercised autocratically. The church is a consensual society, and worship, particularly at a time of change, asks clergy to be persuaders and educators. Clergy frequently find it pastorally wise if liturgical decision making is exercised distributively and the preparation of liturgy approached collaboratively—not only because the tasks (from preparing and reading Scripture lessons to arranging flowers) are many, but because worship is the business of the community of faith.

Many congregations have a *worship committee* that is an extension of the pastoral responsibility that by canon is given to the cleric. This committee considers general questions of the personnel, budgeting, direction and quality of liturgy. Such a committee understands that the week-to-week preparation of liturgical events falls to a more specific *task group.*

The *worship committee* asks such questions as: "Should there be a group of lectors in this congregation? How should its members be selected, organized and trained?" The *task group* asks such questions as: "What biblical readings are appointed for this week? Why were they chosen? How can they best be presented?"

Perhaps small congregations (and in the Episcopal Church that means most congregations) cannot think in terms of two groups, and the functions spoken of here will in considerable measure be combined. The important thing is the functions, which the organizational structure should serve with some economy.

The *worship committee* does not prepare and clean the communion vessels, write intercessions, select choir anthems, or preach sermons. But it supports those who can do these things. It is desirable that such a committee include persons beyond the professional or volunteer liturgical leaders. They are not consulted because they have training and expertise but because, as representatives of the congregation, they seek to create conditions whereby those who do have special gifts and positions in the worship life of the parish can carry out their tasks most satisfactorily. If they are given real responsibility, such persons can provide general guidance; help interpret the liturgy to the congregation; and represent the congregation to those who are doing the weekly preparing.

The openness of membership in such a committee is based on the recognition that the worshiping unit is the congregation. Members of the congregation are part of the liturgy by reason of their baptism and their week-by-week participation. As part of the praying, singing, offering and receiving congregation, they may, if they wish, take part in the deliberate shaping of liturgy. Their role should not be more passive than they choose it to be. Perhaps, however, there is something vocational about membership in a worship committee. Some people will take to the role as soon as it is explained and opened to them, while others will think that their gifts and interests lie elsewhere. Persons of ability may create a more-or-less regular place for themselves, but they should not shut out others.

Members of a worship committee can bring ideas, cautions and wisdom, sometimes moderating the unrealistic professional enthusiasms of celebrants, officiants and musicians, and sometimes catching those enthusiasms and interpreting them to others. These persons also play a significant role in such evaluation as may take place after the liturgy and in discovering and reporting the congregation's response.

Participation in such a committee can be educative. Most members will have attended church for years with little grasp of what the preacher was seeking to do in the sermon or what the liturgy, its whole or its parts, intended. If they knew that they liked or did not like certain things, they could not have explained why. The consideration of liturgy is not just a functional business of setting the music budget or clarifying lines of authority where groups seem confused about who has responsibility for what. It is an exploration into the mystery of worship. It is an unending spiritual and intellectual challenge. Persons who become part of discussing and preparing liturgy engage in corporate discovery. They gain sophistication and understanding. Perhaps for the first time they grasp what liturgy and proclamation are about. They can take part in worship with informed sympathy and explain their new understanding to others. If membership in a worship committee is on a rotating basis, such understanding can raise the general level of participation in the faithful worship of God.

However shared the discussion of and responsibility for worship may be, the actual preparation of liturgy each week falls to a small, intentional *task group* that must make determinations and see that they are carried out. In speaking of this group and its processes, a disclaimer concerning the discussion that follows and a word of caution about committees that prepare liturgy may be offered at the start, lest readers entertain mistaken expectations:

As to the disclaimer, the sketch presented here will not provide a neat "how-to" program for shaping liturgical events. The circumstances in which preparers of liturgy work are diverse and each occasion of worship is, in some respects, unique; directions that were too prescriptive would tend to cut off, rather than to encourage, creativity. So the intention here is to be specific enough to provide some ideas, but loose enough to credit planners with the ability to take responsibility on their own. Groups preparing liturgical events will no doubt develop habits of work that are more specific than this chapter can be. Some such groups may devise and print their own forms (simple forms, one hopes) for capturing the ideas that emerge in discussion and for preserving records of what is actually done. But no such forms will be found here.

A note of realism and caution may also be entered here at the start. A committee that prepares and carries out worship can, like any other committee, become politicized. Since worship is, to a marked extent, a matter of judgment, the taste and level of discrimination of the individual members of the committee become quite apparent; and there are likely to be disagreements. Certain members can insist that their ideas or preferences prevail. The group will usually begin with no agreed-upon criteria. Since worship is a many-sided action whose general quality is determined by attention to details, this committee can become preoccupied with trivialities and miss the large pastoral and theological issues with which the discussion of worship ought to be concerned. But, like any other committee, a group responsible for liturgy can identify such flaws in its own processes. It can discipline its ways of working, clarify its tasks and agenda, set limits to meeting times, and remind itself of its reason for being.

The following pages are written as though for a group that meets weekly for preparing a Sunday or Feast Day liturgy. Many parish committees that consider worship do not prepare so specifically, and therefore need not meet that often, but some preparation necessarily takes place every week. And groups that are charged with responsibility for worship will meet fairly regularly (if not weekly) to project new ideas and to evaluate past experience. The thought processes described here can be adapted by worship committees that do their work along more general lines and on other than weekly schedules.

• The Group •

How shall the group that is charged with specific preparation of liturgy be comprised? Just who and how many may take part and how their work is organized are things that depend, of course, on the size and resources of the congregation. But a few things may be remarked about the composition and purpose of the group.

The group members should possess recognized training and gifts. Some of them may be salaried employees of the parish. But some may be persons whose previously undiscovered skills have been identified as responsibility for worship comes to involve more members of the congregation. There is a role for the expert in something as complex and exacting as liturgy. But the expertise of these group members must be rooted in their identity as worshipers. Whatever special competences anyone brings, and however those competences may be affirmed, in the humbling business of prayer and the praise of God all believers retain their amateur status.

> **The Celebrant:** The gathering of persons to prepare liturgy should always, and from the start, include the principal celebrant. Perhaps this rule is so obvious that it should go without saying. In most parishes it would hardly be conceivable that the rector or curate (or whoever is to celebrate) would not be a basic member of the preparing team. But at conferences or schools where there are a number of possible celebrants, it is not unknown for a group to take initiative in shaping a liturgical event with a quite definite intention or a strong musical character and then to search for a celebrant who would be willing to go along with these fairly developed plans. The design and style of the event should not be of a sort that takes the principal minister by surprise and makes him or her feel uncomfortable. A celebrant who is put in an awkward position is so conspicuous in the ministry of word and sacrament that her or his discomfort cannot be altogether concealed. The strengths and limitations, the inner satisfactions and constraints of the liturgical presider are among the first things for the preparers to take into account. Ministers are full of surprises; they may in fact like things they were expected to dislike, and they may want to try things that it was supposed they would not. The fair and gracious thing is to have the presider present throughout the preparation process to speak for him- or herself.

Perhaps the greater danger is that a group meeting to prepare a liturgy will defer habitually to the principal celebrant, or that the celebrant (intentionally or not) will manipulate the work of the planning group so that it achieves what he or she had in mind from the start. Needless to say, there may be times when the celebrant's ideas should prevail. As a rule, the clergy are the ones with specific training in liturgy and Scripture. (Such expertise cannot be taken for granted. Clergy, especially younger clergy, are often startled by the demands of the weekly liturgical schedule, and they wish they had given such matters more attention during seminary days. Help is sometimes available in workshops or conferences, but it is not always easy to come by when it is wanted.) Clergy will often have insights into the character of a liturgical occasion or the flow of a season. The celebrant should not take a passive role in the preparation process, but neither should she nor he dominate it. If the members of the group designated to prepare a liturgical event come to feel that they are disregarded, the effort at collaborative preparation will fail. The clergy, many of whom have taken the shaping of liturgy to be their unique prerogative, must share the task of preparation from a conviction that the involvement of many in what has hitherto been the task of one, promises advantages, advantages for liturgy and for the spiritual growth of the congregation. The group members who have had no prior experience in thinking critically about worship will, through the preparation process, learn new roles. But so will many of the clergy.

> **The Leader of the Music:** Beside the principal celebrant, there should be someone who represents music. This would ordinarily be the organist and choir director. It needs to be someone who knows what the choir members and instrumentalists take pleasure in doing and do well, and who knows also what new challenges are manageable enough to be found rewarding. Of course there are churches that have no choir and no music library, and in some cases no organ. So the planning group must include someone who knows the musical resources of the congregation and who is alert to new vocal and instrumental possibilities. The music will do more than anything else to establish the character of the liturgical event as a whole, and it dare not be an afterthought.

Others: In addition to the above two persons, the preparing group should include, if possible:

— the person(s) who will read the Scriptures,

— the person who will preach (who in most instances will be the celebrant),

— the person who will prepare and lead the intercessions,

— someone who represents servers, and others who take part in such matters as the movement of persons or the decoration and lighting of the liturgical space,

— someone (or several people) who is (are) aware of the pastoral needs of the congregation. (This will, of course, include the rector. But there may be others who are doing visiting and who are alert to the life of the parish.)

Liturgists: Some large parishes, principally in the Roman church, where congregations often must have multiple celebrations on Sundays, have engaged a salaried liturgical director. Such a commitment indicates that the congregation accords a high priority to worship and recognizes the complexity of the work that lies behind each smoothly executed liturgical event. Such a person keeps abreast of musical resources and is generally informed on liturgical matters. She or he would, of course, always be part of the planning group, and might be its convener and record-keeper. This person sees to it that the decisions arrived at by the committee are in fact carried through. Only a few congregations, Roman or non-Roman, have been able to employ such a staff member, and perhaps the parishes that can do so will remain relatively few. Yet there seems to be a genuine need, and there are persons of gifts and training who could fill the role capably.

Although this group may take initiative for setting the preparation going in a certain direction, as soon as something comes up concerning visual, musical, or ceremonial matters, the appropriate persons should be brought into the process (if they are not already there). Who has ideas about light and color? about space and the movement of people? about the involvement of children? The best ideas and competences of the congregation should be sought.

It should perhaps be said that the group charged with preparation for worship is not a democracy. It does not seek a least common denominator consensus. That is the way to dull liturgy. Its task is, in part, to discover the gifts that are present in the local faith community and to make room for them to be exercised collaboratively.

• The Group Convenes •

As a rule, the preparing group should begin its work with prayer or silence, or both. We tend to rush to our meetings from our busy lives elsewhere, and we are not ready to focus on the important tasks at hand until we have made an emotional and mental transition. Our silence and our prayer express an openness or readiness to be led. For centuries the Anglican Eucharist has begun with Cranmer's "Collect for Purity" which says, in effect, that it is only through God that we are enabled to worship God. The point is applicable to the task of liturgical preparation. There is, of course, a technical side to shaping good liturgy, and persons who prepare it want to do their work well. But before these preparers are technicians, they are themselves worshipers. Their credentials are rooted first of all in their awareness of the reality of God and the mystery of worship. We do not set about shaping an act of worship without asking that we and our work be at God's disposal.

• Agenda One: Liturgical Material •

In liturgical preparation, two agendas will come to bear on each other and on the final order of worship. Even though the two will be mixed in the liturgical event itself, they will be put in sequence here for explanation. As a group considers its task, sometimes one of these agendas, sometimes the other will seem more urgent.

One set of factors that goes into the liturgical event is not in doubt: the *liturgical material* that the Prayer Book will bring before the church on a given occasion. Such material is often carried on a liturgical planning calendar. (One that is widely used is the *Episcopal Church Lesson Calendar,* which is published for each year, beginning with Advent, by Morehouse-Barlow; the editing is expertly done.) This material pertinent to the work of preparers can be known in advance.

The first agenda, consisting of liturgical material, may be developed here by questions:

> **The Occasion or Season:** Where are we in the Christian Year? What signs of the season should appear in the liturgy? When the season changes or when seasonal change is anticipated a few weeks in advance, the time of year becomes important for a group preparing liturgy. The season gives a coloration to all that takes place within it, especially in the rapid changes in the half-year between Advent and Pentecost. No particular event can be developed well without attending to the character of the season in which it falls. On many Sundays however, the matter will not call for much discussion: the forthcoming Sunday simply sustains a seasonal tone previously established that runs through several weeks.

> **The Appointed Scriptures:** What Scripture passages will be read? Preparers should not just look up the references in the lectionary or calendar and leave a note for those will mark the Bible on the lectern. The Scriptures for the day are not only important in themselves, they are also basic to many other decisions. Those who are preparing the liturgy as a whole need to examine them with care. The rubrics expect that there will be three readings, and the Sunday lectionary provides accordingly. On some days, the lectionary offers a choice of readings. Which combination would be best for this Sunday? Why?

Someone from the group (often, but not necessarily one of the clergy) should examine the passages prior to the planning meeting so that the group can have an idea of the background and meaning of each. If a prophet, or if St. Paul is arguing, who is the opponent? What is the social setting for a parable of Jesus? Is there anything that should be known about the context in order for the specific verses chosen for reading to be clear? Some passages in the lectionary begin in the middle of a series of events, or they are part of a sustained argument. As read aloud, they should not be baffling to hearers. Are any of the passages part of a sequence from past Sundays? The epistle readings usually are, in fact, continuous from Sunday to Sunday. And the Gospel readings to a great extent follow one another in series. And most important of all, there is usually (not always) a connection between the Gospel reading and the Old Testament reading. What is it?

As the group considers the biblical material, it should not be in a hurry to propose a modern relevance for the passages. If some member of the group urges a point of view about what this biblical material means for us today, it is probably best to receive the suggestion, but to counsel patience until all the passages have been looked at with the necessary care. When we rush to conclude what the point of the biblical material is, we can short-circuit the required openness to the new. We risk telling the Bible what it should tell us.

In this matter of familiarity with the Bible, the business of liturgical preparation may especially be a means of educating the committee members. The liturgical lectionary is not beyond criticism, but it has a fine structure:

- It is built on a three-year coverage of the synoptic Gospels—Years A, B and C; governed by Matthew, Mark and Luke respectively. In each year, the principal events of Jesus' life are told largely between Christmas and Easter, while the remaining portions of each Gospel that relate Jesus' miracles, encounters and teaching are heard on the Sundays of Pentecost. Material that appears in more than one of the Gospel accounts in substantially similar form is usually not repeated.
- The Fourth Gospel is used in all three years to interpret the major festivals of Christ. Chapters 13 through 17, which describe life in Christ and the Church and the Spirit, are drawn on during the weeks of Easter; and certain other parts are used during Pentecost. Although there is no "John year," the Fourth Gospel is used as extensively as any of the synoptics.
- The Epistles are usually read rather consecutively. On the more important days of the Church Year, all three readings will fit the occasion and one another, but on many Sundays, the Epistle reading will simply be the next portion of one of the New Testament letters in sequence.
- The Old Testament readings are very discontinuous. Through most of

the year, they are chosen because they in some way illustrate or parallel the Gospel reading: For example, a New Testament quotation is matched with its Old Testament source (as on Proper 26 in Year B, the Gospel lesson, Mark 12:28–34, contains Jesus' "First and Great Commandment," which is drawn from Deuteronomy 6:1–9, which is the appointed Old Testament reading). Or an event from the Old Testament is paired with a similar event in the life of Jesus (as on Proper 1 in Year B, in the Gospel reading, Mark 1:40–45, Jesus cures a leper, while the Old Testament reading, 2 Kings 5:1–15, is the story of the cure of Naaman by Elisha). On some Sundays, the Old Testament lesson is simply an important passage from the Jewish Scriptures that ought to be familiar to Christian readers and that does not fit in as a New Testament parallel. For example, in Lent, some of the great "call" stories from the Old Testament are read for their own value as paradigmatic accounts, and not because of any specific link with the Gospel reading for the Sunday.

This structure, over its three-year course, gives an extensive coverage of the biblical material, material that in time ought to grow more familiar to what some critics have called our "Bible-starved" American congregations. But it does have the effect of presenting the Bible in short units, suitable for public reading. No part of the Bible was written as a series of short independent passages. In order to understand any portion appointed in the lectionary, one should have a sense of the larger whole in which each one stands. Often it is desirable to identify the section of the writing from which the particular lesson comes. Is this lesson one in a series of Jesus' answers to questions that were meant to trap him (Mark 11:15–12:44)? Is this a part of St. Paul's counsel in matters of Christian conduct that had been referred to him (1 Corinthians 5–16)? And what is the emotional tone of the reading? Is the prophet being sarcastic against idolatry (Isaiah 44:9–20)?

A committee that looks at such questions is likely to want on hand some reference sources such as the *Harper's Dictionary of the Bible*, 1985, edited by Paul Achtemeier; and *A Theological Word Book of the Bible*, 1950, edited by Alan Richardson; or the *Dictionary of Biblical Theology*, 1977, edited by Xavier Leon-Dufour. For questions about the origin and character of a part of the Bible, some basic works of introduction and commentary may be desirable. Of the one-volume Bible commentaries, the *New Jerome Biblical Commentary,* 1990, orig. ed., 1968, written by Roman Catholic exegetes and edited by Raymond Brown, Joseph Fitzmyer, and Roland Murphy is very fine; and the *Harper's Bible Commentary,* 1988, general editor James L. Mays, is full of information. *The Interpreter's Bible,* although it was prepared at a time of shifting emphases in biblical studies, remains generally good, particularly the articles introducing the major biblical sections.

The Prayer Book eucharistic lectionary is the Episcopal Church's adaptation of "the ecumenical lectionary," now in use, with small denominational differences, in several major churches. This lectionary, with its remarkable coverage of Scripture, has been a stimulus to biblical knowledge and to preaching. A considerable literature, from many scholars and publishing houses, representing many churches, has grown up to give comment on the appointed readings. A few such guides are mentioned in the reading list at the end of this book.

One learns how to use such tools for biblical study and what one can expect to find in them, and not find. A great deal of the insight necessary for placing a passage within the context for which it was written, however, can be obtained by an attentive reading of the biblical book as a whole—perhaps several times.

The interior of the biblical literature is its presentation of the redemptive Gospel. There is a great deal in the Bible (and in the portions of the Bible that appear in the lectionary) that is hortatory. A reader feels and is meant to feel subdued and chastened. But that is not the heart of the story told by the Scriptures as they are read over the seasons of the church year.

The essential story is Good News—the long divine seeking, and the binding of a people into God's own purpose; the coming of Jesus; his presentation, in teaching and in mighty works, of the active reign of God; his acts and words of power; his attracting of followers (many of them somewhat disreputable); the enmity against him of those who were self-righteous or set in incomprehension; his crucifixion and resurrection; the coming of the Spirit, and the birth of the Church; the apostolic proclamation and the joyful faith to which it gave rise; the shaping of a community around this new faith; the hope to which the promise of the Good News points. This divine Good News is a summons to radical change on the part of individuals and of human collectivities. It elicits and supports the trusting relation with God. It offers a new and abundant life. Even in penitential seasons, or when the readings emphasize human failure, the Church is a community that can look at sin without despair, for it is in touch with that which transcends sin. Given the complexity of the biblical material, there may be some oversimplification in putting the matter so, but in a sense we have not really heard any part of the Bible until we have heard it in relation to the organizing theme of the biblical literature as a whole: the good news of the victorious love of God in Christ.

Preachers and worship committees often seem to spend a great deal of effort looking for some "common theme" in each Sunday's readings. If they cannot discern a unifying theme, they suppose it is due to dullness on their part. On the major festivals the readings will, of course, suit the day. But on most Sundays there is something serendipitous about the way in which the New Testament Epistle reading fits into the mix. And on every occasion there is a sharp-edged particularity about each biblical passage. The task of the preparers is to see to it that the rich variety of the biblical witness reaches the congregation. When a "theme Eucharist" is drawn from the lectionary, the sort of "point" that is identified for the day is too often some general moral teaching—"good can be made to come out of evil," "doing good to others does good to the doer as well." The Bible is never platitudinous.

Uncovering the particular force of a biblical passage is not solely a matter of looking into its cultural background and literary context. The immediacy of the biblical writings lies in what connects them in their settings with us in our settings. What they said then and there carries power for readers here and now. This life-interpreting contemporaneity is made possible, in considerable measure, through the Bible's appeal to the imagination, often by means of story or image. The group that looks at the Sunday Scriptures should let the texture of the scriptural material speak from imagination to imagination. Often the vividness of the Hebrew idiom will make the Old Testament reading the most graphic of the three readings. How can our out-of-training imaginations hear and respond to the Scriptures? We can be attentive for images or for paradigmatic incidents. We can ask what pictures or associations a unit of the Bible sets going in our own minds. We can wait to speak about the passage until it has spoken to us. There is constant surprise and power in the biblical text, and the first task of liturgical preparation is to be open to the Word of God on its own terms.

The group should not be impatient if readily applicable meanings do not arise quickly from all of the appointed readings. Some parts of the Bible are difficult. Obscurities are not always the result of the inquirers being dense or uninformed. The mystery is there in the biblical source. The necessary familiarity with the Scriptures may be acquired cumulatively. Understanding of the biblical literature can be rewarding even in its rudimentary stages, but, in a lectionary that runs for three years, insight obtained in one year can be the starting point for another later examination of the same configuration of readings. Or learning acquired in the "Mark Year" will illuminate the similarities and differences in the texts encountered in the "Luke Year." Perhaps three years later, when a particularly baffling reading comes around again, the group will be more familiar with the Bible as a whole and clearer about this specific part. Meanwhile it can be read, letting its opacity and suggestiveness fall in the congregation's ears as they will.

These comments will have indicated that a group of preparers will not simply ascertain what Scriptures are appointed. It must also do what it can to see why these were given for the day, how they go together (insofar as they do), and what part they play in presenting the broad panorama of the biblical story of God in redemptive action.

> **Hymn Choice:** A preparing group, taking its direction from the lectionary, must ask at an early point: what shall be sung? Opening and closing hymns set the tone for the entire occasion. A sequence Psalm (using the texts in the eucharistic lectionary) may be sung as a response to the First Reading. Some responsorial Psalm settings engage the congregation by a repeated refrain while placing most of the musical demands on a lead voice. (The *Gradual Psalms,* published by The Church Hymnal Corporation, with one volume for each year of the Prayer Book lectionary, are widely used and musically accessible. The tear-out pages may be duplicated.) A sequence hymn (perhaps with an Alleluia verse) after the second reading and before the Gospel gives further devotional development of the Scriptures. The offertory hymn marks a turn in the eucharistic action. Some congregations like hymns during the Communion, while others regard singing in this location as inevitably intrusive.

Here again, the principal source, the *Hymnal 1982,* is available to be consulted in advance. Some printings of the *Hymnal* carry (on pages 1031–39) an index of Scripture passages matched with hymns. (This index is repeated in the *Service Music:* Accompaniment Edition, Volume 1, pages 703–11.) Some printed calendars and guides have appropriate hymns listed for each liturgical occasion. The *Episcopal Church Lesson Calendar,* noted previously, carries well-thought-out hymn suggestions. Another indispensable reference is *A Liturgical Index to The Hymnal 1982,* by Marion Hatchett (published by The Church Hymnal Corporation as "Hymnal Studies Five.") In one manageable book, persons looking at liturgy in advance are given suggestions for hymns for all three years of the lectionary, for all occasions in the Prayer Book, in *The Book of Occasional Services,* and in *Lesser Feasts and Fasts.*

No one is required to accept the choices of such published sources. Each congregation's preferences, needs and resources are distinct. But a calendar that a committee learns to trust can be a fine starting place. The published resources listed here are prepared by persons who know both the lectionary and the hymnal well. Their skill in noting where hymns pick up themes from the lessons would be hard to match by those whose familiarity with the lectionary and the hymn book is just growing. Some persons may be asked to come to the committee meeting having looked at such sources in advance and having a tentative choice of hymns to propose. The committee members, whose work is making them become familiar with the Bible and the Prayer Book, will also be looking more closely at the contents of *Hymnal 1982* than they ever had before.

For some great festal occasions, a few familiar, expected hymns virtually select themselves. But if there are multiple services at Christmas or Easter, which hymns shall be sung at which hour? Can some less familiar hymns (perhaps new in the 1982 hymn book) which seem unusually appropriate be worked in without raising the congregation's resentment? If not, how and when can new material be introduced? (In this matter, there is wise and practical counsel in Marilyn Keiser's *Teaching Music in Small Churches,* The Church Hymnal Corporation, "Hymnal Studies Three.")

Often hymns will not be picked on a week-to-week basis. The hymns to be used over the span of a season may need to be looked at together so that the selection has some deliberate shape. Easter, for example, is now not a day (nor an octave), but a season of seven weeks. The proportion of hymns suitable for Easter in *The Hymnal 1982* is much enlarged over what it was in *The Hymnal 1940*. (And the proportion of hymns for Lent—and for Passiontide, a week that has been dropped as a specially named period—is somewhat reduced.) But not all of the hymns are equally usable or familiar. Certain great favorites may well be repeated during the season. Some hymns that are newly introduced may be used several Sundays in a row in order to overcome such musical difficulties as they may have and to add them solidly into the congregation's repertoire. (Many seasonal hymns will not be used again for a year, so if they are to return as old favorites a year later, they must have adequate exposure when they are first tried.) The choir may want to rehearse some of the hymns for two or three weeks before they are sung by the congregation, and it may need to help the congregation when the hymn is introduced.

When all or part of the music is determined some time in advance, the committee does not choose what should be sung next Sunday. Rather, it reviews the choices that were made and asks how they can take their part in the liturgical event that is beginning to take shape. At times the committee may want to ask whether or not the hymn selection for the next season of the year is under way.

Committees, working with choir leaders, will develop their own methods of hymn selection. Even the best of the printed liturgical calendars will propose hymns that have, for a specific congregation, insurmountable musical difficulties, or are otherwise unusable. A few suggestions may be useful:

In general, hymns can be thought of in categories of, on the one hand, those that are inward, confessional, subjective, and often in the first-person "I" form (as "Eternal Spirit of the living Christ," [698]); and, on the other hand, those that are occupied with God and the wonder of Christ, are more objective, and are often in the plural "we" form (as "Christ is made the sure foundation," [518]). One does not want to be dogmatic. At times the "I" is a representative shared voice, speaking of the great common things of Christian experience (as "Guide me, O thou great Jehovah," [690]); and sometimes a hymn that is formally in the "we" form can be quite introspective (as Whittier's [563]). Sometimes doctrine and devotion are united (as "Alleluia! Sing to Jesus!" [460/461]). But these rough categories are often useful. In general, it can be recommended that the more objective hymns are better for opening and closing hymns and often for offertories, while the more subjective hymns may suit graduals, or communion hymns. As a rule, if a liturgical event contains one well-chosen, well-located, inward-looking, meditative hymn, it does not want another.

At times, and for some congregations, it may be desirable to look at the words of the hymns to see whether or not they are fully believable. There are sentimental and maudlin hymns in the tradition, including some that are widely liked. *The Hymnal 1982* has removed most of the grave offenders that were in *The Hymnal 1940*, as that hymnal deleted many that had been in *The Hymnal 1916*. People should not have to snap their hymn books shut saying, "I can't sing that!" But neither should twentieth-century worshipers make hasty judgments. There is, in the church's hymnody, with respect to both words and music, a remarkable variety.

Hymns come from many periods and styles of piety: sturdy Lutheran chorales (such as "O sacred head" [169],); metrical Psalms, often from the Reformed tradition (such as "I to the hills will lift mine eyes" [668]); pietistic hymns expressing deep inwardness (such as "God himself is with us" [475]); rather other-worldly Medieval Office Hymns (such as three settings of "Christ, mighty Savior" [33–35]); nineteenth- and twentieth-century hymns of social awareness (such as "Lord, whose love . . . " [610]); simple folk songs (such as "What wondrous love is this" [439]), and many more. Some old words are set effectively to contemporary music (as in George Herbert's seventeenth-century poem matched with Calvin Hampton's wonderful melody and its busy accompaniment [403]). Congregations, often without thinking about it, acquire some versatility in moving from one of these frames of thought and expression to another. Those persons who regularly prepare liturgy should cultivate a fairly general appreciation of this variety, but they should also ask how credible each hymn is for a congregation whose mind they know fairly well.

Hymns provide the somewhat inarticulate worshiper with a vehicle through which to say things beyond his or her present experience or power of expression. He or she may have a pretty good idea of the conviction from which the hymn was written, and accept it as a reminder of a range of devotion and conviction that belongs to this great tradition, but to which he or she is as yet something of a stranger.

Groups that select hymns may want to keep records of their work. It is a good idea to know what hymns have been used and when, so that a few loved and easily sung choices are not overworked. Unless records are kept, persons who attend worship lose track quite easily and think their favorites have not been used for longer than is the case, while they think that some new hymn with which they have not yet come to terms has been used five times in two months. If several persons come to a meeting for liturgical preparation with suggestions for hymns, they are likely to bring more possibilities than can be used. Choices must be made, but the process will have turned up usable hymns that can be noted for future use. In this way, groups can develop lists of hymns that are thought to be suitable for certain functions in the Eucharist, or for certain seasons, for penitential occasions, festal days, saints' days, or for general praise. Some hymns are ideally matched with certain scriptural passages or themes; and the hymns on such a list that are not used this week may be held for another time—in some cases, held for a year. At certain sessions, when some pressing matter dominates the committee's agenda, the group will be glad that it has on hand a classified list of hymns that had previously been considered (and perhaps annotated) and could now be drawn on easily.

> **Choral and Instrumental Music:** While considering music, it may be well to note that choirs must usually prepare anthems some weeks in advance of their use, particularly if the music is new or difficult. Thus, the selections to be sung by the choir can seldom be chosen or changed on short notice. Similarly, special instrumental music will often be in preparation some weeks in advance of its use. Those who choose the choir anthems will want to look at the Prayer Book and the liturgical calendar so that their choices, even though they are made on an independent schedule, will not represent conflicting interpretations of the character of a Sunday and its liturgy.

This body of discussion and preliminary choices—this first agenda—is only part of planning, but it is a basic part. The liturgical material presented by the Prayer Book holds the Christ-saga before the community of faith. The hymns are chosen for their compatibility with the season and the Scriptures. Liturgy is informed by the conviction that human life is not explained out of or redeemed by itself, but in relation to this Person and this redemptive story. When these primary liturgical determinations have become clear, a great deal remains to be done, but a firm direction has been given to the occasion and the committee can approach its other decisions with something to work from.

● Agenda Two: The Current Experience of the Community ●

Earlier or later in the preparation process another body of considerations—*the current experience of the community*—will press for examination. Sometimes it may be quite urgent; at other times less so; but it requires attention by those who prepare liturgy. Its development may draw on members of the group who have not had much to contribute to the former agenda, but who bring wisdom required for this one.

This agenda is not prompted by the Prayer Book nor by liturgical seasons or days that can be placed on a calendar well in advance. It emerges from world, local and parochial events.

It is probably not useful to think in terms of a checklist of questions, but liturgical preparation will be affected by such matters as:

What has been read in the newspapers or seen in television newscasts this week?

What is going on in world and national affairs?

What hopes or apprehensions will the congregation bring to church?

Newsgathering has extended our accessible world. Some of the events that are publicly reported are sources of shock, anxiety, joy, or relief. Sometimes the sympathy of the congregation is genuinely touched by some far-off catastrophe. Sometimes the congregation is not so much impressed by what has taken place as fearful over what may take place. But the news media on which we depend are oddly selective. Someone on the committee may suggest that certain important matters in the modern world have gone largely unreported. (Perhaps they do not make good television pictures, or perhaps news coverage is forbidden.) Knowing that this agenda will be considered is likely to make preparers of liturgy more alert and reflective concerning the news they encounter through the week than they might otherwise be.

The group that is thinking of Christian prayer and worship may want to consider not so much specific events as deep, continuing conditions: What happens to the soul of an officially optimistic society when a great many adults in it become convinced that their children will not be better off than they are themselves? Our collective life—national, international, and local—is often impacted by reminders of the precariousness of our political and civic order. Many people are deeply concerned about what they take to be a decline in that thing which is concretely present but hard to define and measure—the quality of life. The fragility of the natural environment, the pressure on its resources from development around the world, and the consequent threat to humanity are becoming clearer. Many conditions of oppression and stark inequality in American society are so systemic that they are present apart from any specific recent event that may have called public attention to them. But persons who are alert to such pervasive conditions can bring them to awareness.

It hardly needs to be labored that these issues are in great measure theological issues. They go back to what we take to be the nature of the bonds that unite human beings with one another and what we take to be our relation with the natural world. Our attitudes to them reveal our values, priorities, and the myths by which we live. These issues are touched by divine judgment and compassion.

But emphasis on world-scale matters should not suggest that local concerns are not also important: What has happened in the local community and in the congregation?

It is seldom that a week goes by without deep, impacting events that are shared at some level by a Christian congregation. There are births, marriages, deaths; illness and accident. There are individual and shared disruptions. Many marriages are troubled; child-rearing is an uncertain business. Perhaps a local industry is threatening to close, and persons fear loss of work. Or a family may be moving from the congregation. It is good to remember that although family units are important in the parish, the pastoral and prayer agenda should not focus on them too exclusively. Many persons live alone, some by choice and some not by choice, and they sometimes feel overlooked. Other persons in the congregation may be from families that are religiously divided, and the references to families should not assume that all of them are families of the congregation.

Again, it is not so much a matter of specific events as of pervasive factors. How close are these people to suffering, to death, to tasks too hard for them, to the feeling that life is unbearable, to the ultimate mysteries of whence and whither, to the breakdown of internal and external resource?

Some of these events and conditions that are shared among the persons preparing liturgy will not be spoken of in the liturgical act itself, and not everything privately known can be said in the preparing committee. Reticences and confidences must be respected. Some issues and problems are not public matters, and some are difficult to reduce to specific words. On some public matters members of the congregation may conscientiously differ, and liturgy is not the forum in which to argue or take sides. In faithful preaching and prayer and sacramental action the issues beneath the apparent and openly identifiable issues will be touched. The role of the preparing group is to ask about the present experience of the congregation, and seek to bring to awareness features of context for confession, celebration, proclamation and intercession.

The purpose of this "agenda" is to suggest a range of nonliturgical concerns that are ingredients for liturgy. Matters—world, national or local in scope—will arise with differing urgency on different occasions. The use made of this material in the liturgy itself is a matter of judgment. Whether and how specific facts of the collective experience are used will depend on such factors as the size and closeness of the congregation, as well as on how well the material can lend itself to liturgical use. The planning group, however, is looking toward a liturgical event that arises from and refers to a particular time in a social history. God is at work in judgment and redemption in all of life. In deciding the words and actions of corporate worship, the committee needs to open itself to the awareness of the God of the prophets.

• Design for Liturgy •

These two "agendas," Liturgical Material, and The Current Experience of the Community, raise the question for preparers of liturgy: Do the two interact creatively?

What the preparers seek is a liturgy with coherence, unity, and some economy. The liturgical act is not to include all the ideas that committee discussion has brought to attention, but the eventual liturgy will be richer for having considered this wide-ranging body of human concerns.

The two principal places at which the agendas interact are the sermon and the intercessions. The liturgy has a general structure, determined by the Prayer Book and the long tradition in which the Prayer Book stands. There is something universal to which the given structures bear witness. Within those structures, our names, our faith and doubt, our joy and our pain come to expression in what is preached and what is prayed for.

This sketch of the planning process cannot deal with the preparation of the sermon. Other books give general homiletic counsel and speak of the specific opportunities of liturgical preaching. Moreover, each occasion is unique, and general comments run to the obvious. It is perhaps fitting to note, however, that the task for the preacher is to relate the biblical material identified in the first "agenda" with the contemporary condition identified in the second. The committee discussion should inform the preacher and set the development of the sermon going in a certain direction. The work will be developed by a single homilist. (Generally speaking, committees cannot write.) What is said by the homilist will carry the richness, closeness to life, and the authority of the collective discussion from which it took its rise.

Some preachers have developed the disciplined habit of identifying at least the central idea of each sermon some time in advance. The final shaping of the sermon usually takes place in the week prior to its being preached. But some sketches and ideas are prepared ahead of time for the sermons for a season or for a period of weeks. There is much to be said for this practice. The further ahead the focus of a sermon is decided, the more observations, ideas and associations come to notice. When the preacher comes to a preparing group with a pretty good idea of the thesis and direction of the sermon, the group simply takes this report into account as it considers the appointed Scriptures. Needless to say, not only does the preacher's advance planning influence the choices in the liturgy, the liturgical group's discussion of its two agendas influences the final development of the sermon.

As to intercessions, the Prayer Book requires prayer for a short comprehensive list of concerns (rubric in Rite II, p. 359, repeated p. 383, and referred to in Rite I, p. 328). The congregation can and should take the responsibility for developing this prayer. Skill can be acquired in wording prayers in a representative voice, in using forms that bring in the congregation smoothly, and that mix general and specific concerns. Some persons seem to do this sort of thing well from the start. Part of the long-term task of liturgical preparation is to discover and develop such skills in the congregation (see Chapter Six).

The interaction of the two agendas of the preparatory process in these two large components of liturgy, the Sermon and the Intercessions, contributes to the special character of each liturgical event. Once the direction of the two agendas is clear, other decisions must be made, and made in general consistency with the lines taken in the Prayer Book material, the preaching, and the intercessory prayer. Not all of the decisions need to be freshly thought out for each liturgical occasion. A certain way of doing things may be adopted for a season of the year, and hence it will not be up for review for several weeks. Practical factors may make it possible to use the liturgical space only in certain ways, and planners do not want to try something different without reason. It is disconcerting to a congregation if there are too many surprises. But the following list of questions will indicate matters on which decision may be made:

- What of the appearance of the liturgical space when people enter? Are major rearrangements desirable? Will small touches (or even big splashes) of color be useful? Of what sort? Who does this sort of thing well?
- While the people are assembling, should there be silence? Or music? If music, of what kind? This music is not something performed before the liturgy begins. Rather, it is itself the beginning of the liturgy. Carefully chosen and well-played opening and closing instrumental music can be an integral part of the liturgical whole.
- Does the congregation need to rehearse new music, or is before-the-event coaching required? If so, by whom should it be done? (Sometimes the persons who can perform music well are not the ones who can best put it across to the congregation.) How can it be sufficient to put people at ease, but at the same time minimal and unobtrusive?
- What about the parish notices? In some congregations on most Sundays there are none at all. But if there must be such announcements, at what point should they come? It is possible to have them at the very start of the liturgy—as part of a greeting and before the first hymn. At that time they do not interrupt the flow of the liturgy, but they may

seem to create a hesitant, prosaic opening. If that location is not desirable, where else seems best? A rubric of the Prayer Book [407] suggests four possible locations. The choice is a matter of judgment.

• How do the ministers and choir enter the eucharistic room? Most liturgists question the regular use of a hymn in procession to convey the choir in and another to convey it out. Such hymns become "walking music." The ministers and choir can enter by the shortest route while the organ is playing, (their entry being the signal for the congregation to stand), and when they have reached the place from which they can best sing and lead the congregation, an opening hymn may begin. If processions are wanted, they might be used several times a year on something of a grand scale—choir leading the whole congregation around the church, or into the churchyard, with stations and prayers, and congregation and choir returning to their seats. The movement of persons in file, singing, is a powerful gesture. Its power is squandered if it is used Sunday by Sunday simply for entries and exits. Even though this practice, which is hardly more than a century old, is criticized by many liturgists, it is clung to fiercely by most parishes.

An attractive option, allowed by the rubrics of Rite II and proposed by Byron Stuhlman (*Prayer Book Rubrics Expanded,* pp. 62f.), is that the opening acclamations be sung or said before the formal entrance (the Collect for Purity probably omitted), and the ministers enter during the singing of the *Gloria in excelsis* (or *Kyrie, Trisagion,* or other canticle, Psalm, or hymn). The greeting and collect of the day would conclude the entry and begin the Service of the Word.

• What is the character of the first few things that are said or sung? These things center the action and set a tone. Does the event begin on a sombre, reflective "low?" The Prayer Book prints the Penitential Order so that it can be used as a part of the entry rite (pp. 319–21, 351–53). The traditional Anglican pattern has been to begin liturgy with contrition, and there is much to be said for the custom. When this tone is struck, the rite may pass to the *Kyrie* (which was originally not penitential in character, but has become so in common understanding and in most musical settings). From there it can build, through the reading and later music, to a more clearly praiseful tone. But at times it would seem best for the service to begin doxologically or celebrationally and pass quickly to the *Gloria in excelsis* or the *Trisagion.* The rubric (pp. 324, 356) allows for "some other song of praise," requiring the *Gloria* at certain festal periods (fifth rubric, p. 406). Might some other hymn be considered for this location on certain occasions? What hymns? On what occasions? Of course, for an evening Eucharist, An Order of Worship for the Evening (pp. 109–14) is available to serve as an opening. When it is considered, what character is it meant to impart to the opening of the service? How may it be conducted? How flexible is it? What might be sung? What ritual actions are suitable?

Rubrics on pages 36, 74 and 142 allow the Order for Morning or Evening Prayer to be used at a celebration of the Eucharist "in place of all that precedes the Offertory." This use of the Office for the Service of the Word brings a full Psalm into the liturgy, and it supports the readings with canticles. The creed may be the Apostles' Creed or the Nicene Creed. The Lord's Prayer and the versicles following may be omitted. (The Lord's Prayer will follow the Great Thanksgiving.) The prayers following the collect(s) are opened to cover the subjects outlined for the Prayers of the People (p. 383). The rite joins the eucharistic order at the Peace. This combination has much to be said for it. The Office is busy, participatory, and it has grown to be loved through much of Anglicanism. The combination can seem long, however; the joining of the parts can seem awkward, and there are risks of duplications. The whole must be prepared with attention to flow and economy. A rubric on p. 142 allows the sermon to follow the readings (where proclamation arises out of the Scripture lessons) or for it to follow the collects (where the Office formally ended in the first English Prayer Books). How might the sermon fit best with the canticle following the second lesson and with the creed? In short, this use of the Office for the Service of the Word at the Eucharist calls for thought and care. (Byron Stuhlman's *Prayer Book Rubrics Expanded,* pp. 76f., has an outline and some good comments.) This combination often seems better in theory than it does in practice, but when care is given to structure and flow, it can work very well.

• Are there actions related to Christian initiation that figure in a Sunday's Eucharist? (Of course, a bishop's visitation will color the whole liturgy, and it will have been taken into account some weeks in advance.) Is this one of the occasions mandated by the first rubric on p. 312 for Holy Baptism? If so, are there to be baptisms? How will they be worked into the movement of people? the readings? the presence and participation of the children? the prayers on pp. 305f.? the presentation of the bread and wine? If there are no baptisms, the Renewal of Baptismal Vows may take the place of the Nicene Creed in the Eucharist (fourth rubric, p. 312). Are there catechumens preparing for Baptism? How are they recognized in the Sunday liturgy, particularly during the weeks of Lent? The Prayer Book provides ways by which the foundational act of Baptism (and preparation for Baptism) can be held before each congregation. (In such matters, the book *The Baptizing Community* by Theodore Eastman is very fine.)

• What about the day's Scripture readings? Who is appointed to read them? Should they be introduced in any special way? It is often useful to give listeners some clue as to what to listen for in a lesson from the Bible. One does not want to give a precis of the reading—the reading should make its own point. But some background information may be supplied. Some of the church publishers provide sheets with the printed Sunday lessons, from a translation necessarily chosen by the publisher. Some of these printed forms carry terse introductions to the passages, but many lay readers or committees could prepare their own introductions with better results. And lectors might read them with more interest than they generally read the "canned" introductions supplied by the publishing houses. Such leaflets may have some educational value when they are used for private or family reading. But it is surely desirable in the liturgy itself to have members of the congregation listen to the lesson as it is read aloud, rather than have their eyes on printed leaflets.

What Bible translation is best? It need not always be the same one, and it need not be the same one for all the readings. Certain translations seem better in some kinds of biblical literature than they are in others. Should there be a hymn or psalm or Alleluia between them? What of the silence that is to follow each reading? How long is too long, and how short is too short? Who will bring the silence to an end? Is there to be any special treatment of the Gospel reading, such as a procession to the midst of the congregation? (The Gospel Procession, as a ritual gesture, seems strong and desirable when one is thinking of neo-Gothic space, with a deep chancel; it brings the reading of the Gospel into the midst of the people. But it seems less needed if the Scriptures are ordinarily read from a station toward the congregation.)

Or will the Gospel be read from the place from which it will be preached?

- What shall be preached? (This question has been considered above.) Who will preach, and from what place in the eucharistic room? After the sermon, what happens next? Does the congregation stand, on signal, at the end of the sermon for an ascription by the preacher, after which it goes directly to the Creed or the intercessions? Or may the sermon end in such a way as to allow for a period of silence following the Gospel and sermon, like the silences after the readings? If there is to be silence, during which the preacher is seated, who brings this silence to an end?

- At the Prayers of the People, what is prayed about? Who prepares and leads this intercession? (This matter has been spoken of earlier in this chapter, and it will be the subject of Chapter Six.) Should the prayer contain thanksgivings? Is this, rather than the opening of the service, the preferred place for the General Confession? (The Prayer Book prints the confession in this location, see pp. 330–32, 359f, as well as at the opening of the Eucharist.) If this is the better location, how is the penitential material woven into the prayer as a whole? (Form VI, pp. 392f, models a structure that includes thanksgiving and a brief effective confession.) If there is a confession, should it be followed by an absolution? (This matter is not as simple as past Prayer Book practice might make it seem. A note on the place of confession and absolution in the Eucharist is appended to this chapter.)

- At the Peace, what is generally done? Should anything special be done in the light of the character of the day's liturgy as a whole?

- At the Offertory, what is said? The Prayer Book does not confine the sentences from Scripture that bid the offertory to those printed on pages 343f and 376. The gathering of the people's offerings is an obvious place for singing. What is sung? Who prepares and brings the offerings to the holy table? Frequently this task is given to different people in a rotation. The Prayer Book provides words by which the offertory action may be begun, but it associates neither actions nor spoken or sung words with the presentation of the gifts. Is something required at this point? What should it be? What is done with the alms? Why? (Liturgical preparers beware. In many otherwise quite un-ceremonial congregations, this liturgical moment, to which the Prayer Book attaches no great significance, becomes the moment of highest ritual drama. In some congregations the alms, the bread, and the wine are for mystagogic reasons passed through a series of hands before they arrive at the table. Then they are conspicuously elevated.)

• What bread and wine are used? In some congregations, members take turns baking the bread for the eucharist: table bread, which speaks of the holy-common. The Prayer Book (pp. 322, 354) designates the preparation of the table as a function of a deacon, but not all congregations have deacons. How is the table to be prepared? What vessels are used? (Usually they will simply be the best that the church has, often in silver, and conventional in shape. But when new vessels are to be secured, can other designs and other materials be looked into?) A rubric on page 407 commends that one chalice, together with a flagon or some other vessel containing such additional wine as is likely to be required, be on the table at the consecration. Such additional chalices as may be needed for administration would be introduced at the fraction. This direction has in mind more than simplicity, it undoubtedly echoes, also, the early church's emphasis that the unity of the elements spoke of the oneness of the Church. The rubrics, however, say nothing about the bread—a matter on which St. Paul seems to have felt much as the Liturgical Commission felt about the wine (see 1 Cor.10:16–17). Clearly it is desirable to have the bread in a single loaf for all of the same reasons that it is desirable to have the wine in a single chalice.

• What eucharistic prayer shall be used? All of those in the Prayer Book are good, but each has distinctive characteristics. Does the character of the day, as it is taking shape, suggest one of the Great Thanksgiving texts? Prayer A is direct and straightforward, and may be most memorable for the image, derived from the early third-century prayer by Hippolytus, "He stretched out his arms on the cross." Prayer B has many good touches—such as the mention of the calling of Israel and the place for commemorating the saints. Its rhythmic mention of "out of error into truth, out of sin into righteousness, out of death into life" (p. 368), may make it particularly pertinent at occasions of baptism and the recalling of the promises of baptism. Prayer C, by the sweep of its content and its frequent congregational acclamations, is dramatic and participatory; some congregations like it particularly well. But does this fine prayer lose its striking character if it is used too often? Prayer D is very full, making it suitable for theologically important events in the Church Year. It allows for intercessions within it—a challenge for someone from the planning group.

Two of the Great Thanksgiving prayers require a Proper Preface, and two do not. Some Prefaces, as printed, allow for a choice. Which shall it be? How much shall be sung? Clearly if there is any singing in the service, the *Sanctus* should be sung. It is one of the great hymns of the Eucharist. But should the Sursum Corda and the Preface also be sung? The Hymnal gives musical settings for the congregational acclamations (S 132–S 141), for the conclusion of the Eucharistic Prayer and the Amen, for the Lord's Prayer, "Christ Our Passover" at the fraction, and "O Lamb of God." Other texts make it possible for musically competent celebrants to sing the entire eucharistic prayer.

- The manner of receiving communion is often dictated by the space and furnishings of the church. Moreover, even if some variety is possible, this action of the rite is so important to the communicants that it may well be left generally routinized. Distraction and novelty are particularly unwelcome here. But a group engaged in long-term consideration of liturgy might well ask about the general parish practice. A congregation cannot really decide between two or more options until they have been tested fairly. Persons who have always received communion kneeling at a rail may suppose that they would not like receiving while standing at a station. But if they actually did it, some of them might like it, or at least they might grant that it is an acceptable alternative. The use of different ways of receiving the elements can help members of the congregation to acquire some flexibility, useful for ease in the varied practices in an ecumenical era.

- At the conclusion of the administration, there is an old practice of a motet being sung. Is music here a distraction? An interruption? Or is this a desirable location for special music? What is done with the vessels and the remaining consecrated elements? Generally speaking, it seems good to have the holy table empty at the conclusion of the administration, as it was when the liturgy began. The receiving of communion has broken the formation with which the community began the liturgy. Should the ministers stay at the table for the post-communion devotions? Or should they, with the congregation, return to the locations they had at the start of the rite?

- A rubric on page 409 directs that a hymn may be sung either between the communions and the post-communion thanksgiving, or between the post-communion thanksgiving and the dismissal. And in the eucharistic order, this is the last music for which the Prayer Book makes provision. (The rubric in the 1928 Prayer Book that allowed a hymn to be sung before or after any rite is deliberately dropped in the 1979 Book.) This direction intends that the hymn be sung at an appropriate moment in the eucharistic rite and while the choir members are in their best places for singing and leading the congregation. The dismissal should be an honest dismissal, not followed by a "walking music" hymn and further prayers and fussy actions. Can the group that takes a regular look at parish worship decide on a clear economical conclusion? Perhaps, if the building is long and the only real exit for the congregation, the choir and the officiants is from the liturgical west, after the post-communion thanksgiving a hymn might be sung during which the choir and ministers move toward the end of the aisle, and the dismissal be made from the rear of the congregation, near the main door, with the choir still in the eucharistic room. Or the final hymn might be sung and the people dismissed while the choir and clergy are in their places; followed by the orderly exit of the choir by the nearest door, without singing; while the ministers go to the door to greet the departing congregation, if that is their custom.

The priest's concluding blessing had been part of the Prayer Book Eucharist since 1549. It is continued in this place in Holy Eucharist I (p. 339). But in Holy Eucharist II, the text of the blessing is not printed in the rite itself, and the rubric on page 366, which speaks of its possible inclusion before the dismissal, uses the permissive term "may." The blessing seems like a duplication. At the Eucharist one is blessed through receiving the Body and Blood of Christ. The "giving" in the Eucharist brings one into the divine *Shalom* secured in Christ. The inclusion of a priestly blessing as part of the dismissal could seem to imply that no blessing had yet occurred. Such a blessing at the conclusion of the Eucharist has many generations of Anglican use behind it, and the custom has done no demonstrable harm. But it can be seen as a piece of clericalism—one that the Roman Church has seen no need for. And if this act in this place seems to obscure the meaning and shape of the Eucharist, it is doubtless best to set it aside, or at least to use it only on chosen occasions. (The Seasonal Blessings, in *The Book of Occasional Services*, pp. 20–27, may be taken into account by preparers.)

This outline of questions and suggestions indicates the sort of decisions that must be made at each Eucharist, even if they are made by deciding to decide nothing and to do what has become the custom of the congregation. Matters such as these would have to be determined if a group were considering only a simple Sunday Prayer Book Eucharist. If on any Sunday the Eucharist were to be combined with Holy Baptism, or if it were a special occasion in the Church Year or in the life of a parish, new elements would be added to the design for the day's liturgy, and further decisions would of course be required. But the intention here has been to suggest some of the thought processes of the group charged with making adequate preparations. The resourcefulness of such a group can take account of the many exceptional demands that will be placed on the worship routine of any active parish.

Through their work, members of committees that prepare liturgies will become well acquainted with the Bible and the Hymnal, and they will welcome the help that is increasingly available from secondary works. Such committee members will also become knowledgable about the Prayer Book and its rubrics. They will note what directions are prescriptive and what rubrics say "may." They will see what actions or ministers are mandated, what are recommended, and what possibilities are opened. (As guides for this working familiarity with the Episcopal Church's basic liturgical text, several books are suggested in section 3 of "For Further Reading" at the end of this book. Special note might be taken here of *Prayer Book Rubrics Expanded* by Byron Stuhlman. It clarifies rubrical matters; it speaks wisely of ceremonial; and it is sensitive to the place of music.)

● Evaluation ●

When a liturgical event has been completed, those who helped to prepare it or to carry it out will often have quick and definite reactions to it. If these are practical reactions—"This took too long," or "We could save motions there," or "We seemed to be hurrying," or "That seemed arbitrarily stuck into the order of service"—they can be registered at once. But often these persons are so closely involved in the liturgy that they are poor judges of its actual qualities. So a part of good consideration of liturgy is to devise some sort of evaluation. This liturgical self-criticism should not spoil the joy and spontaneity that participation in worship should have. Perhaps some people are by temperament not able to look discriminatingly at worship: "It always spoils it if I have to give an opinion about it." But other people seem to have the peculiar ability to take part in worship wholeheartedly while keeping a critical eye open at the same time. The point of evaluation is not just to hear people say "I liked it" or "I didn't like it." The point is, rather, to accomplish at least these things:

—to develop in the congregation and among the preparers serious criteria for what is good worship (and, by implication, some way of identifying what is not good),

—to see an act of worship as part of a continuing, developing liturgical life, by which the congregation is built up into the common faith, and

—to identify and retain the good features of anything that has been done well.

These pages describe a process of liturgical preparation whose general intent is simple, but which in practice can become quite detailed. No doubt most groups that begin such a process will at first do rather less than is outlined here, but they may eventually find themselves doing more than has been considered here and doing it easily. Even quite complicated tasks can become manageable through routine and familiarity. Think of an orchestra playing Beethoven's *Seventh Symphony*—and doing so with ease and joy!

Groups that recognize the desirability of such preparation and give it a serious try often report a risk, which takes them by surprise. When something has been done quite well on one Sunday, that success raises the question "How can we equal (or even top) this effort next week?" But such a driving, self-important, competitive attitude belongs to athletic performances, to theatre, and perhaps to civic extravaganzas—not to liturgy. Can a congregation become more conscious and intentional about its worship than it has been while avoiding the "producer" mentality? A liturgy fails if it sets out to be dramatic or impressive, rather than being simply faithful.

There is an essential modesty about Christian liturgy: A group gathers for the public reading of the Scriptures, for praise and prayer; followed by the family meal of the people of God. A prepared liturgy need not be complex. In fact, well-prepared liturgies will often commend themselves by reason of their restraint. They will, however, show care and focus. Out of a great many things that might be done, and out of many imaginative ideas that may be proposed, a few are selected that show forth the glory of God and that contribute to what Paul was always concerned about: the building up of the Body of Christ.

• Note: The Place of Confession and Absolution in the Eucharist •

The conviction that a devout communicant should come to the Eucharist by way of confession and absolution, and not otherwise, lies very deep in Western piety.

In the Anglican tradition, in 1548, the year before the first Prayer Book, the Church of England authorized a brief form called "The Order of the Communion" that inserted corporate public confession and absolution, in English, into the Latin Mass after the priest had completed the consecration and before the people's communion. Those who intended to receive were bidden to come into the choir of the church ("draw near") where they made a General Confession, led by the priest. An absolution by the priest followed. Some appropriate Scripture passages (the "Comfortable Words") led to the receiving of communion, both the bread and the wine. This short insertion into the familiar Mass would no doubt have been the first feature of the English liturgical reformation to reach most worshipers. It would have signified that the leaders of this movement were concerned that the language be the people's language, that the people receive the Eucharist in both kinds, and that each communicant make a confession (not private, but in community) and receive absolution prior to partaking communion.

When, in the following year, a full Prayer Book was issued, this ritual sequence was incorporated into the English service of Holy Communion—the long 1549 consecration prayer was followed by the 1548 penitential devotions, which led to communion. This sequence was changed when, in the Prayer Book that was issued in 1552, the Confession, absolution and Comfortable Words were placed after the Prayer for the Church and before the Sursum Corda, where they did not separate consecration from communion. Though the first two Prayer Books differed in the order in which these acts were set, in both of them a communicant was led to communion by way of confession and absolution. Subsequent Anglican Prayer Books maintained this sequence.

For many centuries, before and after the Reformation, the Roman Church required private confession and absolution before going to Mass. Clearly one was not fit to "assist at Mass" or to make "a good communion" (as it was spoken of then) without this penitential preparation.

In some Reformed Churches, "Sacrament Sunday" was preceded by a preparatory service, usually on a Saturday evening. This service was of a deeply serious and penitential character. By this means, or by others, many Protestant churches have sought to give form to Paul's warning against eating and drinking at the Lord's Supper "in an unworthy manner" (1 Cor.11:27–32).

It has been widely understood in the Christian West that there should be some ritual dealing with sin—either corporate or individual, either public or private, either prior to the Eucharist or within it—but prior to receiving the Body and Blood of Christ. Any eucharistic practice that lacked such a regular discipline would have seemed defective, without proper seriousness concerning sin.

But this deep, widespread religious intuition carries less historical and theological authority than one might suppose. Although the early church took seriously the reality of sin among the baptized, none of the early eucharistic liturgies contains a confession and absolution. In certain early periods and places, moral discipline required that a person who had brought disgrace on the congregation and who had been excommunicated, but who sought to return, be put in a group of "penitents" who were dismissed from the Eucharist, with the catechumens, after the Service of the Word, without receiving communion. In the weeks before Easter a penitent might stand at the church door, asking the forgiveness of the congregation. At Easter such a penitent might be readmitted. Some students of the history of penance think that for less serious and public sins the kiss of peace was taken to be a time to make right what was not right, a gesture of a reconciled community. The practice of regular private confession and absolution prior to Mass was not early but Medieval, an adoption throughout the West of a custom that had Celtic origins.

The practice of the West—Roman, Anglican and Reformed—has seemed to require that one go to confession and absolution *in order to qualify to receive communion.* One then went to communion as a sinner forgiven. To have gone otherwise would have seemed a violation of an important discipline and to run a risk of incurring an "eating and drinking" judgment on oneself.

But this idea that confession and absolution form a necessary preparation for communion is open to significant question:

One of the meanings of the Eucharist is that it (like Baptism) is "for the forgiveness of sins." This meaning has regularly been articulated in liturgies and in doctrinal accounts of the sacrament. See BCP, p. 335, where Eucharistic Prayer I (which is the prayer of 1928 and its American predecessors) says:

> . . . most humbly beseeching thee to grant that, by the
> merits and death of thy Son Jesus Christ, and through faith
> in his blood, we, and all thy whole Church, may obtain
> remission of our sins and all other benefits of his passion.

See also the question and answer in "The Outline of the Faith":

> Q. What are the benefits we receive in the Lord's Supper?
> A. The benefits we receive are the forgiveness of our
> sins . . ."

As Baptism is "for the forgiveness of sins," and is given to each Christian once, so the Holy Communion is a frequently repeated restoration of the baptismal condition. Each of the two great sacraments of salvation represents this fundamental divine act of cleansing and renewal, though they enact it in different and complementary ways.

The question can then be put quite concisely: *If the Eucharist is itself absolution, should it be prepared for by an absolution?* A liturgy in which one goes to an absolution by way of an absolution seems clearly redundant. To put the matter in quite personal terms, does one go to the Communion as a sinner who has previously sought and received ritual absolution? Or does one go as a sinner who, in the eucharistic action itself, finds absolution?

The problem is not so much with the appropriateness of recognizing and confessing sin in the Eucharist as with absolution. It might be well, in connection with the church's prayers, to speak honestly of sin: the sin of the world, of the believing community, and of each person. Indeed, one might ask how we can, in our interconnected society, pray, in our General Intercessions, for the poor without acknowledging the complicity of us all in maintaining a poverty culture in an affluent society. Can we pray realistically and honestly for the sick without taking some account of the inequitable delivery of health services in our society? Can we ask God's mercy for the homeless without inquiring how long it has been since we contended for the public building of low-cost housing? The collective sins of our time trace to the fact that most people are similar to us. We shield and justify our common self-interests, and we share our moral blind spots. We are sinful persons in the midst of a sinful people. Thus the confession of sin should not be just one item among others on the agenda of an intercessory prayer. Sin is a systemic, pervasive factor in human life, and honest prayer should say as much.

If the Eucharist is a fresh enactment, in our midst, of the gracious divine acceptance in Christ and his cross, we should approach it with the gratitude that arises from an awareness of our alienation and our undeserving. It is from such awareness that we come to the Table. We do not deal with sin and failure first and then come to communion; we come to communion in order to deal with sin and failure. We come, and unfailingly we find grace.

The practice of coming to communion by way of contrition tends to suggest that the efficacy of the sacrament depends, at least in some measure, on the sincerity and thoroughness of our repentance. Inadequate recognition of one's sin: limited grace in the Eucharist. But is God's acceptance of us governed by our acceptability—or by whether we suppose ourselves to be sufficiently acceptable? Is the reality of the Eucharist dependent on how we happen to feel at the time about the Eucharist or about ourselves? Luther, in one of his bold and wonderful moments, remarked, "I sometimes rush to the altar and receive the sacrament without confession as a way of making clear to myself that whether or not I feel a certain way about it has nothing to do with God's act of grace for me."

This question about the dispensability of confession and absolution for the devout communicant has been raised by a few Anglican theologians.

(Roman theologians are also dealing with the relation of penance to Eucharist, but they do so from their own special sacramental tradition.) In the present Prayer Book, rubrics (pp. 330 and 359) permit the Confession to be omitted on occasion. And in the Prayers of the People, Form VI contains a well-worded confession of sin, but the rubric allows for the intercessions in this Form to conclude with "a suitable Collect," rather than with an absolution. These possibilities, of an adequate Eucharist in which there is no confession and absolution, and of a confession prayer in the Eucharist that is not followed at once by a formal absolution, are departures from long Anglican practice. But they are made in recognition of the varieties of historical precedent and the desirability of having more than one theological understanding of the relation of penance and Eucharist.

•

CHAPTER SIX

The Prayers of the People

In the sequence of the Eucharist, no matter which rite is used, after the readings, the sermon and the creed are ended, and before the action moves to the holy table, the community engages in corporate interces- ✓ sion. The Prayer Book gives several usable forms to guide these prayers, but it also opens possibilities for creativity and independence here, possibilities which, in considerable measure, seem to go unrecognized and unfulfilled.

The skills required to carry out imaginatively what the rite makes possible are perhaps not at once in hand. Since 1979 (or 1976) there has not been much time, modeling or training for the clergy or for the lay preparers of liturgy who may now shape The Prayers of the People to an extent without precedent in Anglican Prayer Books.

In earlier chapters of this book, when The Prayers of the People were mentioned, the reader was referred ahead to this chapter. Although we shall speak largely of the people's prayers within the Eucharist, the forms and principles discussed here would apply to any act of participatory prayer on a range of subjects.

• "The Prayers of the Faithful": Historical Sketch •

To begin with history, there are suggestions in the New Testament itself that one of the things the Christians did when they assembled was to offer common prayers. A late subapostolic letter says:

First of all, then, I urge that:
supplications, prayers, intercessions, and
thanksgivings be made
for all people,
for kings and all who are in high positions,
that we may lead a quiet and peaceable life,
godly and respectful in every way.
(1 Tim.2:1f).

This brief passage seems like the beginning of a formal agenda for prayer, an agenda that began with the most comprehensive social and political unit, the Empire. But the author's "first of all" does not begin a continued series, almost as though he had lost the train of his thought. Did the usual topics for prayer already have a somewhat agreed order, at least in the Pauline churches? How did they continue? Did the sequence move from the more general and inclusive toward the more local and close-at-hand? Persons evidently prayed with their hands raised and extended (vs.8)—a posture illustrated by the "orant" figures in early Christian art. A lengthy prayer from this early period can be found in 1 Clement, chs. 59–61. Whether or not it exemplifies what came to be the prayers of the faithful, it gives a pattern of subjects and a style of formal official prayer. The inclusion of intercession within Christian worship would have had a model in the Eighteen Benedictions of the synagogue liturgy.

When the Christian Sunday liturgy acquired its classic shape (first documented in the second century), the prayers seem to have begun the service of "the faithful." The catechumens (persons under instruction and not yet baptized) were present for the readings and the preaching. When they were dismissed, and only the baptized remained, the "faithful" exchanged the kiss of peace and engaged in common prayers, two acts expressing the life shared in Christ. The prayers would ordinarily have been said with the people standing and their arms outstretched.

At least one early form of intercession would appear to have comprised: *bidding,* probably by a deacon, to focus prayer on a subject; *silence,* for unspoken prayer by all present; followed by a *collect,* by the bishop, gathering up in general, compressed, oral form the silent prayer. This form: bidding, silence, collect . . . , bidding, silence, collect . . . , would have been flexible, specific and participatory. The content would seem to have included the emperor and the civic structure (even when the Empire was a source of persecution), and it is hard to suppose that intercession did not also include the church, its witness in the world, and the concerns of the local congregation. The Good Friday collects in the Latin Missal preserved this form of biddings and collects. The "Solemn Collects" of Good Friday, BCP pp. 277–80, restore this ancient form to the twentieth-century Episcopal Church.

Later, when there were no longer catechumens, the prayers could be located earlier in the liturgy. The classic written liturgies of the East have litanies—short prayers, in series, made by a leader; each followed by a brief constant response. Several litanies were and are used after the preparatory rite in the Divine Liturgy of the Orthodox churches.

In the West, with the clericalization of the Mass, the people's prayers dropped out. In the Latin Mass, the Greek litany response, *Kyrie eleison,* became an opening hymn. At a later point in the Mass, following the creed, the priest said *"oremus,"* ("let us pray"). But what followed was not prayer, but the beginning of the offertory. This nonfunctional invitation to prayer was probably a vestigial indication of the place once occupied by common prayers.

But intercession, which had dropped out of its earlier location, was developed in the West as part of the consecration. In the Latin canon, prior to the narrative of institution, prayer was made for the living in a section called the *memento;* and after it there was prayer for the departed, the *memento etiam.*

In the late Middle Ages the need for prayers for specific local needs was met by a vernacular service called, in England, the Prone, which might be used in the Sunday Mass at the time of the sermon. It was the kind of extempore, variable devotion that does not leave behind much record. It seems, however, to have included elementary instructions, simple popular devotions, and a "bidding prayer." This prayer, variable in length and content, was in the form "I bid you pray for. . . ."

The first English Prayer Book, 1549, kept intercession in the prayer of consecration; but all of the intercessory material was brought into one flowing, comprehensive unit, which stood at the beginning of the consecration, immediately after the Sanctus. Since this intercession was part of the liturgy of a state church, it prayed for the commonwealth. In fuller terms than those of the medieval model, prayer was made for the monarch and those who govern, for the hierarchy of the church, for the persons present, for those in need, and for those in the life beyond. In form, the intercessions were a monologue by the priest; but books were not everywhere in hand; few people in towns and villages could read; and there was no habit of oral participation or response. So we may guess that few people felt excluded.

The Prayer Book of 1552 removed the intercessions from the consecration and placed them in a unit by themselves, following the creed, sermon, and the gathering of the alms, and before the penitential material that led to the consecration and communion. Perhaps Justin Martyr's *Apology* (c. 150 CE), which was in Cranmer's library, had indicated that this was approximately their early location. In response to a Reformed conviction that prayer for the departed lacked biblical warrant and should therefore be excluded, the 1552 intercession made no mention of the saints or the faithful departed; and it was introduced almost argumentatively: "Let us pray for the whole state of Christ's church militant here in earth."

The Prayer Books of the Episcopal Church from 1789 to 1928 followed the 1552 location of the intercessions. In the English revision of 1662, a *commemoration of* the departed had been entered in the intercessions, and American books followed the English in that matter. In the 1928 American revision, a brief explicit *petition for* the departed was added to the Prayer for the Whole State of Christ's Church: ". . . beseeching thee to grant them continual growth in thy love and service."

These Prayer Book intercessions did not wear well. Their strength was in their comprehensiveness. Through well-defined categories, they covered the civic and ecclesiastical order. But even in this matter, the terms in which the state and the church were described seem to belong to another age. The civil order was divided into the rulers (Christian rulers, whose task was to promote religion and virtue and to punish wickedness and vice) and the ruled. The ecclesiastical order consisted of the clergy, who ministered the word and sacraments, and the obedient laity, whose task was to serve God truly and devoutly. The prayer had the marks of late Medieval Christendom. Yet it was used for two centuries in the eucharistic liturgy of the Episcopal Church—a church with participatory, representative polity, set in a society in which government derived its just powers from the consent of the governed. The problem was not that the prayer was written as it was in the sixteenth century, but that it continued to be used, unchanged, even though the conditions for which it was fully appropriate had all but disappeared. Not only was its content not fully applicable, but the Prayer for the Whole State of Christ's Church was, in form, an invariable clerical monologue. By custom, this prayer was said by an officiant standing at the remotest point in the eucharistic room, with his back to the congregation. The Prayer for the Whole State of Christ's Church was, in sum, one of the least satisfactory parts of the 1928 Prayer Book. But it had to be used, just as it stood, at each public Eucharist.

I enter a personal note at this point, suspecting that it catches a useful observation concerning liturgy. I worried during the 1950s and early 1960s about the confining character of this prayer. Like some other clergy, I indicated my restlessness with it by occasionally proposing special intentions before the prayer or between its sections or by entering "remembering especially . . ." interpolations in its text. But now that we pray through flexible wordings that are well adapted to today's situation, I realize that the old practice was not as bad as I, in my left-brained way, had taken it to be. Most worshipers, as I see it now, were not using the terms of the prayer of intercession literally. Rather, through those familiar, somewhat incantatory words, they were praying their real-life agenda. If this was the place for praying what was on the minds of Christian people, those things would be prayed. But one prayed for one's twentieth-century, American, Episcopalian world and church somewhat against the resistant sixteenth-century, Church of England wording of *The Book of Common Prayer*.

When the 1965 Anglican document on the structure and content of the Eucharist, which was cited in Chapter Four, spoke of intercession, it commended the litany form, as making for greater participation. As to substance, it proposed prayer "not only for the church but for the world the church is to serve." This counsel fits the situation of modern churches. Christians and the general citizenry are not the same body of people, only seen from different angles of vision. (The Tudor and Stuart dream of Christian commonwealth became unattainable not long after it had been articulated.) The church is in the world, for the world—and at times against the world. When the church-world relation is so conceived, the laity, who were described passively in the intercessions of 1928 and before, come into their own; for the church's ministry in and for the world is largely carried out through lay persons. Much of God's work is done in and through the world's work, and the laity are God's people engaged in the work of the world.

The 1967 "trial use" Eucharist, "The Liturgy of the Lord's Supper," was the first text authorized in the Episcopal Church that pioneered new language, form and substance. The rather lengthy intercession, in litany form, ranged widely, speaking of work: ". . . those who bear authority . . . who labor in commerce and industry . . . who keep house and train children, . . . for those whose work is dangerous or burdensome." It contained a valuable ecological petition: "For those who farm the fields and tend the woods; for all who gather the harvest of the lands and of the waters; and for our faithful use of thy creative bounty." Although it prayed specifically for the world, it projected a somewhat romantic view of an ordered, responsible, interconnected world. Everyone had a niche in things and performed useful tasks in a conscientious way. But the later 1960s were a time of social conflict and unrest: the young *vs* the old; blacks *vs* whites; doves *vs* hawks. Rather than general satisfaction with the social order, it was a time of penetrating criticism and the rhetoric of revolution. It seems ironic that, in its intercession, the church introduced this vision of harmony at a time of prophetic protest and terrible division.

Such shortcomings in the prayer that had been in the Prayer Book for four centuries and in the first text by which the Episcopal Church sought to replace it indicate that to pray comprehensively for the accomplishment of God's will in "the bent world" is not a simple task.

• The Joy and Burden of Intercession •

How shall we pray for the church and the world? It will not do to say, "We just follow the Prayer Book wordings," for, as we shall observe, those wordings are open to creative adaptation. Moreover, even to use them just as they stand and to enter them sympathetically, one must have some idea of their intention. One must try to do oneself the sort of thing the Prayer Book does in order to cooperate freely with the words of the authorized liturgy. The church's prayers are not to displace our own; rather, we are to pray with and through them.

When we set out to form intercessions for a range of things, consulting our own innermost convictions, we find the task unexpectedly difficult. Of course, some prayer, usually for things close to us, seems to arise specifically and spontaneously. The words are virtually given us with the experience itself as we open it to God. The prayer may be very good in its brevity and authenticity; or we may blurt out words we remember later with regret. Such prayer is not, at the time, a subject of reflection. But if such unreflective prayer is not easy to manage, neither is the prayer that is more conscious and intentional. Issues are complex and our views are limited. The ways of providence are baffling, and yet we are convinced that God is not unpartisan, and we do not pray dispassionately. Despite its difficulty, the task of prayer, in part a theological and intellectual task, may be regarded as the first task of the life of faith. It is deeply educative. Perhaps we do not understand God, or ourselves, or what is expected of us in the world until we have tried to frame such understandings in prayer.

On the Large Scale: The problem of right praying comes up in certain very obvious ways on those occasions when we seek to speak in prayer of the large, public world. The God of the prophetic faith—the God of righteousness, judgment and compassion—is concerned and active in the life of nations and the stir of history. It is a part of the grace of comprehensive intercession that we are reminded of our involvement in systemic, and in some cases seemingly remote issues. In seeking to identify with such issues, we are delivered from our provincialism. We can enter an agenda for prayer larger than that to which we would be drawn by our immediate impulses. In our deeply interconnected world, the well-being of many people is bound up with such things as political and economic decisions, technological capabilities, scientific knowledge, or control of the principal media of communication. In prayer we may well give attention to the creative and destructive forces through whose power large numbers of people are fulfilled, or else diminished. How shall we, in praying, name and describe great human collectivities? In the complex swirl of events, events in which we are ourselves caught up, what may we reverently ask for?

Intercession inevitably makes a political statement. If we do not pray for conditions to change, we pray, by our silence, for them to remain as they are. But how do prayer and politics mix? It is easy to think of ways in which they have been badly confected—not so much because the persons leading in prayer were thoughtless as because the problems are complex, and few traditions have given much critical thought to the wording of public prayer. In the conflicts of the social order, for one side to prevail or gain, ordinarily means that another side loses, often at great social and personal cost. Perhaps, as peace-loving, reconciling persons, Christians seek the good of society in which there are no losers. We are convinced that oppression harms those who inflict it, and freedom for the oppressed would also free the oppressors. Most often such hopes are starry-eyed. Structures of injustice are not remedied without pain. In many social divisions, we are not presented with clear good vs evil, but with mixed conditions and difficult choices. It is part of Christian political wisdom not to see things in simplistic, moralistic ways. But how can we identify social and political conflicts for purposes of praying?

To begin to answer by a negation, we must express our commitments without arrogance. In public intercession we must resist the temptation to use the fashioning of prayer as an occasion to exhort, correct, or instruct. To lead in prayer can give into one person's hands an opportunity for tyranny. One can unload one's own convictions—which are voiced as though they were God's convictions—on a group, without its consent. A prayer becomes a charge or an argument. This tendency is endemic in much popular prayer in many traditions. Formally, words, such as "O God, make us mindful that we ought . . ." or "Help us to recognize . . . ," are addressed to God, but no one mistakes the extent to which they are directed to the congregation. Generally speaking, the Prayer Book has kept such "homiletic prayer" out of Anglican liturgies, but now that more initiative can be taken in forming the prayers of the people, Episcopalians are no brighter and no better than others. The clergy, for the most part, have had little training in writing prayers, but they have been taught to preach, and they have years of practice in the art. It is easy for a lengthy prayer to take on the sound of a sermon. This subversion of intercessory prayer can occur when any of us who has not considered the matter adequately gets a chance to word the prayer of a congregation.

At times hortatory prayer seems not to be a matter of inadvertence; it is not hard to recall when in the deeply divisive issues of the 1960s, some persons wanted to take charge of an occasion of prayer in order to beat drums for a cause. Inevitably, in such cases, the opinions of a few are foisted on the many; what "we" pray for or the failings that "we" confess are determined rather dictatorially. Such prayer can be resented. Sacralizing (perhaps shrilly) one side of a cause can seem to cast others who do not agree with the leader's words or tone as being terribly in the wrong. Whether intended or not, prayer can sound like an accusation.

Except at the most general level (at which peace is to be preferred to war, justice is better than injustice, and kindness better than cruelty) issues are complex. Good and thoughtful people differ, differ so strongly that often it is hard for one side to credit the humanity or the good will of the other. But a "pro" prayer from one partisan invites a "con" prayer from another; and soon neither is a prayer at all.

Behind all intercessory prayer must be an informing sense of the mystery of things. Much pain is undeserved and unrelieved. Many persons prosper through exploiting others. The Christian revelation relativizes all demon theories and all messiah theories—including one's own. Some good things are accomplished in the political realm by some not very good people; and other people with the best of intentions make a botch of things. Steps that are generally praised often have unwanted and unforeseen consequences. Hopeful, well-meant social or technical solutions have created new problems and left a legacy of dismay. Moral people are especially open to self-deception in matters of public policy. They are taken in by piety or apparent good will. Honest intercession cannot be based on political naivete. The first axiom of such prayer is that we do not see as God sees. But if this awareness moderates the dogmatism with which intercession might be expressed, it should not lead to indecision. In a moral world, sides must be taken. Christians, out of their profoundest beliefs concerning God's creative and redemptive purpose, will be people of conviction and passionate commitment. In a world in which good and evil interpenetrate, we have an absolute duty to do our relative best. And prayer will arise out of the confusion and clarity, the struggle, the passions and vocational involvements of a praying group seeking to know and follow the will of God.

As a general counsel, it seems best to avoid praying for abstractions. It is usually not helpful to pray for "peace" or for "cooperation." Such wishes are so vague that it is hard to know exactly what is being asked and how one would know that it had in fact come about. Abstractions can be general terms that unite us around great hopes or visions, even though we might disagree about how such dreams might be approximated. But such terms should not stand alone. A colleague recently said that instead of praying somewhat innocuously for "the President of the United States," he would like to pray the equivalent of the old petition "Open the King of England's eyes." We need to articulate our intentions in prayer by being specific and by associating verbs and relative clauses with our nouns. If we are going to pray for peace, it is best to say something like ". . . and for God's guidance for those who will conduct the disarmament talks which begin this week," or ". . . for peace, and for strength and wisdom for those who, in the great affairs of the world, must pursue it." The point is not, of course, that we should be too specific and prescriptive, but that we should say what it is that we seek for the President of the United States or for the relation among nations.

There can be surprises when one seeks suitable words for the intercessions of a particular congregation. Members may need a forum in which the terms that are used can be questioned and clarified. I recall once, in a small group, using a prayer that had been written by someone else. I thought that it was a model of good intercessory prayer. It mentioned specifically "planners" who work for the community's good. I was thinking of such things as the staff at a county office which made sure that streets in new subdivisions that were going to join or cross other streets were all put through at the same grade level, and that houses were not built where utilities were inadequate. One man in the group found the word offensive; it spoke to him of a collectivist society. What he thought I sought was not what I sought; what he feared was not in fact in the intention of the prayer; and what was actually intended would probably have been acceptable to him. If a little more had been said about the intent of the word in the prayer the misunderstanding might have been avoided. Yet too many explanatory phrases would have flawed the prayer too. As a somewhat isolated noun, "planners" was a scare word in one person's mythology, and its use set off unprayerful reactions.

Our own words can sound so acceptable to us that we assume that they will be equally acceptable to everyone. But if, when we write, we also listen in on how our words will sound to others, we can be caught up short. The words we thought innocent enough can sound overbearing or didactic. To pray, in a fairly well-to-do group, for peace and a resolution of current conflicts can sound, at least to some persons (and to the group itself, if it is hearing itself as others will hear it) as a plea that a community will quiet down so that things may again be about as they had been, with their hidden cruelties once again unprotested. In many situations of perceived aggrievement, one group's "peace" may be another group's "perpetuation of injustice." When wording prayer for a diversified group, which represents in its prayer a portion of Christ's catholic church, one needs to think about something seldom mentioned in manuals on prayer: the sociology of language.

These general remarks may have suggested the complexity of public intercession. We must say enough in our prayers to engage persons in real petition, but not so much as to seem to persuade the congregation or to give God instructions. The task is intrinsically difficult, and most of us who undertake it will probably do it imperfectly—although most of us can learn to do it better than we do at first. Here especially we need to pray for wisdom in praying. A prayer by E. Milner White expresses the spirit in which one approaches the preparation of the Prayers of the People:

> O Lord God
> when we pray unto thee
>   desiring well and meaning truly,
> if thou seest a better way
>   to thy glory and our good,
> then thy will be done,
>   and not ours:
> as with thy dear Son
>   in the Garden of Agony,
> even Jesus Christ our Lord.
>   (*The Oxford Book of Prayer,* no. 303)

On the Small Scale: Intercession, which deals with large concerns, deals also with specific close-at-hand concerns. The intercession will be voiced in a particular congregation, with

its own history, common experience, and present-day situation. The prayers of the people are this group's opportunity
to articulate its own agenda for prayer.

The eucharistic liturgy puts us in touch with great catholic collective
sources; Scripture readings recall the redemptive saga; eucharistic action
has a universal, traditional character; the terms of the great hymns,
prayers and structural units of the Eucharist do not expressly interpret
the particulars of modern existence. In two portions of the liturgy,
however, the hereness and nowness of life under God can be developed:
the sermon, which seeks to relate the biblical faith to the contemporary
condition, and the Prayers of the People, which brings to expression the
names, circumstances, hopes and fears of a praying group.

Among the close-at-hand matters may be civic concerns of the local
community: a local election; a rash of drunk-driving accidents; the closing of a major industry; the sudden awareness of hidden poverty among
the elderly; the difficulty of guiding the young; and the difficulty for the
young of growing up in today's world. . . . Some of these matters will
be general problems in American (or world) society, but they will be felt
locally, specifically, and sometimes shockingly.

Prayer can make us aware of universal human issues that are always
near, but are often pushed to the edges of awareness: the fragility of
marriage; the uncertainty of the future; the nearness of suffering and
death; the speed of change. . . . These things press about us constantly,
and we have ways of shielding ourselves from them. But the very fact
of prayer, an act that implies our limitedness and dependence, puts us
in a posture in which they can be recognized, without despair.

These matters do not need to be brought into the prayer agenda as
though they were extraneous. At times the room where the congregation
is gathered can seem thick with them. Any act of worship that does not,
in a measured and appropriate way, bring these things to articulateness
fails the community of faith.

The praying group is usually a congregation with a continuous history
and a God-given reason for being. But it does not live alone; other
groups share a similar history and the same call of God. No congregation's life of prayer should fail to take account of its near relations. It is
bound to other congregations in the familial ties of deanery and diocese,

and it stands in ecumenical relation with neighboring churches. In addition, in communities where there are Jewish congregations, there may be considerable cordiality between Christians and Jews. The Christian churches are, in faith and obedience, deeply related to the Jewish community, and it seems desirable that their life of prayer give voice to that fact. Perhaps, especially at those times when the Jewish community celebrates its holy days (which on some occasions coincide with Christian festivals), the Prayers of the People might include the Christian church's elder generation in the faith.

The congregation represents people who are bound up in one another's well-being. Much that its members do as Christians, they will do together. The parish is a school of mutual cooperation, service, forbearance, listening and forgiving. The intercessory prayers should arise from and speak for the internal life of the congregation as it sets about the complex and difficult task of following Christ in today's world. When the congregation prays for itself, it will think of the structured life of the parish, usually mentioning the clergy and others in positions of leadership. But the basic component of the congregation's life is the baptized people, and prayer should take account of the collective tasks of worshipping, witnessing, caring, learning and ministering.

Within the congregation, attention will often be on individuals with whom others weep and rejoice. There are things to celebrate, as there are persons in sorrow or special need.

The ways of bringing names and occasions into the Prayers of the People must take account of practical things such as the size of the congregation and of the room. Perhaps particular prayers or requests for prayer can be spoken from the congregation and be heard by all, but perhaps they will have to be given in writing before the liturgy to the person who will lead. Beyond such practical matters, prayers for individuals (however they are entered in the spoken prayers) must weigh the difficult tension between circumstantiality and reticence. Often prayer will be made for persons who are themselves not fully known in the congregation. When collective prayer is sought, it is usually not helpful to hear de-contextualized names. There may be some danger of public intercession becoming a local gossip column. Most congregations will recognize the problem of urgently requesting prayer, but at the same time avoiding chattiness and preserving confidences. (The common difficulty is of freeing people to speak, not of guarding lest they say too much.) A few words are usually appreciated: ". . . for Andrea, and for her mother, who has suffered a stroke"; ". . . for George, who is recovering from injury at work this week."

Sometimes the reason for seeking prayer requires careful statement. Much depends on the closeness of the congregation and the character of the need. In some places, the loss of a job might be mentioned openly, but in other settings, it might have associations of something like shame and could only be spoken of kindly if it were spoken of indirectly or perhaps anonymously. Clearly the wishes and sensitivities of the person or family to be prayed for must be taken into account. Some conditions, known to a few, are of such a private nature that they must be specified reticently, if at all: a marriage in trouble; a case of deep depression; a struggle with addiction; or a spiritual crisis. Wordings such as ". . . for a person seeking inner strength" or ". . . for a person who seeks the prayers of this congregation" will be sufficient to insert the need and will betray no confidences. Members of the congregation soon learn how to enter such a prayer sympathetically. The request can be eloquent by reason of what it withholds.

• The Prayer Book Provision •

With these general remarks about the calling of the church to be intercessor, and about the complexity of that calling, some attention may be directed to the specific provision and expectation in the Prayer Book. The Church's liturgy provides two ways of developing the people's prayers.

1. The Prayer Book contains some printed forms for eucharistic intercessions. There is one form for Holy Eucharist I (pp. 328–30); six are provided for Holy Eucharist II (pp. 383–93); in addition, the very fine Litany for Ordinations, omitting the parts that refer specifically to the ordinands, "may be used for the Prayers of the People at the Eucharist," (pp. 548–51). "The Great Litany" (pp. 148–53) is suggested by rubric for use "before the Eucharist." In that case it would surely take the place of any full form of intercession and confession in the midst of the rite, although perhaps some particular prayers might be desirable following the Creed and before The Peace.

These printed forms have various features:

Some are largely monologue. The prayer on pp. 328–31 is an adapted form of the Prayer for the Whole State of Christ's Church from earlier Prayer Books, and it is a monologue. But a rubric (p. 328) allows for insertions by the people after each paragraph. Form II (pp. 385–86) is a bidding prayer (of which more will be said a little later), and in its printed form it is all by a leader.

Several of the intercessions are litanies:

Forms I, IV, V, and The Litany for Ordinations, have a constant response throughout, making it unnecessary for the congregation to follow a printed text. (Although in Forms I and V and in The Litany for Ordinations the last response does change, there is a verbal cue in each case.)

Others of the prayers are in litany form with a changing response: Forms III, VI, and The Great Litany. In the case of Forms III and VI, the congregational response is appropriate to the petition with which it is matched and serves to advance the thought. In the Great Litany, the changing of the response indicates passage from one large unit of content to the next.

Some of these forms make openings for insertions. Form II asks for prayer from the members of the congregation, and it allows room for it to be spoken. Forms III and VI create spaces for prayer from the congregation. Two forms expressly invite the leader to add (Form V, and the "especially _____" phrases in The Prayers of the People for Rite I).

Some of the prayers include thanksgivings (Forms II and VI), and some weave confession of sin into the prayer as a whole (Forms I, V and VI, The Great Litany, and The Litany for Ordinations).

Most of these forms of intercession end with a summary collect, either provided in the prayer itself or to be taken from the group on pp. 394–95. The concluding collect may be one appropriate to the season or the occasion, or it may be a Collect for the Mission of the Church (rubric p. 394). The prayer in Rite I has a final summary petition. Form VI, which ends with a confession prayed by all, may be brought to its conclusion by an absolution.

Although these prayers involve the voice of the congregation in varying degrees, they are all meant to be The Prayers of the People. A rubric (p. 322) commends the leading of intercession as a liturgical role for a

Deacon, but a later direction on the same page opens the role to appointed "lay persons." This role of leading the prayers of the *laos* is not a clerical prerogative.

All of these printed forms are good comprehensive prayers. All of them can guide a congregation in the God-given priestly task of representing humanity before God. Stylistically these Prayer Book forms contain many graceful wordings, yet they are general enough and cautious enough so that they seem to wear well. The Episcopal Church has been admirably served by these texts.

But many congregations seem to use one of the printed forms just about as it stands. (The mind-set of the Prayer Books from 1549 through 1928 lingers.) On occasion one finds congregations in which, at the time of the People's Prayers, one of the Prayer Book forms is used, followed by a series, sometimes quite lengthy, of biddings and special prayers or collects—for the sick, for the troubled, for memorials, for the departed and the bereaved. It is as though the congregation (or the minister) does not really trust the adequacy of the printed forms, but thinks it necessary to supplement them with specifically chosen material. The result is a lack of shape and economy. Too much time is spent on intercession, and the time includes sprawling redundancies.

The rubrics at the beginning of the section of printed prayers (p. 383) encourage creativity and imagination in the use of the forms provided. One note says "The Celebrant may introduce the Prayers with a sentence of invitation related to the occasion, or the season, or the Proper of the Day." By such words of introduction, the fixed forms can be varied, and a transition can be provided from the readings, sermon and creed to the prayers. Another rubric says that in the course of the forms provided "Adaptations or insertions suitable to the occasion may be made."

It is thus possible, with faithfulness to the Prayer Book, to use the printed forms with thoughtful editing and interpolations. The treatment of the period of prayer may be somewhat free, yet if the authorized and familiar forms are the basis of what is done, the congregation can follow and take part easily. The leader may weave "especially for . . ." phrases into the general terms of the prayers, while respecting the shape of the act as a whole. Not everything needs be prayed for in particular on every Sunday, but the forms and headings provided by the Prayer Book give structure and comprehensiveness to the whole, while a sensitive leader can weave appropriate, urgent emphases into the spoken text.

2. But the Prayer Book does not confine the people's prayers at the Eucharist to these printed forms. It invites a congregation to prepare its own intercessions. In Holy Eucharist II, following the Creed, the rubric says, "Prayer is offered with intercession for . . ." Then it gives a list of concerns. The list, in effect, says, "Pray. And when you pray, do not forget the large systemic issues. But do not forget the close-at-hand particulars either." When the rubric says, "See the forms beginning on page 383," it commends these forms, but it does not say, "On pain of ecclesiastical penalties and divine disfavor, turn to pages 383 and following and use the forms you will find there, without addition or deletion." The Prayer Book says, "pray"—implying, "Take this occasion into your own hands. No one else is competent to tell you what you should pray about today. Trust the Spirit." But the rubric suggests a range of themes, and the models printed in the Prayer Book give forms and wordings that should be of help in the demanding liturgical task. (This provision, which is developed for Holy Eucharist II is, by a rubric on p. 328, opened to users of Holy Eucharist I as well.)

The Prayer Book seems to say that while prayer, its range and content, is important, and while set forms are provided, these forms are not themselves essential to the people's prayers. In other words, in addition to using or adapting the forms of intercession given in the Prayer Book itself, this action of the Eucharist is open to creative development by the local community. Fresh thought and wording may be prepared, perhaps so specific to the occasion that today's intercession material may never be used again with just the wording that seemed best for today.

No task of the preparing group is more responsible than the shaping of the community's intercessions. There is profound spiritual challenge in seeking to bring to audible words the deep latent prayers of the congregation—prayers that, in some matters, may not be fully clear to the members themselves.

But there is also a professional challenge. Can an individual or a group that prepares intercessions write clearly and in intelligible sequence, so that others can share the flow of thought and petition? Can the worded prayer say enough without saying too much?

When the Prayer Book is used as a general guide but not as a source of specific wordings, gifts of what St. Paul called "utterance," as well as criteria for self-criticism (Pauline "discernment," 1 Cor. 12:10) must be discovered in the community of faith. Congregations and groups have found that, once the community is open to seek and recognize it, some persons turn out to be good at this sort of thing. A single person working alone can coin phrases and identify themes that give richness and specificity to an occasion of prayer. Sometimes this person's work must be edited by others who can soften such idiosyncratic features as an early draft may show, for even though, as a rule, groups cannot write, the voice of intercession needs to be a representative voice. The initial drafter may begin with a unifying theme from the day's Scriptures, and then divide its content. Or this writer may begin with a list of things to be prayed about, and then order them, group them, and determine what is to be said about each. Eventually what is sought is an instrument of words whose parts and whole—comprehension, focus, dignity, and closeness to life—will carry the united prayer of the congregation.

• Some Forms for Intercession •

There is a technical, rhetorical side to the drafting of prayers. The most satisfactory prayers are those in which something that urgently needs to be prayed about is matched with wording that adequately expresses the content. No one would long be satisfied in public prayer with elegant form that had nothing to say, or with reverent impulse toward prayer that could not find adequate articulation. The inside and the outside of prayer are so united that a great deal can be learned about the act as a whole by struggling with the obstinate details of trying to make words behave and seeking forms that actively engage a diversified congregation.

So we turn to matters of technique. First there will be five general notes, followed by a consideration of several usable forms.

> **A Note on Structure:** If a praying group is large and diversified, it is necessary (and it may be desirable in any other setting as well) that prayer have structure and sequence. A prayer that seeks to cover a large range of concerns cannot name very many of these concerns; they must be grouped in some intelligible way and identified by general cover terms. A structured prayer suggests by its divisions and movement an inclusiveness beyond the matters that are expressly mentioned. When we pray for government and those in authority, we cannot specify

all the levels of government nor all of the matters of public concern, but when the civil order is named, many specific prayers in the congregation are prompted by the words and silences of the leader.

The prayer needs to move in spoken time by some fairly obvious divisions. When people grasp the scheme, they know how to cooperate with the prayer, even if they have never heard it before. People's participation is helped if they are given a clear sense of where they have been, where they are, and where they might be going.

The rubric of the Prayer Book that directs the structure of intercessory prayer at the Eucharist (p. 359, repeated p. 383, referred to on p. 328) suggests:

> move from the large units of civil life to those more close at hand;
>
> move from the larger church to the local congregation and its members;
>
> move from the church in this life to the church in the life beyond.

This simple progression has probably been internalized by many Episcopalians so that it seems inevitable. But there can be others. The gifted Dutch poet and writer of prayers Huub Oosterhuis has a splendid "Prayer of Petition: For All Ages" (*Your Word is Near,* pp. 49–52) that moves through the stages of life, from infancy to old age, and thus includes everyone. This prayer is vindicated by the principle on which it is organized as much as by the sensitive character of its petitions. Having used it in a number of settings, I can report that people seem to be carried along by its sequence. The same author has another prayer (*ibid.,* pp. 125–27) that alternates between big concerns and events ("newspapers full of news") and intimate uncelebrated matters. This prayer lends itself to being divided (and duplicated so that all can speak it), with two sides of the room praying it antiphonally. Again the principle of organization is easy to catch at once.

These are suggestions. Other kinds of structure may come to mind, appropriate to specific occasions, and the basic, durable Prayer Book forms can accept many variations. In prayer, form is not the enemy of inwardness and grace. Rather, structured prayer receives and contains the things we came to church wanting to pray about, and it unites our prayer for these things with the prayer of others. But structured prayer, by its comprehensiveness, also reminds us of forgotten things. It enlarges and extends our individual prayers as we participate in the church's prayers.

Note on Style: The intercessions are to be spoken aloud and taken in through hearing. If they are freshly composed, and if a written text is desirable, the wording must be free, concrete, uncomplicated—like speech. Rhythm can be established by lists or items in series or by clusters of phrases. Cranmer's Great Litany (BCP, pp. 148–55) is a miracle of rhythm. He avoided the tiresome staccato of his medieval models. Abstract words or complex sentences are best avoided. Although written and spoken language are often quite different one from the other, it is possible to write in such a way as to *hear* the words on the page as speech. If the prayer is to be led by someone other than the person who wrote it, the leader should be given the text in advance so that its expressions can become familiar. The person who will lead the prayer should be permitted to insert connectives, or otherwise alter the rhythm, so that the text suits her or his mode of speaking. There are some guides to "writing for the ear," but the matter is quite individual, and the techniques for doing it well cannot be reduced to neat rules. Some persons can write and lead their own prayers very effectively, but when someone else tries to use those same prayer texts orally, they sound like tongue-twisters. The intercessory prayers in the Prayer Book (pp. 383–93) are set out on the page in loose lines that indicate the structure of their ideas and the movement of the words in breatheable units. Persons who prepare intercessions for congregations may find it useful to set out their text on the page in lines each one phrase or breath long.

Note on Instructions: In a group that meets often and usually does things in about the same way, custom prevails and explanations are unnecessary. But when such conditions are not present and when there is no printed text for all, if it is desired that people participate freely, they must know the terms of the contract with the leader of the prayer. What will be provided for the congregation? What may it do? When? Instructions are a matter of courtesy and fairness; without them an occasion of prayer can seem like a demand whose terms are imposed. Or it may seem baffling—a missed opportunity. "If only I had known at the start what I knew at the end." People can be put at ease if a litany is introduced by saying something like: "The Prayers of the People today are in the form of a litany. Each petition ends 'O God, in your mercy.' The congregation's response throughout is 'Hear our prayer.' Near the conclusion of the prayer, there will be an opening for free intercessions."

Note on Collects: The collect form is inherited from the Latin tradition, as its conciseness of wording might suggest. This form is familiar to Christians in the Western liturgical traditions, but unfamiliar to millions of American Christians who are at home with the more loose associational, conversational (is it unjust to say "garrulous?") modes of prayer-rhetoric.

The collect probably functioned at first as a summary prayer; it says much in little. It usually has just one point, although the point may be complex. The commonest form begins with an address to God, usually brief. The address is followed by a clause or idea citing some aspect of God's character, actions or promises, something about God that is the basis for what will be asked for ourselves. (For many generations this part of the collect more often than not took the form of a relative clause beginning with "who . . ."—as "Almighty God who art more ready to hear than we to ask . . ." But with the change of prayer speech to modern pronouns, the affirmation concerning God must avoid the "yoo-hoo" construction. So most collects now follow the address with a "you" sentence that affirms something about God.) A petition, simple or compound, comes next, followed by some statement of the intention or result that is sought, which also may be simple or compound:

> ". . . that we may perfectly love you, and
> worthily magnify your holy name."

This form of prayer exhibits care and economy in wording. But so much is said so quickly that the content may be missed by those who are not accustomed to the kind of listening that such wording requires. Modern communication media may, among their other cultural effects, erode our ability to hear and use the collect form. Our brief communications—"thirty-second breaks" and "sound bites"—are terribly obvious; while the collect is subtle and involuted.

At the same time, just because the expression in a collect is so compressed, persons who are familiar with such prayers in the liturgy know that they can return to them repeatedly and not tire of them. They are not prayers that one is finished with after a single hearing. They are for a lifetime.

In general it is clear that it is not a good idea to try to cover extended comprehensive intercessions by a string of collects. Good collects are short lapidary statements that detract from one another if several of them are set in series.

> **Note on Silence:** Although the 1979 Prayer Book has provision for it, many Episcopalians remain unaccustomed to liturgical silence. They feel awkward and ill at ease during it, and they need coaching as to how to use it. As silence has, by rubric and by custom, become more common in Prayer Book worship, one hears remarks about Episcopalian congregations becoming Quaker meetings. The understandable remark invites a clarification. In Quaker practice, silence precedes speech. Words arise out of preparedness and expectancy created by silence. This use of silence is valuable and is familiar to many Episcopalians. In addition to the private practice of collectedness, the Prayer Book uses silence before prayers of confession (pp. 41, 360, 393, for instance), at the fraction (p. 364), or before the central prayer of ordination (pp. 520, 533, 544). But the form of silence that is most often called for in the rubrics of the Prayer Book is silence *after* something has been said. It opens time in which to reflect inwardly, undistractedly on something important.

Prayer Book rubrics suggest silence after Scripture readings (pp. 47, 65, 84, 119, 326, 357). Some congregations have introduced it after the

Gospel and sermon. In prayers, silence may come after a subject for petition or thanksgiving has been bidden (Form II, pp. 385–86), or it may come at the end of a litany (Form V, p. 391). During such silence, the prayer continues, although the leader is silent. The congregation, in a time that is simultaneously very private and inward and very shared, prays while saying nothing aloud.

This practice is still foreign to persons who have had little experience of retreats or monastic discipline. One dare not assume that nothing is happening even though nothing is said aloud. Liturgical leaders must learn not to feel compulsive about saying something to cover the silence. Perhaps Episcopalians have come to feel that liturgy must be impelled from the outside. (Some other groups need to learn that worship can, in fact, be prompted from the outside.) When the external prompting voice falls silent, they cannot relax.

In our noisy culture, we are so unfamiliar with silence that we can be made uncomfortable by it. Can one conjecture an internal monologue? "Oh, the speaking has stopped. What am I to think about? My mind wandered during the last things that were read or said. It is now a total blank. How stupid of me! I now am in a period when my attention has no focus. Is that really useful? Why doesn't somebody say something?"

It is not required that one think about the last thing that was said aloud. That would make worship a series of demands. Perhaps one missed the last thing that was said because of associations set off by something that had been said some moments before. At one level, one is still back there doing interior business with that phrase or image. But why not? A great deal happens in a well-formed liturgical unit. No one is meant to follow every word intensely. One rides loose to the part and is caught up in the movement of the whole. During periods of silence, even though something will have been said that merits thought, one's mind is unruly and it is brought under control only with some training, and imperfectly then. Silence is not an occasion for burdening the inner life with a feeling of guilt, inadequacy, or missed opportunity. In liturgical silence one's mind may move where it will.

But if attention has failed prior to a silence, and the silence has made one notice the lapse, attention will soon be called back. The spoken prayer will resume. Meanwhile, how often does one have a moment of sheer undistracted quietness?

Now, to describe and illustrate some longer forms of prayer that are suitable for general intercessions:

> **Free Oral Prayers by Members of the Group:** If a worshipping group is small, so that words spoken in a conversational tone can be heard by all, and if the group is fairly united, corporate intercessions may be carried forward by random freely offered prayers by members of the group who are inwardly prompted to pray. Such prayer will have little order or formal completeness, and it may have some duplication. Not every occasion requires that prayer for an inclusive range of subjects be arranged in linear sequence, although, inevitably, things will be left out, what is said will be deeply felt. (It is desirable to allow time for unformed intentions to come to articulateness. Impatience is the enemy of this sort of prayer.) Yet the act can leave the sense of a satisfactory whole. It may be best to have some summing-up by a leader at the end.

There is a tendency in groups that have no practice at this sort of thing for several members in turn to offer fairly comprehensive prayers, all covering much the same ground, each rendering the others unnecessary. Regulation needs to be supplied by courtesy and listening. There must be attention to the others who are contributing and to the common act in which all take part. Such communal prayer is fully as much an exercise in listening as it is in speaking. Each contribution may be quite pointed.

If persons are speaking in a slow ruminative fashion, there may be pauses in their thought and speech. It may be desirable to inject a little formality into this style. If each contribution begins with a form such as ". . . for (this need and that)" and ends with some such formal phrase as "Let us pray to the Lord," others will know that the person who has been speaking aloud is finished. Sometimes a competent person can be put in charge of bringing each individual petition to an end in such a way as to let others make a response and to prepare some readiness for the next person's entry.

This simple way of corporate prayer can be powerful. Individuals are free to contribute orally, or they can identify with the others who speak. The act is deeply shared, even though it is not directed by a text or a presiding voice.

This way is, however, not suitable without the right setting. The group must not be so large that people cannot easily hear one another, and at least some persons in it should have already become at ease in contributing aloud in such a group. But when the conditions support it, this is a natural and convincing form for community intercessions.

Guided Prayer—A Series of Biddings: In this form a leader carries the group along, but not by praying (unless there is a concluding collect) but by guiding the group through a series of subjects for prayer. (This is the manner of prayer used by Form II in the Prayer Book, pp. 385–86. It appeared in former Prayer Books as the Bidding Prayer. This prayer had medieval precedent and was printed on pp. 47–48 of the 1928 revision. It was widely used in the early centuries of the Prayer Book tradition, but in modern American practice it had dropped out of common use.) In this manner of prayer each new topic is introduced by some formula such as "I bid your prayer for . . . ," or "I ask . . . ," or "Let us offer our prayer for. . . ."

If this form were to be used at the intercessions of the Eucharist, it might well be introduced in such a way as to provide a transition from the Scripture readings and the sermon (and creed) to the intercessions. In Advent, for instance, one might make a bridge something like, "As the people of Christ, living by memory and hope, I bid you pray for the well-being of the church and the world." A prayer in this form might continue, basing each bidding on the outline in the rubric on pp. 359 and 383, with a few words of special intention expanding each topic. Something like an "in order that" idea or two can give point to a bidding, and an "especially for . . ." can give desirable specificity. But these enlargements should not be so full as to take away the initiative from the group members by doing everything for them.

Following each bidding there may be silence. If the leader is expecting spoken additions from group members in those silences, the pace must not be too rapid. The group is moving together through a sequence of intercessions, and spoken words and inner associations are to carry along thoughtfully.

The insertion of silences that allow for unspoken prayer after each bidding has the advantage of making time for active group participation. But the alternation of speech and silence can create an unwanted habit of mind. These openings for unspoken prayer can suggest that praying is something that takes place inwardly and essentially privately *between* the biddings or prayers of the leader. It is easy for people to think, "I cannot pray as long as someone else is talking." But clearly one of the skills required in this and other forms of corporate prayer is to pray *with* the leader and *by means of* the biddings spoken by someone else.

This form is very flexible. It can be developed at any length on any subject or series of subjects. It can be prepared or extemporized as a rewording of material from the Prayer Book outline (pp. 359, 383). In character, it can be formal or conversational.

The task of this form is to lead or prompt the prayer of the congregation. The leader is talking to the people, not talking in their name to God. Yet through the well-worded pointed biddings, a community engages in sustained corporate prayer.

Here, as an example, is a prayer in bidding form around the theme of peace:

Good Christian friends,
    I bid you pray to God for peace—for the peace from above—that it may prevail in our world, among peoples and nations, and within our own lives.

    I bid you pray for God's comfort for the victims of wars—for those who are now suffering, especially those those in _____, and _____, and _____—for those who bear the wounds of old wars, for refugees, the bereaved, and the emotionally scarred.

    I bid you pray for divine wisdom for the leaders of the nations—that they may practice restraint in speech and actions, that they may seek mutual accommodation, and may find national strength in the quest for justice and liberty.

    Pray too for discretion for the people of our nation, and of all nations, that they may withhold consent when priorities are mistaken, opinion is manipulated, and by reckless public words and acts their lives are put at risk.

I bid your prayer too for the churches, that with courage and consistency they may speak and act on the side of peace, understanding and generosity.

Let us pray also for ourselves—that our hostilities toward, and our small tyrannies over others may be overcome in the grace of Christ.

Let us ask God for the absolution and remission of our sins and offenses.

Let us pray that in compassion God will defend, deliver and protect us.
[concluding collect]

Eternal God, in whose perfect kingdom no sword is drawn but the sword of righteousness, no strength known but the strength of love: So mightily spread abroad your Spirit, that all peoples may be gathered, as children of one family, under the banner of the Prince of Peace, to whom be glory and dominion, now and for ever. *Amen.*

Biddings and Short Prayers: This form is much like the previous one; but it is not bidding, perhaps followed by silence, and then by the next subject; it is bidding, silence, brief spoken prayer, and then next topic. The spoken prayer may be by the "bidder" or by someone else.

Each short prayer gives voice in public petition to the theme asked in the bidding. If there is a problem with the bidding prayer form discussed above, it is that it has become so unfamiliar that many persons, on hearing it, may hardly think of it as prayer at all. In this form, biddings are mixed with petitions.

(Something like this manner of formal prayer is used in Form IV in the Prayer Book, pp. 388–89. Its order is brief prayer, followed by silence, which is ended by versicle and response. The "Solemn Collects" in the Good Friday liturgy (pp. 277–80) reproduce this ancient form of intercession.)

This form, like the previous one, leads a group in united prayer. It enables the congregation to follow and participate, silently or aloud. If the room and the congregation are so large that voices from the congregation would be hard to hear, this form would be eminently usable.

Here is an example of this form. It was drafted for an Easter Vigil service at which the congregation was made up largely of intelligent devout Christians who did not ordinarily worship together.

> **Leader's announcement:** On this night which is different from all other nights, prayer will be bidden for concerns of the church and the world. In the silence after each bidding, you are invited to add your own petitions, silently or aloud.
>
> The silence will be ended by the versicle "God, in your mercy." The congregation's response is "Hear our prayer."
>
> I bid your prayers for all of Christ's people throughout the world, for their steadfastness in faith, for their increase in love, and for their progress toward unity.
>
> [silence]
>
> God, in your mercy,
> *Hear our prayer.*
>
> Lord, let the blessing of your peace always be upon your people, and through us upon your world. *Amen.*

*

I bid your prayers for peace among nations, for leaders who work for the common good, for wise choices in the care of the earth.

> [silence]
>
> God, in your mercy,
> *Hear our prayer.*
>
> Lord God, bring your wisdom to supplant our small vision and shortsightedness. *Amen.*

*

I bid your prayers for the Jewish community which today enters upon its observance of Passover.

[silence]
God, in your mercy,
Hear our prayer.

Lord, may Israel know your peace. *Amen.*

*

I bid your prayers for those who are ill, troubled or oppressed.

[silence]

God, in your mercy,
Hear our prayer.

Send, O Lord, your healing, freeing power among us, and help us, for our part, to discern and side with life. *Amen.*

*

I bid you remember before God our sins, our selfishness, our justifying of that which has no justification.

[silence]
God, in your mercy,
Hear our prayer.

Lord, we confess our sins, negligences and ignorances, confident always in your abounding grace. *Amen.*

*

I bid you commend to God's everlasting love those who have died.

[silence]

God, in your mercy,
Hear our prayer.

O God, you have heard our requests, spoken and unspoken. Grant what has been truly prayed—not according to our wisdom in asking, nor according to our deserving, but according to your gracious will which you have made known to us in Our Lord and Saviour, Jesus Christ. AMEN.

The Litany: This familiar form can be lengthy or short; quite specific in theme and tone, or quite varied and comprehensive. It is participatory—that is its strength. In the sixteenth century, the Puritans sought to trivialize this prayer form by complaining that it was like a tennis game, with the ball going from one side of the net to the other. But of course! This is an act in which there are no spectators or mere auditors.

It is sometimes commented that the leader "gets all the good lines." While the leader's lines change and advance the thought of the prayer, the congregation's response is usually short and repetitive, either constant throughout the litany, or else unchanged through substantial sections of it.

This unvaried, or relatively unvaried, response lends a rhythm to a litany in actual use, a characteristic that is particularly clear when a litany is sung. (The Hymnal provides settings for several of the eucharistic intercessions [S 106–S109] and for the Great Litany [S 67]. The simple music for Form I [S 106] is particularly effective. The congregation can sustain the final note or chord of the response with a wordless hum beneath the next petition sung by the cantor. The cantor's final "Lord" can also be the start of the "Lord have mercy" of the congregation.) A momentum catches up the parts of the prayer into a unified, paced whole whose essential beats are established by the alternation between the leader and the congregation. This rhythmic character requires that the leader's lines have brevity, along with some variety. Thomas Cranmer was particularly skillful in clustering a number of noun phrases in the leader's petitions, giving them cadence, pulse and interest. More than is the case with some of the other forms identified previously, the litany does not depend on members of the congregation following it thoughtfully and making their own contributions. Many litanies make their impact as spiritually engaging prayer through the sweep and flow of the large unit. The prayer, even in its complexity, is a single act. Of course, not all litanies are alike, and they will not always be used in the same way. But this sense of tempo and of rhythmic alternation between leader and people is more important in litanies than in the other forms of prayer discussed here.

If the drafters of a litany want the congregation to take an active part throughout the prayer, either the congregational response must be announced at the beginning and then remain constant, or else there must be a duplicated text from which everyone can read or sing. If the drafters want changing responses, there may be a different response following each petition (as in Form III, p. 387f) to advance or complete the thought of the leader's line, or else a change in the response to indicate the large units of the prayer's structure (as in The Great Litany, pp. 148–55).

A litany, particularly if it is long and complex, requires care and skill in the writing. There must be unity, with flow and sequence. There must be sections of contrasting character and a feel for emotional climax. Congregations feel an unmistakable fulfillment in taking part in a well-conceived act of prayer. Perhaps the vocabulary, religious depth, and spiritual passion of a good litany prayer are not something that most persons could produce themselves, but they are glad to take its words on their lips—as in singing a great hymn.

Since the litany form lends itself to an indefinite number of topics and tonalities, if it is used often for eucharistic intercessions, each occasion can have a theme suggested by the season, the occasion, or the propers of the day.

The following brief litany was used as the Prayers of the People on a day in which the propers and the sermon made use of the theme of the Word of God—leading one to reflect on words and their human importance.

>**Leader's announcement:**
>>The Prayers of the People are in litany form.
>>Each petition ends with "O God, in your mercy."
>>The response is *"Hear our prayer."*

>O God,
>>Eternal Word,
>>Eternal Listener,

>We pray that your Word may prevail in the great affairs of peoples and nations—judging and setting free, casting down and raising up—and that your righteous rule may be established throughout the earth.
>>O God, in your mercy,
>>*Hear our prayer.*

>We pray that your church may be attentive to your life-giving, informing, correcting, redeeming Word—that

there may be among us no famine of hearing the Word of God—and that we may faithfully proclaim what we hear.

O God, in your mercy,
Hear our prayer.

We pray for grace to hear Jesus, your Word, in the voices of the poor and oppressed, in the stir of events, in the prophets of art and culture, in our study, in our friends, our neighbors, and in those with whom we disagree.

O God, in your mercy,
Hear our prayer.

O God, send your Word to illuminate the dark mystery of ourselves.

O God, in your mercy,
Hear our prayer.

We pray that your word of comfort, kindness and support will touch the poor, the sick, the suffering, and the bereaved.

O God, in your mercy,
Hear our prayer.

We confess our sin, and we claim your Word of forgiveness.

O God, in your mercy,
Hear our prayer.

We praise you for your Word of Christ, a Word that sounds in heaven and earth. We pray that we may celebrate it here with all those who have gone before us and now see him face to face.

O God, in your mercy,
Hear our prayer.

Let us pray for our own needs and those of others.

[silence]

[concluding collect, by the celebrant]

O God, you speak by the Spirit which searches your own depths, and you speak into the deep places of our humanity. Grant that in the din of noise and the clamor of competing words, we may discern your voice and follow it with faithfulness and courage; through Jesus Christ, to whom we listen and through whom we pray. AMEN.

Note on the Use of Lectionary Material: Intercessions can draw on lectionary material. The following prayer was written for the Seventh Sunday after Epiphany in Year B. The Old Testament reading was Isaiah 43:18–25, which suggested the theme of newness. The Psalm was 32, from which the response lines came. The Epistle was 2 Corinthians 1:18–22, with its idea of Christ as God's "Yes." The Gospel was Mark 2:1–12, of Jesus meeting the paralyzed young man who was brought to him. Jesus first said "Your sins are forgiven," and later "Rise, and walk." Since the leader gives no verbal cue for the congregational response, this prayer as written here would require a printed text for everyone. Local circumstances might suggest other petitions or other wordings; intercessions would not always want to be as tight and linear, nor perhaps as explanatory as this example is; but it indicates the possibilities in turning the scriptures into prayer:

(**Leader:**) We have heard God's voice saying through the ancient prophet "I am doing a new thing." As we celebrate the new thing done in Jesus Christ and in the church, by the Spirit, let us pray for a new thing to be done in our world, in the church, and in ourselves:

O God, we pray for our world,
　resourceful in solving small things,
　　but inclined towards self-destruction,
　　　and set in habits of folly.
Bring to this world a fresh touch of your life-giving Spirit.
　Bring a way in the wilderness,
　and rivers in the desert.

We pray for those whose skill and training are at work for the human good:

—for healers of the soul, for those who lift emotional
burdens, for those who are called by you to say to
others, "Your sins are forgiven,"

—for healers of the body, who say "Stand up and walk,"

—for those who work to relieve the pain of unjust social
orders,

—for those who struggle against ancient ills of mind,
body or society, and do not always prevail.

Give them wisdom and courage.
Bring a way in the wilderness,
and rivers in the desert.

We pray for the church, the people you have formed and
called to be a voice of your everlasting praise:

—You have promised that you will not remember its
sins.

Grant that we not keep remembering them
against ourselves.

—You have established it in Christ and given the
guarantee of the Spirit.

Grant that we do not quench the Spirit.
Bring a way in the wilderness,
and rivers in the desert.

We pray for ourselves,

—that your own ever-fresh life may quicken and heal
our inner weariness,

—that we may find our truest life by finding and
sharing yours.

Bring a way in the wilderness,
and rivers in the desert.

In silence or aloud, let us pray for our own needs and
those of others.

[silence]

Let us remember before God those persons known and
loved by us who have died.

[silence]

Everlasting God, you have given Jesus Christ as your "Yes" to us—the security of all your promises. Grant that in the "no" we hear around us and from within ourselves, we may hold in life and death to that faithful yes: Jesus Christ, through whom we utter our "Amen" to your eternal glory. *Amen.*

Note on the Use of Commemoration Days: Brief collects, response lines for a litany, or a larger act of prayer such as the Prayers of the People can draw on the work of those persons in the calendar who have left us a record in words. We can adapt for our own intercessions the sermons, meditative prose, theological works, and actual prayers of the persons who are brought before us in the church's calendar. One thinks of the possibilities in the writings of such persons as John Donne, Augustine, W.P. DuBose, Charles Wesley, Lady Julian of Norwich, or Lancelot Andrewes.

Augustine's thought was shared with and addressed to God; in a sense the entire *Confessions* is a long prayer. Moreover, it contains many brief and often beautiful passages that are expressed as prayer, and it contains ideas that can be adapted as prayers. Here is a brief prayer adapted from *Confessions,* I.20:

O Our God,
   in whom is our delight,
      our glory,
      and our trust,
we thank you for your gifts
and ask you to preserve and keep them for us.

Keep us too,
   and so our gifts will grow
      and reach perfection,
   and we shall be with you ourselves,
for we should not even exist
   if it were not by your gift—

—your gift secured to us
   through Jesus Christ, our Lord. *Amen.*

If one cannot, with the resources at one's disposal, draw an entire litany from their works, it might at times be possible to find an effective congregational response to be worked into a litany. Perhaps, for the right prayer and the right occasion, liturgical use might be made of Lady Julian's haunting lines:

> But all shall be well,
> and all shall be well,
> and all manner of thing shall be well.
> (*Showings,* ch. xvii)

To move to a somewhat unlikely illustration, William Laud, who was Archbishop of Canterbury under Charles I and executed in 1645, has had a generally bad press. Although he was austere and unyielding, as critics and biographers have said, he was a man of high principle. He left little in the way of memorable preaching or writing. But his own interior religion is discoverable in some daily devotions that he prepared for his own use. They show his largeness of spirit, his humility, and his genuine compassion. On William Laud's Day, January 10, a few years ago, I adapted this litany from his work and used it (keeping the period rhetoric) at a noonday Eucharist in a seminary chapel:

Leader's announcement: The Prayers of the People are adapted from the *Daily Devotions* of William Laud.

Each section ends with "Let Thy ways be known upon earth." The congregation's response is *"Thy saving health among all nations."*

O eternal God and merciful Father,
　　we humbly beseech Thee,
　　　　bless Thy holy Catholic Church,
　　　　　　wheresoever it is spread abroad upon the face of the
　　　　　　　　whole earth.
Good Lord,
　　purge it from all atheism, heresy, schism, superstition,
　　　　factious maintenance of groundless opinions;

that one Faith, one Lord, one Baptism, may in all places
  be professed—as Thy Church is, and can be but one.
And grant, good Lord, that we may be, and continue,
  faithful, living, and working members
    under Christ the Head,
  in that Church, the Body,
  all the days of our life,
  and through the hour of our death,
    through the merits, and by the grace,
      of the same Jesus Christ, our Lord and only Saviour.

Let Thy way be known upon earth;
Thy saving health among all nations.

O merciful God,
  bless the particular Church in which we live;
  make it, and all members of it,
    sound in faith,
      and holy in life,
  that they may serve Thee,
    and Thou bless them.

Let Thy way be known upon earth;
Thy saving health among all nations.

Lord, bless all those who govern the civil state,
  that righteousness and peace may kiss each other,
  and that we serve and honor Thee for ever.

Let Thy way be known upon earth;
Thy saving health among all nations.

Good Lord,
  bless all the places to which Thou hast made each of us
    have nearer reference,
  the place where we were born,
    and the places where we have lived and worked;
  bless every soul contained in any of these,
    all our friends, kindred, acquaintance,
      any unto whom Thou hast made us any way
      beholding.

Lord, we beseech Thee,
  forgive us and them all our sins,
    and continue us Thy servants both in life and death.

Let Thy way be known upon earth;
Thy saving health among all nations.

O Lord,
  bless all the afflicted members of the body of Thy Son,
    wheresoever, howsoever afflicted
      [especially those we name. . . .]
  Send them constant patience or speedy deliverance,
    as seems best to Thee
      and is best for them.

Let Thy way be known upon earth;
Thy saving health among all nations.

O Lord,
  against heaven and against Thee
    have we sinned and committed transgressions.
  But we beseech Thee,
    wipe them out of the book of remembrance
      which Thou hast written,
    through our Lord and Saviour.

Let Thy way be known upon earth;
Thy saving health among all nations.

Lord, here we are,
  do with us as seems best in Thine own eyes;
  only give us each a penitent and a patient spirit
    to expect Thee.

Let Thy way be known upon earth;
Thy saving health among all nations.

Celebrant:
  Gracious Father,
we humbly beseech Thee for Thy holy Catholic Church;
  fill it with all truth,
    with all peace.

Where it is corrupt, purge it;
where it is in error, direct it;
where it is superstitious, rectify it;
where anything is amiss, reform it;
where it is right, strengthen and confirm it;
where it is in want, furnish it;
where it is divided and rent asunder,
  make up the breaches of it;
    O Thou Holy One of Israel. *Amen.*

CHAPTER SEVEN

•

Gender-Conscious Editing

• The Current Situation •

For the most part, only second-place roles, as roles are measured by public power or status, have been open to women. Historical studies are showing that patterns of discrimination are age-old, and alerted consciousness notes that they persist. This subordination of women has, to a marked extent, been formed and supported by language, language that articulates a view of reality. Insofar as securing equality for women is a matter of language, it is of concern to the wordsmiths who prepare liturgical events for today's faith communities.

There are now in Episcopalian congregations many edited versions of Scripture readings, hymns, and liturgical wordings, penciled in the margins of lectern Bibles and noted in choir anthems and in hymn books. Individuals or congregations have undertaken such revisions on their own in order to deal with the practice, endemic in the sources, of designating both human and divine reality in masculine terms.

Worshipers, however, come upon this matter with different initial understandings and sympathies. Some people may dismiss any local editing that seeks to take account of the issue: "Authoritative texts should not be tampered with, at least not by us, in this congregation, with our limited expertise." Other people may think that whatever is done is too little: "The language problem is systemic, indicating a fundamental wrong direction in the tradition of words, images, and the implied order of reality. Our piecemeal editing can only begin to address it." Convictions, even within a single congregation, may be strong and in conflict.

In the late months of 1989, the Standing Liturgical Commission of the Episcopal church issued some alternative forms in *Supplemental Liturgical Texts:* Prayer Book Studies 30. The texts, that were in preparation for many months, represent a considered initial attempt to address officially the widely felt need for more inclusive liturgical wordings. They are published in two forms: a brief booklet, usable by congregations, containing liturgical texts and musical settings; and a longer booklet that contains, in addition to the texts themselves, a "Commentary" (a good statement of why such supplemental texts are desirable), and a study guide for introducing them. The Committee which drafted these Supplemental Texts drew on the work of an ecumenical English Language Liturgical Consultation, the ELLC, which was formed in 1985. The texts of Prayer Book Studies 30 do not comprise a substitute Prayer Book; they include only the basic daily Offices and the Holy Eucharist; and many rubrics suggest ways of combining them with the Prayer Book. They are not to replace *The Book of Common Prayer,* but are supplemental texts which hold authority in the church for a limited time. The Liturgical Commission does not put them forward as the last word, but as an initial published draft which is subject to further "refinement."

No doubt some users will wish the editors of the texts had done less than they have and done it differently, while other users will wish that the drafters had done more. If these texts are to be given a fair hearing, new, untried wordings cannot be compared with familiar, internalized wordings. Two fairly familiar texts need to be looked at together, and familiarity can only be acquired by consistent use. Although some users may wish that different words had been chosen here or there, these supplemental texts are to be used as they stand. They are not to be altered nor to be duplicated (except as allowed on the page opposite the title page of the booklet) without permission of the copyright holder.

One cannot simply examine and use these texts; one must examine the issue which they are meant to address. Since this issue is complex, and since the texts that are put forward in response to it will, to a great extent, be matters of judgment, it is important that whatever is done or not done in any congregation have behind it some thought-out reasons and that intelligent worshippers not become locked into reactive positions that cannot be reviewed.

The issue covers: (1) language for speaking of humanity, and (2) language for speaking of God. No doubt the first is the easier.

• Designations of Humanity •

The use of "man" or "men" or "anyone . . . he" to refer generically to humanity has a long history in Western languages. It appears not only in Bible translations and liturgical texts, but also in the literatures of hymnody, homily and devotion: "What is *man* that thou art mindful of *him?*" "If anyone thirsts, let *him* come to me . . . ," ". . . God in *man* made manifest," ". . . for us *men* and for our salvation," *"Nature, Man and God."*

This mode of expression has been accepted and used for many centuries, by women speakers and writers as well as by men. When positive reference was made to the rationality or dignity of "man," or to the rights with which all "men" were endowed, women were entitled to think themselves included (even though those who articulated the American proposition that certain rights belong inalienably to "all men" held generally that slaves, women, and men without property were less equal than others). Of course, women should not exclude themselves from the universal negative references that fit, such as "fallible man." But when expressions that used "man" generically were in regular use, women could understandably suppose that common speech simply excluded them from the principal pronouncements about humanity and set them in a subordinate place in the order of reality. They had to speak of themselves and think of themselves through masculine terms, while men did not in the same way find themselves left out of the generic forms of English speech. "Man" often included men and women, but "woman" excluded men. This common reference to the entire human reality, half male and half female, as "man" was not just a convention of language, it reflected patterns of ideas, social exclusion and power.

Since this issue came into popular awareness in the late 1960s and early 1970s, most journals, newspapers, and publishing houses have simply stopped using generic "man." It is usually retained in quoting an author, long past or relatively recent, who wrote in that style. However, some writers and publishers will change the language of a source, usually indicating that they are doing so.

Churches, in their lectionaries, hymnals, and forms of prayer and praise, make extensive public use of older texts. With respect to readings from Scripture, the Bible translations now in use were made before this issue had arisen, so to read the appointed lessons as they stand on the page can at times offend present day hearers. A canon (II.2) approves certain Bible translations for liturgical reading and by implication, rejects others. Does a congregation, or does a lector have the right to adapt the biblical text?

Several considerations come to mind: The English translations of the Bible that are in widest use are good, but they are not above criticism. Their function is to bring to present-day English-speaking readers an equivalent of what was written in Hebrew or Greek. But in some instances, not in all, translators have supplied a gratuitous "man" or "he." To cite three examples:

(1) John 14:21a reads in RSV, "He who has my commandments and keeps them, he it is who loves me; and he who loves me will be loved by my Father . . ."—three "he's" designating persons who stand related to Jesus in a love that opens one to the Father's love. The pronouns are so insistent that it almost seems in English as though John's Gospel were making a point of the privileged role of males. But the Greek terms are the indefinite or generic "whoever," from a participle, which by convention carries a masculine ending, and the demonstrative "that one" (*ekeinos,* grammatically masculine, to agree with the foregoing). Such endings are a matter of gender, not of sex (a distinction which is clear in many languages, and unclear in English). A translation might go something like "One who has my commandments and keeps them, that one (or such a one) loves me; and the one who loves me will be loved by my Father." The literal "one" and "that one" may not be felicitous English, and better wordings can be sought; but the sex-specific pronouns are an intrusion. No point is being made of the maleness of the ones to whom Jesus will be self-manifested, even though a reader of the RSV might suppose that to be the case.

(2) In 2 Corinthians 5:17, the AV read "If any man be in Christ, he is a new creature. . . ." The RSV improved the matter by translating: "If any one is in Christ, he is a new creature. . . ." But neither the "man" of the AV version nor the "he" of AV and RSV is in the Greek. There might be more than one way in which to bring the original into good English, but there is no need to import masculine pronouns into a text

that lacks them in the original. "Anyone who is in Christ is a new creation *(ktisis)*" seems an obvious possibility.

(3) In 1 Peter 2:16, where the RSV has "Live as free men," the "men" is without basis in the original.

Where the necessary competences are at hand, local authorities can double-check the translators to see whether, in this matter, their work can be bettered. In 1946, when the RSV New Testament was issued (and of course in 1611, the date of the Authorized Version) the translators, writing as they did, thought of their words as inclusive, and readers would have understood them in that way. But we can be confident that they would not translate in the same way if they were doing their work today. (It is to be regretted that *The Revised English Bible,* 1989, a revision of NEB which has just come to hand, is frequently disappointing in this matter.)

The task of translators is to put a text from one language into a good current form of another. But a few years ago this generic use of masculine pronouns stopped being acceptable English. One assumes that when, for public reading, lectors make adaptations from the RSV, the NEB, or other translations, adaptations that turn the words into what is understood to be good English today, they are not subverting, but carrying out in a changed linguistic situation, the translators' intentions.

Generic "man" has not yet been totally dropped by writers, editors and publishers in the English-speaking world. Where it has been dropped, not everyone dropped it at the same time (even though, as such changes go, this one was quite general and rapid). Following such a change old, established and often copyrighted texts cannot all be altered at once to bring them into conformity with new usage. Perhaps some of them should not be altered at all.

At worship, texts of Scripture, canticle, hymn, and prayer are not lodged in their original settings, where they might be preserved to satisfy the concerns of historians of language and ideas; they are read as living utterances. Can we use as our own texts that may mislead or give unintended offense? Obviously not, but help is at hand:

It is possible, although not always easy, for careful lectors to find graceful ways of opening the pronouns in our usual biblical translations. Singulars can be made plural, so that "Anyone . . . he" becomes "All those who . . ." "All men" can be changed to "all people" or sometimes to "all" without abridging the author's intent. "Anyone . . . their," once given low marks by grammarians, seems on the way to acceptance, replacing "Anyone . . . his."

It is common for a person who is preparing a reading to substitute "he or she" or "her and his" for an exclusive "he" or "his" in the text. But too many "he or she" constructions coming rapidly upon one another can divert a hearer's attention from what the text is about and to what a scrupulous lector has done to it. (The change may be conspicuous if members of the congregation are following the oral reading with their eyes on a printed text.) This "he or she" device should be used sparingly. Persons who enter such substitutions must look at entire sentences. If a noun or pronoun subject is changed from singular to plural, the verb, and perhaps other subordinate grammatical units, may also need to be altered. Similarly, when the term "brother" or "brothers" (which may have been less exclusive in New Testament Greek than the English equivalents sound) is changed to "brother and sister," the intentional change is likely to call attention to itself, especially if the words are repeated within a passage. When "brothers" are addressed, the term can sometimes be changed to "you" or to something like "my dear fellow believers." Rules are wooden; the matter requires judgment and an ear for language.

In a patrilineal society, ancestry was commonly spoken of in terms of "sons" and "fathers." But the collaboration of men and women in bringing children into the world can be assumed to have prevailed in antiquity, as now. When collective terms are used, "fathers" can be changed to "ancestors" or "fathers and mothers," and "forefathers" can become "forebears" without violence to the idea. When villagers are spoken of as "the men" of the village, change is not difficult. But when men are identified as "son of" (as repeatedly in such places as the public credit lines of Nehemiah 3; or in the genealogies, consisting of exclusively male names in series, that mark the Jewish Scriptures), a simple change will not do. Such genealogies are the vital statistics of ancient Israel, and we lack the information from which to supply the names of both parents. Should such passages be abridged? Or can we read them as they are, understanding them much as one might understand tribal or familial boasting in Homer or in *Beowulf*?

A reader's thought processes might go something like: "That is the way people thought and talked then. The recalled names must have provided a sense of roots, even though the exclusion of women from the remembered account no doubt did some psychic damage to both men and women. The text is part of history, and part of our heritage. The very biblical material which, in certain of its literary strata, preserves this ancient style of thought also, in other strata, gives us a way of transcending its limitedness. We do not have to think or speak now as people did millennia ago, but, somewhat in the manner of an historical ethnologist, we can recognize that they spoke as they did. We can read or hear their language without its impairing us."

The Psalms in the Prayer Book translation have handled the generic masculine with care. In Psalm 1:1, for instance, "Blessed is the man who . . ." of AV/RSV has become "Happy are those who . . ." The "he" of the tradition was probably *not* meant generically. Meditating day and night in the divine Torah was considered an occupation for men. But the opening of the pronoun of Psalm 1 for twentieth century worship expresses also the opening of roles within the Jewish and Christian communities. Some sex-specific terms do remain in the Psalter. When a Psalm refers to social roles that would clearly be those of a man or of a woman, the sex-specific pronouns are sustained in the Prayer Book Psalter. Occasionally, when the central figure of a Psalm has been understood, either by New Testament quotation or by a long tradition of typological interpretation, to refer to Christ, the "he" has been kept. With such exceptions, the generic "he" no longer stands in the Psalms of the Prayer Book.

In matters of inclusive designations of humanity, and in other linguistic matters as well, two books can help with the Scripture readings that are included in the eucharistic lectionary. One is the ecumenically prepared *Inclusive Language Lectionary,* issued for the A, B and C years. Although it is a serious work, speaking only as one reader, I find it rather doctrinaire and inattentive to differences in words and phrases as they appear in distinctive contexts. The other is *Lectionary for the Christian People,* prepared by Lutheran editors, Gordon Lathrop and Gail Ramshaw, and similarly issued in separate volumes for the three lectionary years. (The sturdily bound, attractively printed paperback volumes are suitable for public use.) This work is keyed to the Lutheran, Roman and Episcopalian lectionaries, and is skillfully done. It seeks to avoid telling the biblical writers what they ought to have said; at the same time, it is responsive to today's raised linguistic consciousness.

In following the Daily Office lectionary, that draws on more of the

Bible, one can learn principles to guide as one edits on one's own from style manuals that some publishers have issued. (Some basic suggestions can be found in Robert Bennett's Occasional Paper "The Power and Promise of Language in Worship," written for the Standing Liturgical Commission.) The fabric of Scripture is complex, and more systemic help is needed. The long-anticipated *New Revised Standard Version* with inclusive language was recently published and may help to resolve many of these issues.

When it comes to hymn texts, the editors of the Hymnal 1982 have helped with many of the instances of the generic "man" or of "brothers," but not with all of them. (Sometimes copyright restrictions made change impossible.) Many parishes, perhaps most, will accept the words of the hymns just as they stand. Such reservations as congregations or liturgy committees may have are less important than is their gratitude for a fine, considered, varied body of hymns.

Legal and moral issues arise when one seeks to alter an author's work. Each author wrote what she or he intended, and, in the case of living authors, changes should not be made in that work without the writer's consent. The texts of the Hymnal 1982 are copyrighted, and are not to be reproduced or altered without advance written permission of the copyright holder and the publisher. Many copyright holders have given The Church Hymnal Corporation permission to allow the reproduction of texts as they currently appear in the hymnal, and permission to use the texts in an altered form is often granted. Indeed, some authors have revised their own texts to remove gender bias since the Hymnal 1982 was compiled. Seeking such permission allows living writers the chance to authorize changes that they deem suitable, thereby sparing them the shock of seeing random, and at times graceless, alterations of their work.

The texts as they stand in the hymnal will not be to everyone's satisfaction in the matter of masculine designations for humanity and images for God. Some congregations may simply regard certain hymns as unusable. Despite the fact that it abridges copyright, some further editing is likely to be undertaken in some places; and if it is done, it should be done well. All stanzas of all hymns must be examined, for sometimes a hymn that gets off to a promising start has a surprise in its later stanzas. (For instance "When morning gilds the skies," [427] after three unexceptional stanzas has "Ye nations of *mankind.*") When the problem wording is in a single stanza, omission of the offending stanza may sometimes flaw the idea-structure of the text. (The fourth stanza of Hymn 427 is the one that refers to the sociopolitical order; without it the hymn is weakened.)

Some problem wordings are fairly easily dealt with, but some are stubborn. Alterations must, at a minimum, respect the author's rhythm and rhyme scheme. (In the fourth stanza of Hymn 427, ". . . of mankind" rhymes with ". . . concord find." A satisfactory substitute wording is hard to come by.) Atrocities in this matter have been committed. It should not be necessary to have to choose between sexism and barbarism.

But hymns differ. A fairly pedestrian hymn, especially if it was originally in a language other than English, may seem to allow a critical look. If the hymn has the status of an English classic, a change will inevitably call attention to itself. Alterations in known and loved sung texts can bring one's edited version very close to parody. Shall one offend by making no changes, or offend by making changes? There may be times when the best decision may be to use the hymn as it stands, as something of a period piece—as the light-hearted eighteenth-century English carol "God rest ye merry, Gentlemen" [105]—or else not use that hymn at all. A well-intentioned change in an a classic, widely known hymn can be as awkward and as conspicuous as an actor trying to improve Shakespeare's line "What a work of God is man!"

Even when the desired changes have been determined, how may they be introduced? Alterations that are announced orally will be forgotten when the hymn is sung; those that are inked in will draw attention to the changes.

Ultimately what is needed is for repair work on old hymns to be matched by the writing of new hymns that not only break out of such constriction as may have attached to past understandings of divine and human reality but which also, by their style and their theological depth, commend themselves widely in the Christian community.

• Designations for God •

The God-language of liturgy is a more difficult matter. For present purposes, we may identify two issues: (a) pronouns for the divine, and (b) image terms.

1. Pronouns for the Divine: Although by long-standing convention, the third-person pronouns for God have been masculine—"he," "his," and "him,"—sophisticated believers have doubtless understood that God is neither masculine nor feminine, but is the one in whom our selfhood, feminine and masculine, is rooted. But God is personal, and the only pronouns we have for personal reality are human, and hence gender-specific, pronouns. Often, when change is sought, the "he" and "his" can be changed to "God" and "God's." This simple change is usually unobtrusive and meets much of the discomfort that readers and hearers feel. The rejection of any obvious personal third-person pronoun can be a theological witness that God is personal, but transcends gender. But when the "he," "his," and "him" pronouns are frequent in a passage, the reiterated substitute "God" or "God's" can seem like a series of mallet blows. (The *Venite,* for example, uses "he" or "his" or "him" ten times in one brief canticle. A change to "God" or "God's" produces monotony. After such repetition, one realizes why the English language has pronouns.) Substitute terms such as "the Divine" or "the Eternal," or "the Almighty," terms that are gotten by turning adjectives into nouns, are usable, although they seem more abstract than "God." Such words resemble the Jewish use of expressions such as "heaven" in order to avoid speaking the name of God. The pronoun problem is heightened in passages, common in the Jewish Scriptures, that speak intensively of God in forms such as "he, himself . . ." (correlative of "I, myself" or "you, yourselves"). It is sometimes proposed that a distinctive form, "Godself," be used. It can be understood as a personal designation, but unique to God. Despite a few years of use in some places, this neologism seems not to have established itself in the church's vocabulary. Perhaps in many cases something like "God, God alone . . ." would do.

The proposal is sometimes made that feminine third-person pronouns, "she" or "her" or "hers," be used for God. Indeed, the proposal is often put into effect. A similar proposal is that feminine and masculine pronouns be used more or less alternately. It is at least as defensible to recognize God's personal quality by using feminine pronouns as it is to do so by using masculine pronouns. Opinions in the matter will no doubt differ, but in the judgment of one listener, this linguistic strategem seems to call attention to a problem more than to contribute to its solution.

A related issue arises as to what pronoun should be used in speaking of the ascended living Christ. It is argued that however appropriate it is to speak of Jesus, the Galilean rabbi, as a man, which he surely was, the ascended Christ should not be spoken of as "he." The present, reigning Christ is universalized and is not sex-specific. To be sure, this universalized figure was one of us—sharing our life, though not our sin. Incarnation means particularity; the Word made flesh had to be sex-specific, and he was a man; he had to be of a time, a place, and a people, and he was a first-century Palestinian Jew. But what was essential to his work for us was his humanity, not his male humanity nor his first-century Jewish humanity. "What was not entered was not redeemed." As Richard Hooker once put it: "Wisdom, to the end she might save many built her house of that Nature which is common unto all" (*E.P.,* V.lii.3). Because the Eternal Logos participated in humanity (not one-half of humanity), humanity (not one-half of it) can through him participate in the life of God. What is carried (as the profound, but necessarily indirect scriptural imagery has it) to "God's right hand" is the character that was shared with human beings—the humanity common to both sexes.

This argument has force; words must be used with care. But language in this matter defies exactness. We cannot make sharp linguistic distinctions in a matter in which realities are mingled. The *Kyrios* who lives now "in the heavenly places" is the same Jesus who lived in first-century Palestine. The experience of a human life, in its time-place specificity, its limitedness, its joy, and its pain, was, so to speak, caught up into the redemptive work of God. The figure of earth and history and the figure of heaven and faith are not separate. The Epistle to the Hebrews, the New Testament document that has the most to say about the present, living Jesus, uses the symbolic speech that the matter requires and depicts Jesus as "at the right hand" of God. But Hebrews emphasizes that the royal high priest can be touched with human frailty, for he himself was tempted, cried for deliverance, and learned obedience through suffering (Heb. 2:9;5:7f). It would cut the nerve of Christological doctrine and faith if the living Christ and the historical Jesus were separated. The glory and the scandal of the Gospel is that the two are, in fact, one. An early christological hymn speaks of "the name of Jesus" as carrying final, cosmic significance (Phil.2:10). Many hymns in active use, some of them of great tenderness, are addressed to "Jesus" or "Jesu." The "lord of glory" carries a name given by Mary and Joseph, a name by which he is still addressable (see Acts 7:59;9:5,17). The consequences of rejecting the pronoun "he" are at least as troubling as are the consequences of accepting the traditional "he" designation unthinkingly.

(Do some of the same complexities carry over to pronouns for the devil? Is the reality of evil to be thought of as personal? Not all theologians would say so. But if so, is this personal Adversary sex-specific? Who has inside information on the matter? If the devil is personal, but cannot be determined to be sex-specific, should not the common designation "he" be questioned?)

These troublesome pronouns, it should be noted, come up in our third-person speech *about* God or *about* the living Christ. Prayer and praise are heavily carried by second-person speech *to* God or *to* Christ. In such speech the problem all but vanishes, for in English, we use "you" for both men and women, and for both individuals and groups. In many languages the rhetoric of prayer would have problems, not only of which gender to use in addressing God, but also of what nuance of social relation to express. Should God be addressed formally or intimately? as one older than the speaker, or younger?

Some texts can be dealt with by a paraphrase in which the third-person terms are changed to second-person address. The *Venite,* which was cited above as having many "he" or "his" terms in a few lines, may be mentioned here again. It speaks in the third person (about God) throughout; but its content and tone might be maintained in a cautious paraphrase which would shift consistently to second-person address to God. One notes that the Commission which prepared the *Supplemental Liturgical Texts* did not make such a change, see p. 15; but it introduced an alternative morning canticle "Deus, Deus meus," which is all in second-person form. In Evening Prayer, however, the "Magnificat" (which is also Canticle 15a at Morning Prayer) is changed to second person throughout, following the lead of the English Language Liturgical Consultation.

The sum of these things is that, with respect to pronouns for God, there are difficulties in going on doing what English-speaking churches have done; but there are difficulties as well with many of the proposals for change. The matter is complex, and no solution has yet won wide consent. For the present, and doubtless for some time to come, the English-speaking Christian community will have to live with differing judgments and practices.

2. Image Terms: The terms at issue are not just the third-person pronouns; they are also the principal metaphors for God, which run heavily to masculine terms: father, lord, king, shepherd, warrior, judge, and many more. There are some feminine metaphors. (To cite a few: God as a mother carrying her child, Num.11:12; or watching over a child and teaching it to walk, Hos.11:1,3,4,9; a comforting mother, Isa.66:12f, Psa.131:1f; a woman giving birth, Deut.32:18, and the Holy Spirit as birth-giver, John 3:5–8.) Many nature-derived images, such as light, storm, rock, water, are not sex-specific. Personal images—images of kingship, dominion and splendor, drawn on for doxology; and images of father and son, heavily used in the declaration of redemption—are mostly masculine.

It can seem, at first glance, that, in the sources of the biblical faith, a patriarchal society and a monarchial political order were simply projected into the realm of the divine. But such essentially aesthetic "mirroring" seems more characteristic of Greek or Hellenistic religion and myth than of the Jewish way of thinking of God. The biblical faith was so aware of the uniqueness and holiness of God that such human material as was inevitably drawn on in speaking of God was always understood to be like, and at the same time radically unlike the divine. One thinks of Jesus' pattern of model and qualifier: "If you, being evil, know how to give good gifts to your children, *how much more* shall your Father in heaven . . ." (Luke 11:13). There are enough similarities so that humanity, made in God's image, can illustrate God. The dissimilarities are equally important if one is not to be misled. Humanity is not the measure of God. The biblical faith is both a maker and a breaker of images.

The heavily masculine biblical (and hence liturgical) images do not speak of divine maleness, a theologically appalling thought. Rather, they use role words taken from human societies. The biblical terms arose in cultures in which acting, leading roles were generally held by men. Metaphors for speaking of Israel's God, "the God who acts," drew on the doing, initiating roles in ancient societies—kings, emperors, householders, fathers, masters. But in modern society role-words that formerly designated men do not inevitably do so. Heads of state, heads of households, CEOs, thinkers and scholars, judges, military officers— the doers of society—may be women as well as men. At the same time, nurses, elementary schoolteachers, and airline flight attendants can be men as well as women. Women who may devote some years of their lives principally to the business of child rearing, often have a longer subsequent period during which they follow a second career. Mothers can be engaged in business, politics, the skilled professions, and public life, while fathers can be responsibly involved in child care and housekeeping. Can the church, in this altered social situation, speak of "the God who acts," using terms that are not sex-specific? Yes, but with some care. "Parent," which one sometimes hears, insofar as it seems more like a general category than "father," is unsuitable for address—one does not speak (at least one does not speak intimately) to categories. Similarly "monarch" seems more abstract than "king," although "reign," which is genderless, may be thought to be as concrete a term as is the gender-specific "kingdom."

Moreover, the Bible depicts God not only as an initiator and doer, but also as listener, responder, helper and supporter. God loves and receives love. These responding roles also should be open to depiction through metaphors which employ social roles that can be filled by both women and men. Language should not imply that men are invariably objective, diagnostic, aggressive and competitive, while women are always spontaneous, sympathetic and cooperative. The aim is to reduce, not to continue stereotyping and its psychic damage.

The predominantly masculine terms for God do not mean to say that God is closer to or more imitable by men than women. When Jesus tells his hearers to be like the Father in heaven, he speaks of such divine characteristics as love and impartiality (for example Mt.5:43–48) characteristics that are as attainable by women as by men, and as difficult for men as for women. Jesus' term "Father" ranged widely: if it signified judgment and demand, it signified also intimacy, tenderness and faithfulness; the one who is judge of the nations is also present in the fall of a sparrow (Mt.10:29). Shall we continue to use the term and seek to recover its biblical richness? Or, since such a tactic might seem to exclude women's experience and to swallow up all perceptions of the divine in a male term, shall we enlarge the designation of God with images of motherhood? Or can we do some of both?

While the vocabulary of the Christian community may have some givenness, uniting the present with a history, it also may grant some authority to the present and its uniqueness. When modern experience raises incisive questions about the past and asserts unmistakable newness, it may be, at least in some measure, an expression of the Spirit. It is implied in a revelation which comes through history that no point is exempt from specific cultural limitations. Words and ideas, however involved they may be in revelatory events, must come through the small spaces of social and terminological particularity. That particularity may at some point become confining, if not actually falsifying. When that happens, can one generation of Christians look at the terms of the past—even the terms of its own formative events—and ask what such terms intended to say, and then ask whether those things, insofar as they should still be said, might not be better said in different terms? This question sets a serious task for theologians and liturgists for decades to come.

We can and do select and alter terms and images. We are not required to use language that, in a changed social situation, has come to mislead or give offense. Before we either entertain substitute terms or thoughtlessly sustain traditional usage, we must examine the language of scripture and liturgy closely, lest we be offended by or else accepting of words and metaphors we have not looked into deeply.

Some of the persisting image material comes from the fact that the Christian faith has its roots in times and places, historic events reported in historic witness literature. One can well ask: Are there terms that are so bound up with events and their time-place specificity, and with the power of those events as divine disclosure that to change or drop the terms would change or qualify the reality to which they refer? References to ancient personages and to remote bits of geography, such as Pharaoh and Egypt, or the wilderness, or Moses, David, the River Jordan, Jerusalem, or Calvary, become symbols which are held in living religious traditions. The biblical revelation arose in a shepherding culture, and even a society which has little first hand knowledge of sheep could hardly part with the image of the Divine Shepherd. The redemptive events took place in a world of monarchial political order. If many parts of the modern West have no experience of autocratic rulers, is that true of the past, or of most of the world even today? Is it true of the imagination? Can we do without the use of political experience in speaking of God? Or in a world of injustice and political duplicity and corruption is it still important to affirm faith in an ultimate righteous rule? Jesus spoke intimately to and of the Father in heaven and of himself as the Father's son. Can we delete his terms? modify them? or set other terms alongside them on an equivalent level of authority? Or are there image-terms which are bound up with and not really separable from the events which gave rise to them or came to expression through them? This question, like the contrary question a few paragraphs above, is not one which all right-thinking people will answer in the same way, but it too is a question which needs to be raised.

A partial answer would be that if there are such terms, they would be select, central terms, rather than an entire fabric of speech. Moreover, there are many terms for God, nature-derived metaphors, for instance, that can be readily understood in all periods of culture and are not sex-specific. And some sexually nonspecific social roles, such as "friend," may carry underutilized expressive power.

But there may be indispensable terms in the God-talk of the biblical tradition. It is a basic, immediate activity of faith to characterize the object of faith, even though one knows that the reality of the divine is not captured by any human expression. Faith, as recognition, might be thought of as a union between active trust, on the one hand and, on the other, the witness-bearing characterization of God that springs from that trust. Although faith itself is preverbal, its immediate expressions give it form and communicability. Once the faith has been given expression, the expressive terms can help other persons to "recognize," as the original "recognizer" did. Terms that arose from an original revelatory insight become factors in forming and sustaining a tradition. And, held in the tradition, those terms become in turn elemental, formative components of the religious consciousness of persons within that tradition.

The expressions that bring faith to articulation will perforce use the material of the available culture, material that will be culture-specific and that in time will be dated. Although the faith may be thought to be universal, it is only accessible in its culture-bound packages of expression. Now, the question for persons who, in prayer and praise, use as their own an ancient body of speech in which faith has come to utterance is: Does the faith, by its very character, carry with it references to time-and-place-specific social worlds—worlds that each generation of Christians must, in some measure, learn and inhabit? Or can we break the unity between the faith and its expression and suppose that we can keep the continuity of faith even in an altered body of images? It would be difficult to argue that some disentangling is not possible; interpreters (including good preachers) do a great deal of it. But it would seem presumptuous, except with the utmost caution, to introduce in public worship discontinuity of central images while seeking to maintain continuity in faith.

Biblically derived speech will employ terms representing old social forms: monarchy, patriarchal family structure, nomadism, animal sacrifice, and the like. But more importantly such speech also preserves a record of the creative, reshaping impact that the redemptive events had on language. The historical, incarnational biblical message uses images derived from specific cultures but, significantly, in using those images it does something to the image material. The Good News takes its material from sin-structured social orders, no other human material being available. But in using this material to express the Gospel of a crucified Messiah, a God whose power is shown in weakness and vulnerability, the material is radically restructured. By an act of imagination, human relationships—such as king and subject, emperor ("lord") and citizen, parent and child, master and servant, judge and accused, and others—are radically refashioned. Images of power and status are reconstituted in a new, alternative reality. Paradoxically the material derived from unjust, oppressive, and at times degrading social structures is made the material through which a freeing, dignifying, humanizing message is expressed, proclaimed and lived. But these images, left in what might be called their natural order, could not be bearer of such a message. They have to undergo a conversion, a conversion of images being the correlative of a conversion of the imagination. In a sense, however, the power of these images in their restructured form depends on the continued availability of the unrestructured social material on which they worked dramatically. The terminology carries a record of the revolutionary thing that happened to it.

To be less general: Jesus, speaking in a patriarchal society, told a story (Lk.15:11–32) of a father who, rather than run his son's life for him, gave him his inheritance, set him free without conditions and, when the son brought his life to ruin, took him back joyfully and without recrimination. The story speaks of grace because it did not have to go that way. If we were to lose sight of the unreconstructed order that the story assumes, its surprising modification of that order would lose its dramatic power. The old terms must remain at hand so that their radical alteration, when it comes, can be understood.

Most importantly, persons who work with ancient images that speak of divine character and action must avoid reductionism. When we take traditional terms in hand and remove their strangeness, otherness, and discomfort-making features, we bring them into forms set by contemporary congenial culture and ideas, forms that tell us what we already know and confirm us in attitudes and opinions in which we are already set. Middle-class Americans (conservative or liberal) are likely to use their middle-class American speech and categories to describe a God who is surprisingly like a middle-class American (sometimes more conservative, sometimes more liberal). Persons who trim basic images to an ideology can hardly feel gratified when they find that the resultant image system supports their ideology.

The only language we have for speaking to or about God is indirect speech, the language of metaphor, image, or picture. Persons of faith, in the biblical traditions, have ventured their very souls on such speech or, more correctly, on the reality that is mediated through such speech. It is not the case that the faith community works from a body of discursive *meaning,* out of which, through a process of *symbolization,* it brings resultant concrete *symbol.* In such a route the symbol is little more than an illustration of the idea with which the process began. There is no openness; the beginning has predetermined and closed off the end. The process must be described in quite different terms. The community begins with *symbol*—symbol laden with what Paul Ricoeur has called a "surplus of meaning." Through a process of *interpretation* the symbol yields *meaning;* but such meaning is always partial and provisional. The interpreter may return to the symbol repeatedly and find new unexplored meaning. As the interpreter addresses the symbol, the symbol opens the self to itself. Thus, alongside any modern critique of inherited symbols, there must be an awe or respect for the basic irreplaceable material of the God-talk of the biblical tradition. We cannot be judged or redeemed, or even kept interested for very long, by symbols of our own devising.

These cautionary remarks are not meant to imply that, in our urgent and changing situation, we can and should do nothing with our inherited images. We choose among terms, retire shopworn terms, rediscover terms, and even coin terms all the time. (The 1979 Prayer Book substantially reduced the high proportion of monarchial imagery that had been in Anglican liturgies since the sixteenth century.) New deep understandings give birth to new terminology and require a reappraisal of old terminology. But the process is not fully intentional. We are seeking to determine, at least in part, the thing that, at least in part, determines us.

Symbols, as Paul Tillich observed, are not so much invented as discovered. One cannot, on demand, coin a new image and suppose that everyone who comes upon it will immediately find it authoritative. This complex, largely uncontrolled process of questioning and reworking basic terms, a process conspicuous in the theological discourse of the last half of the twentieth century, is a sign of vitality at least as much as it is a sign of confusion.

Translating or adapting ancient metaphors or proposing new ones depends on some hermeneutical processes that may not be very explicit. How much openly interpretive work belongs in the fabric of liturgy? Clearly the explanation and interpretation of old terms and the exploration of new terms are activities that belong in the teaching life of the church, but liturgy is most at home with somewhat naive, unreflective terms, taken from authoritative, largely prediscursive sources. Although in other contexts we may step back from our language and ask what we have meant by it, in prayer and praise the power and authority of our language depend to a considerable extent on its traditional character and its immediacy.

These summary comments on a large subject are meant to say that the matter is complex, and practices, and argumentation in support of practice, are in continuous change. Facile solutions are not appropriate. The challenge to inherited images is serious. It would be a counsel of despair to say that nothing can or should be done; it would also be reckless to seek to take wholesale terminological change into one's own control. If what is sought is a richer, more whole understanding of human and divine reality, it will not be achieved by closing off either the future or the past.

CHAPTER EIGHT

Corporate Preparation of Liturgy: "An Order for Celebrating the Holy Eucharist"

The service called "An Order for Celebrating the Holy Eucharist," on pages 400–05 of the Prayer Book, consists of a two-page outline of ritual events—things to be done, with generously permissive words in the rubrical directions—followed by a partial text of two consecration prayers, "Form 1" and "Form 2." That is all. Nothing comparable can be found in any previous book in the tradition.

The text, which is not fully worded, is obviously the result of a special conception both of the eucharistic rite and of the needs and competences that are present in the late twentieth-century church. The Holy Communion is thought of as a sequence of acts or events that are named and minimally described. These actions are largely carried out using words; they are somewhat flexible, and may be true to themselves even while being articulated in a wide variety of wordings.

Despite the scant material provided by the Prayer Book, a Eucharist celebrated using this Order is not meant to be trivial, casual, or necessarily short. (The church does not authorize a rite that it is understood will be second rate.) When standards of substance and style are not externally imposed, it becomes crucial that anyone using this liturgical opportunity do so with rigorous interiorized criteria. The Prayer Book assumes the ability on the part of presiders and communities to fill this structure: to sense the intentions of its skeletal outline, and to give unity, flow, consistency, theological adequacy, and verbal richness to a complex of actions whose parts are listed by little more than titles.

The Prayer Book directs that this Order "is not intended for use at

the principal Sunday or weekly celebration of the Holy Eucharist"—
leaving it up to a worshiping community, recognizing this negation, to
determine for what occasions it might be used. The flexibility and economy of the Order suggest its possible use for a regular daily Eucharist.
Rubrics on pages 437 and 506 of the Prayer Book open this Order for
use at a marriage or a burial. The references, in the partially worded
Forms 1 and 2, to "the particular occasion being celebrated" suggest that
the Order is suitable for eucharistic gatherings of persons who have
special pastoral or social concerns in mind, and who would welcome this
freedom and accept these liturgical restraints. The looseness of the official provision invites the congregation, or those persons who plan for it,
to develop the liturgical event in such a way that the style of the community or the circumstances of the occasion come to expression.

The directions printed in the rite focus attention on the essentials
required for liturgical integrity. The minimal character of these directions opens the rite to freedom, variety and creativity. This combination
of freedom on the one hand with limits on the other requires that the
Order be carried out with plan, intentionality and thought. Unless one
is willing to fall back on customs and formulas (things this rite is not well
served by), one cannot simply decide, on a moment's notice, to *do* an
Order for Celebrating the Holy Eucharist. The opening rubric counsels:
"This rite requires careful preparation by the Priest and other participants."

The headings and directions name and describe actions. Many of them
are quite ordinary actions: gathering in a common space, reading aloud
from a book, greeting other persons, preparing food at a table. . . . The
actions are not silent (although at worship silence can be a benign curb
on the tendency to talkativeness). They are enactments of meaning; they
serve a given Christian intention. Hence words are important: words in
liturgy do not simply clothe actions, they are themselves actions. Philoso-
phers like J.L. Austin and John Searle and literary critics like Kenneth
Burke and Stanley Fish have spoken of "verbal actions." We "do things
with words." Language is used performatively in liturgy. It does not
merely describe what we are doing, but is itself a mode of doing.

Because the church has not prescribed a complete form of words in
this Order for the Eucharist, it should not be concluded that any words
will do. Rather, a great variety of wordings might carry out the intent
of this elemental Christian act; and it could, of course, be flawed by

ill-chosen, inappropriate words, words that fall below the realism of a Christian sacramental intention. Thus those who use this Prayer Book provision are simultaneously set free and placed under constraints. They must, to the extent they can, understand the meaning of the Christian Eucharist (for any Eucharist is a traditioned act), be open to the situation of *now* (for this group and this occasion are unique), and then shape a fabric of acts and words giving voice to faith.

• Gather in the Lord's Name •

The first and most basic liturgical action is the assembling of the community. Most of the time the church is not visible or apprehensible as church. Its members are scattered, doing God's work insofar as God's work is done in and through the world's work. But the church has its significant times of "gathering in the Lord's name." In writing about worship, Paul identified moments "when you assemble as church" (1 Cor.11:18). As Christian persons leave their homes and places of employment and gather, the church becomes present to itself, visible and audible, standing before God to do its characteristic shared work.

This act of gathering is self-evidently the basis and precondition of all that follows. But it should not be thought of as taking place before the liturgy begins, but rather as being itself the beginning of the liturgy. Attention needs to be given to the conditions of the assembling. The act of entering the eucharistic room (or of coming to the appointed place, if the Eucharist is outdoors) is the beginning of congregation-making. It moves individuals toward a collective unity. It provides a transition from the many agendas of work, home, witness and service to the common agenda of worship. It creates (or can create) an attitude of preparedness or expectancy.

The act of gathering, needless to say, does not accomplish these things automatically, and sometimes they are not accomplished at all. The conditions of gathering can be examined: Can the tasks of preparation be carried out in advance? Should there be silence in the room, or music? Music can help define the room and the transition into it. If there is to be music, of what sort should it be? What is provided for people to see in the eucharistic space? Might incense be burning in the room? What can the act of gathering do to begin to form the group into a congregation? Can the physical space itself bring people into a measure of unity, and can it order them appropriately for the functions that will follow?

When last-minute preparation of the space is unavoidable, or when some music must be given a final rehearsal just before a service is to begin (as often happens at a liturgy that brings congregation and ministers together at some distance from their homes), the preparatory actions can be brought to a deliberate stop before the formal liturgy opens, and a period of silence and preparedness can be created.

If a group has a history of prior meetings, or if its members bring common understandings or expectations, usually introductory spoken directions are not needed. If they are not needed they should be avoided. When the group cannot count on custom, some things may need to be established at the outset. Some welcome may be expressed. There is often a measure of anxiety in coming to worship in an unfamiliar setting. At an "experimental" rite or a service announced as using the Order for Celebrating the Holy Eucharist, often the people will know in advance only what is *not* going to be said and done. They may feel insecure about what is going to happen. (It is one of the paradoxes of worship that formality and predictability in the liturgy can be releasing for the worshiper, while "freedom" exercised by planners and leaders can strike the worshiper either as tyranny or else as an occasion of vague apprehension.)

People need to be taken into the confidence of those who have given the liturgy its specific character; and they need to know what will be expected of them. Any music that is new will probably need to be rehearsed. If responses or special actions are expected, people need to be informed, and perhaps coached. A few remarks to put people at ease, to establish the leadership of the occasion, and to set the tone may well be a part of "gathering in the name of the Lord."

• Proclaim and Respond to the Word of God •

This liturgical outline gives no direction for the opening of the formal spoken liturgy. Presumably something happens before a passage from the Bible is read; most people would not be ready at once for attentive listening. Those opening words or acts build on but are not part of the act of gathering. Perhaps ministers will enter; or if they are already at their places, they may stand (and signal whether all are to stand with them); or perhaps the principal celebrant will simply begin to speak.

These first words ought to be given thought. They are greeting; they are unifying; and they establish an emotional tone. They should be more than the "Good Morning" (or "Good Evening") that one occasionally hears. They should in some way express the corporate engagement with God. An ascription of praise is appropriate, as are singing and spoken prayer.

When the group is ready to listen to the Word of God and to make response, the rubric allows great flexibility. At a minimum, there might be one reading from one of the Gospels. (Every Eucharist is a feast of Christ, and the New Testament Gospels are our essential sources.) After the reading, there would be some form of response: homily, meditation, shared reflections, directed silence, song, or other. The rubric suggests; it does not say too much, lest it seem to limit.

Several readings are possible, including readings from nonbiblical sources. When one ventures into readings outside the Bible, the range of potentially usable material is very large, and somewhat untested; discretion in its use must be supplied by the judgment of local persons who prepare and lead. If the group is small and a generally conversational tone prevails, somewhat inward or meditative passages might be used. For a larger group something more objective (not necessarily less deeply felt or less expressive) would suit. Not everything that is good is good for oral reading in a diversified group in a spacious room. If this provision for nonbiblical readings were to be used often, a large supply of material would need to be gathered. Ordinarily, for every reading that is used, several that looked promising must be considered and rejected.

As the liturgy directs our attention to something God is saying—to the wonder of God's gracious actions or the searching character of divine judgments—our response, as the rubric proposes, may take varied imaginative forms. Homily or meditation, or shared reflections have been mentioned. But there might be music, or dance, or mime. In the biblical idiom, the "hearing" of the Word of God is inward, deep and transforming. Our response needs to be a clear expression of faith; but in declaring the meaning of what has been heard, the response might well point to the excess of meaning that lies in our sources, beyond our ability to explain. The mystery of God and ourselves can be suggested in liturgy by a sensitive mingling of the verbal and the nonverbal, the discursive and the imaginative.

• Prayer for the World and the Church •

Intercession is an integral part of the eucharistic action. Nothing is said in the directions for the Order for Eucharist as to who voices the prayers, how they are organized, nor how they are made participatory. Such matters are important, but none of them comes up in any special way when this Order is being used. (The task of shaping appropriate corporate intercessions at the Eucharist is covered in Chapter Six of this book.)

• Exchange the Peace •

Nothing is said in this Order as to how the Peace is to be bidden or carried out, and the directions in Rites I and II (and the rubric on p. 407) provide only slight guidance. A cautionary note: The exchange of the Peace, as it is bidden by a leader and passed among the worshipers, ought to keep a "theistic" orientation explicit. This is not simply a cordial group giving expression to its friendliness. Its peace is a divine gift—the *shalom elohim*. What is in its midst and between its members is the peace of Christ. Christians share in a life that is and is not their own. The point is easily forgotten in gregarious bourgeois Christianity.

The rubric suggests, rather vaguely, that the exchange of the Peace may come "here or elsewhere." This location, following the service of the Word and before the focus turns to the table, is ancient. In the Sunday Eucharist in the early church, after the catechumens who were not yet baptized were dismissed and only the faithful remained, this gesture spoke of their commonality as a reconciled people. But many persons today will have some experience of the peace coming after the consecration and before receiving communion. This is its usual location in Roman practice, and it is allowed in this place in Rites I and II by a rubric on page 407. The peace coming after the consecration and before communion, when one is not prepared for it, can seem to interrupt. But in close proximity to the communion, it can associate a "horizontal" awareness of others with the sometimes rather individualistic act of receiving the body and blood of Christ. When the communion is followed at once by a meal or some other common action, the peace can sometimes be effective at the close of the liturgy where it seems rather like a mutual benediction among the worshipers.

• Prepare the Table •

Until this point there has been no ritual focus on the table nor on the character of the event as a meal. The table may or may not have been visually central, but it has been nonfunctional and it should have been empty. Now bread and wine are brought to the table, which becomes both focal and functional. The elements are brought from the congregation. They are signs of ourselves, of our life, our dependence on the things of the earth.

The rubric suggests that "other offerings" can be associated with the bread and wine. Obviously an offering of money, our common medium of exchange, is often presented. Gifts of food for the needy are sometimes brought. Other things can, on occasion, be offered: tokens of work, of school, of fields and gardens, and doubtless many more, but this ritual possibility must be used with restraint. It can invite romantic indulgence. The offertory can acquire drama that overpowers the subsequent rather modest actions at the table with the bread and wine. One needs to be able to answer such questions as: Why are these "other offerings" being brought at this occasion? What connection do they have with the Eucharist? Ritually, what will be done with them after they are presented?

This preparation of the table is an important turn in the eucharistic action. But it has no words that carry deep associations with it. It is an opportunity to express what one takes to be the character of this ritual moment. (Note A at the conclusion of this chapter suggests some words that may interpret this action.)

• Make Eucharist •

The skeletal directions in An Order for Celebrating the Holy Eucharist bring us to the central action of the rite. For the consecration, Forms 1 and 2 are provided, and the rubric on p. 402 permits any other consecration prayer from the Prayer Book to be used. But both Form 1 and Form

2 contain, along with with fully worded sections that are required, other fully worded passages that are optional, and rubrics identify major portions of the prayer for which no express wording is given. There is obviously some effort on the part of the drafters of the Prayer Book to mix freedom with control. The Order for Eucharist on the one hand trusts the Spirit and on the other hand creates a hedge against idiosyncrasy. This provision opens an opportunity beyond that in any previous Prayer Book. The liturgical president (or the person who has prepared the text) is invited to take the wording of the central thanksgiving into his or her own hands, but the opportunity is not without some limits.

The liturgical president seeks language that is sharp and concrete but which can speak for a community. Integrity of theological substance and of rhetorical style is not externally imposed. Yet a liturgical presider intends at this point not to do something catchy or deviative, but to do what the church does. The competences expected by this Order are partly a matter of gift, judgment and taste, and partly a matter of information. What is a consecration prayer? It is obviously a complex unity. What goes into it? What is its function and intent?

One cannot answer with one definitive description or list of components. An examination of any gathering of eucharistic prayers from the tradition (such as R.C.D. Jasper and G.J. Cuming's *Prayers of the Eucharist:* Early and Reformed, or Max Thurian and Geoffrey Wainwright's, *Baptism and Eucharist:* Ecumenical Convergence in Celebration) will indicate a remarkable variety. In inquiring after criteria and essentials, various scholars and traditions formulate their findings differently. However, in recent decades, there has come all but universal consensus (at least among the more liturgical communions) on two aspects: the general tone; and, the principal elements of the eucharistic prayer—what Louis Bouyer called the *anima* and the *schema* of eucharistic prayer.

> **The Eucharistic Tonality:** The Prayer Book title for the consecration prayer is "The Great Thanksgiving." This sacramental act is an occasion for responding to God in thanks. Christians might be described as those who share something specific to be thankful for. To put the point somewhat differently, the Christian identity of one's theology is validated as it comes to expression in thanks and praise. "Great liturgy arises from a great gospel, greatly apprehended."

The basis of this mode of response to God lies in the Jewish prayers of *berakah*, or blessing. For the devout Jew, life was threaded by evidences of divine activity—and hence with occasions for blessing. The blessing was not of things; rather, it was a blessing of God, occasioned by things. Something was seen or noticed or met (usually, but not always, something pleasant) that was recognized as a sign of God. The devout believer turned to praiseful acknowledgment. In the thing seen or noticed, the good Jew recognized the One who is in and behind all. The habit of blessing was thus a sanctification of life. One's day was not filled with self-existent things or events, but rather with occasions for spoken communion with God.

The *berakah* prayers may be very short, rather like devout exclamations:

> *On hearing thunder:*
> "Blessed art thou, O Lord our God,
>   King of the universe,
> whose strength and might fill the world."

> *At the start of a meal:*
> "Blessed art thou, O Lord our God,
>   King of the universe,
> who bringest forth bread from the earth."

But the form is flexible, and some prayers of the type are more extended: blessing God for the good things of life, for the call of Israel, the giving of the covenant, the sending of the prophets, for preserving the people, and for the promise for the future.

The Christians were heirs of this Jewish habit of devotion. Two Greek verbs are used of Jesus' prayer in the Upper Room: "he blessed *(eulogeo)* . . .," and "he gave thanks *(eucharisteo)* . . ." But the two terms are not very different from one another, and doubtless they both refer to this Jewish mode of praying. In the first-century church, when Paul counsels readers to give thanks in everything (1 Th.5:17, and see Phil.4:6), he is the disciple of Gamaliel and of Jesus.

Words of thanksgiving, for the early Christians, were performative, consecratory words. When they were pronounced, things were no longer just things. Even if they were things that had been terribly abused (for instance, meat that had been introduced into a false order of reality at a pagan temple), they could be reclaimed. They were God's good things, and through thanksgiving they could again be rightly related to the Giver and the receiver (1 Tim.4:4f).

The liturgical Eucharist has been, in the Christian community, a continuation and development of this tradition. A leader stands in the midst of the gathered faithful, voicing their central act of thanksgiving. The praiseful, celebrational tone is, or should be, pervasive. Perhaps the occasion is one of joy when praise seems to come easily. But the habit of thanksgiving is not the habit of deluding oneself that things are good when, in fact, they are not. Christian Eucharist is always spoken in the midst of human sin and failure, and sometimes in conditions of extremity and suffering. The central thanksgiving is kerygmatic. Its form is, in important respects, narrative or dramatic, deriving from the story-telling manner of the Bible. It centers on the thing for which Christians are supremely grateful—the redemptive engagement of God in humanity. That act in the midst of history deals with history's finalities, with beginnings and endings. Regardless of the circumstances in which it is spoken, our thanksgiving links us here and now with the cross and resurrection and with the ultimate triumph of God.

> **The Elements and Form:** Consecration is by prayer, not by formula. It is by a prayer of thanksgiving, and by a whole prayer of thanksgiving. We should not ask (although it has been asked) which part of the prayer is the operative part—the other parts being of secondary importance. Nor should we ask how little there can be in a valid consecration prayer (although some good prayers have been quite brief). "The Great Thanksgiving" is a full unit, with proportion, flow, consecutiveness and shape; it is a whole compounded of identifiable parts.

The components of the consecration prayer are variously named, and there are several traditional patterns of sequence. A usable list might be:

1. introductory dialogue and opening doxology
2. thanksgiving for creation, leading, through a preface, to the *Sanctus*
3. anamnesis of redemption

4. narrative of Jesus' institution of the Lord's Supper
5. epiclesis, or prayer for the action of the Holy Spirit
6. offertory
[7. intercession]
8. the intention or benefits of the communion
9. closing doxology and Amen
Lord's Prayer

It is apparent that if each of these features were developed, a consecration prayer could be quite long. But not every such prayer says, or should try to say, everything. Each should demonstrate economy, focus and emphasis. And even a short canon can be complete.

Some discussion of each of these elements is in order:

1. *Introductory dialogue and opening address:* All of the eucharistic prayers of Rites I and II and Form 1 of "An Order for Celebrating the Holy Eucharist" approach the consecration by way of the familiar dialogue: "The Lord be with you" / *"And also with you,"* (or *". . . and with thy spirit."*). This exchange is a greeting, shared in God, between the liturgical president and the people as they turn to a significant act of prayer. (The same form is used in other offices as a transition to prayer.) The leader, in effect, asks the community's permission to lead its thanksgiving, and the people give their consent.

In Form 2 the leader begins with 2 Cor.13:14, a Pauline verse often referred to as "the grace." It is the last verse of a long epistle, and it has had a liturgical history at the end of Morning and Evening Prayer. But it makes a fine beginning, and the response "and also with you" follows it neatly. There is precedent in Eastern liturgies for this liturgical use of these words.

All of the eucharistic prayers continue with: "Lift up your hearts. / *We lift them to the Lord.* / Let us give thanks to the Lord our God. / *It is right to give him thanks and praise."* These elements appear in the earliest surviving eucharistic text (Hippolytus, *Apostolic Tradition,* c.215 CE); they were commented on by several early Christian writers, and their use over the generations is one of the most notable verbal marks of continuity and universality in Christian eucharistic worship.

The familiar summons "Lift up your hearts" is, with other phrases, culminating in the *Sanctus,* a call to unite our worship with that of heaven. It says that in worship we join for a moment a cosmic activity that is always in progress.

The exchange "Let us give thanks to the Lord our God. / *It is right to give him thanks and praise*" traces to the Jewish prayer over the "cup of blessing." It identifies at the outset the praiseful, grateful character of the prayer that now begins.

The Presidential Prayer itself opens with a doxological address to God. Neither Form 1 nor Form 2 gives a text at this point. By tradition, this opening of the eucharistic prayer is addressed to God the Father. In the classic prayers, especially those of the daily offices, the term "Father" was used sparingly. It seems to have been reserved for a few places, of which the opening of the Great Thanksgiving was one.

Today there are times when groups using this Order will be seeking to reduce, relativize, or to avoid altogether the use of this designation for God. When something of the sort is being attempted here, it is important to have in mind the general trinitarian structure of the eucharistic prayer. The wording ought to begin in a way that will correlate with later passages that speak of Christ and the Spirit. These opening words should affirm that the redemptive work, which will be described in the unfolding prayer, is a work rooted in the eternal divine purpose.

The prayer need not hurry. It is celebratory, and people caught up in celebrating are not impatient to get on to the next thing. In general, the liturgies of the West (including the Anglican Prayer Books) begin the consecration with a brief address to God and quickly pass on. The Eastern liturgies pause to celebrate the eternal divine being:

> It is fitting and right to sing to You, to bless You, to
> praise You, to give thanks to You, to worship You in
> every place of your dominion: For You are God, beyond
> description, beyond understanding, invisible,
> incomprehensible, always existing, always the same. . . .

A celebrant using An Order for Celebrating the Holy Eucharist may not want to be so effusive—certainly not if it would seem out of proportion and false to one's own voice and style. But there is occasion here to express in prayer *to* God some pertinent fragment of what the church can in faith affirm *about* God. The opening may linger over the wonder of God and the joy in the divine presence.

2. *Thanksgiving for creation:* The consecration prayers in Western litur-

gies have passed to sin and redemption quickly, but, as liturgists have increasingly realized, an emphasis on creation is desirable. All of the Prayer Book texts except Prayer I (which, in this matter, represents the 1928 Prayer Book and all of its American and English predecessors) have some mention of creation.

This emphasis is theologically important. The Creator is—personally, and at cost—the Redeemer. Conversely, the one who redeems is no one other than or less than the one who has created. The work of redemption is rooted in creation, not outside it, nor against it. We are related to God through the things of the natural world. Our awe and respect for them, our joy in them, our gratitude and responsibility for them, and our sense of dependence on them are all parts of a biblical theism. Therefore, our recalling of God's mighty works begins appropriately in recalling the creative acts and our place within the divinely ordered world.

The point can be made briefly and yet adequately in a consecration prayer. But if one's imagination would like to run at this point a Psalm such as 148 (BCP, pp. 805f.) or a canticle like *A Song of Creation* (pp. 47ff.;88ff.) provide models for the celebration of the natural world. And in Prayer C (pp. 369ff., especially the upper half of p. 370) we have a wonderfully innovative twentieth-century account of creation that turns our sense of cosmic space and evolutionary time into prayer.

A rubric suggests (in both Form 1 and Form 2) that, at appropriate times, the prayer may recall before God the particular occasion being celebrated. Since the Order for Eucharist "is not intended for use at the principal Sunday or weekly celebration of the Holy Eucharist," (rubric, p. 400) its use, rather than being routine, will often be associated with some event. The sense of occasion that is present in the minds of the worshipers and that may have been developed earlier in the service of Scripture, preaching and intercession can be voiced as prayer here.

A rubric points next to a "preface." The term is quasi-technical, not referring to an introductory passage before the main text begins, but rather to an opening passage that is an integral part of the whole—a proclamation not a prelude. Often the theme of the preface is suggested by a day or season in the church year (hence "proper" preface). It identifies a moment in the divine work. Always it speaks of God's character and acts. The rubric of the "Order for Eucharist" does not require one of the printed prefaces (BCP, pp. 344–49 and 377–82), although one of them might be used. The intent of the directions here would be fulfilled by any wording that secures this liturgical action of ours in some element in the great prior actions of God.

The preface leads to the *Sanctus;* often by way of something like the familiar "Therefore with angels. . . ." The first part of this hymn is based on Isaiah 6:3 (with the third-person pronouns changed to second-person direct address). While he was in the Temple, Isaiah had a vision in which heaven, ultimate things, was seen and overheard as a realm of praise. The same hymn is repeated in a vision of heaven by a first-century Christian prophet in Revelation 4:8. In these sources, heaven is conceived as ongoing worship. The cosmic powers celebrate the holiness— the otherness, mystery and wonder—of God. Earthly worship is taken to be an echo of or participation in this continuous celebratory act, a uniting of earth with heaven.

The *Sanctus* entered the Christian eucharistic prayer by at least the late second century. (Although the earliest surviving liturgical texts lack it, its appearance in Revelation 4:8, in a passage full of liturgical allusions, may indicate its very early use in parts of the church.) It was soon linked with a second element, the *Benedictus Qui Venit*—"Blessed is he who comes in the name of the Lord. / *Hosanna in the highest.*" This part of the hymn derives from the acclamation of Jesus at his entry into Jerusalem at the start of the passion events (Mark 11:9 and parallels). Behind the words of the crowd that day were the words of Psalm 118:26. The people, seeing Jesus coming into Jerusalem, used great words, but largely without comprehension. Their acclamation has been taken up by the church in this eucharistic hymn. Thus the *Sanctus,* in its two parts, unites the eternal glory of God with the historic redemptive vocation of the Christ.

The *Sanctus* is one of the great hymns of the Eucharist, and if anything in the liturgy is sung, it should be sung. Moreover, it should be sung by rather than for the congregation. Some settings, such as the one by Powel [Hymnal, S 129], are widely known and liked, but require keyboard accompaniment. The Order for the Holy Eucharist may often be used in places where no instruments or players are at hand. The Hymnal settings S 121–S 125 can be managed unaccompanied, and soon worshipers should not even need to follow the printed music. (Note B at the end of this chapter has some discussion and other examples.)

The rubrics of the Order do not require the use of the *Sanctus* itself, although the printing of the text in both Form 1 and Form 2 suggests that it would often be used. If it is not used, the planners who decide not to use it should understand the function it fills in the symbolic action of the Great Thanksgiving, and such substitutes as may be proposed (perhaps Hymn 324, "Let all mortal flesh keep silence") should be tested by the adequacy with which they do what the *Sanctus* does.

3. *Anamnesis of redemption:* Christian faith and community take their rise from events; hence the importance of memory and recital in creed and ritual. Since the events are seen as divinely-charged, revelatory, and transforming, the church's actions of recital take the form and tone of doxology, acknowledgment, or confession of faith. In this central prayer, the community of faith tells the story by which it is constituted.

The crucial event is, of course, the life, death and resurrection of Jesus Christ. Jesus appears in the context of two communities and two histories: Israel and the Church. With so much potential material, the recalling that is suitable in a eucharistic prayer must be selective and focused—a precis of a panoramic story—but it need not be skimpy or ill-balanced.

Eucharistic prayers in the Western tradition tend to center on Jesus' death and resurrection. (In the case of Anglican liturgies in the tradition of 1552, the resurrection is often slighted.) In this matter, those prayers are like the creed or the writings of Paul. This single-mindedness is not necessarily a grave deficiency. The cross is central in the New Testament account of Christ, and it is a sign of triumph, rather than of defeat.

Most writers of eucharistic prayers today, when they remember the figure of Jesus Christ, seek to give point to the passion and resurrection by placing them in the context of Jesus' life and mission. Thus the Great Thanksgiving can expand to speak of Jesus who was born as one of us yet fully God; who inaugurated the active reign of God; who summoned persons to radical repentance; who healed, sided with the poor, loved his friends, took to himself the marginalized persons of his society, challenged self-righteousness; and held the purposes of God over against the alienated, sin-structured orders of human life; and who stirred such enmity that he was put to death. In the Prayer Book, Prayer D (the section at the top of p. 376) is a model for eloquent but restrained enlargement of this theme.

Rather similarly, many consecration prayers fail to carry the work of Christ through to the Ascension. They stop short of celebrating the present, living, triumphant Christ, Head over all. (The Prayer Books of the 1552/1662 tradition are grave offenders in this matter.) The present life and worship of the church are grounded in a participation in the living Christ. The Eucharist is a claiming now of a victory actualized in Christ and pledged for all in the final consummation. The thanksgiving prayer should at least tell the story of "the salvation of the world through Jesus Christ our Lord" to the point where his link with the faith, the struggle and suffering, the sin, and the joy of today is made explicit.

The traditional prayers have centered on the Gospel history to the exclusion of all else. It is not a mistake to hold the wonder of this graced event central in the articulated memory of the church, but the recalling of Jesus, the Spirit-anointed man from Nazareth, can be enlarged to include the memory of Israel. The early preaching of the Christian story began by affirming "The promises are fulfilled," implying that one cannot know the meaning of Jesus' story apart from a prior story. Even the touch of this recognition in Prayer B (p. 370), "in the calling of Israel to be your people," is a considerable enrichment; these few words imply much. Prayer C (pp. 372 and 374) speaks more fully of the saga of the Old Testament as a sustained appeal by God for the restoration of alienated humanity. One would not want to argue that it is necessary that the eucharistic anamnesis weave the story of Israel into the story of Christ, redemption, and the church; for most of the prayers of the tradition have lacked it. However, when one is wording a consecration prayer today, the prayer, in its whole and in its parts, puts questions to one's theology. If one holds theologically that Christianity cannot be understood apart from Judaism, both as a formative historical factor and as a living faith today, the inclusion of Israel in the Christian prayed memory may be more than optional or decorative. It may be a matter of theological integrity.

Among some of the early thinkers of the church, the story of redemption included the story of the church, from the apostles' time to their own. Writers who roughed out a sense of the providential design of God—Eusebius, Augustine, Orosius, Socrates, Theodoret and others—thought in such terms. I know of no eucharistic prayer that includes in its anamnesis a summary account of the church. Perhaps there is something presumptuous in attempting to describe in prayer a pattern in history. The angle from which any person or tradition sees is sure to lead to the misjudgment of many things. We are all embedded in history and cannot comprehend it fairly or whole.

Perhaps we should just confine ourselves to the biblical account of the originating events of the Christian faith and community. Yet, greatly daring, might one think of the biblical story as an informing base from which to look at history? To the extent that we live in an ecumenical era, we can narrate the story of Christian flawedness and heroism generously and without polemics. The process that H. Richard Niebuhr described as "the conversion of the memory" (in *The Meaning of Revelation,* pp. 111–21) has made some headway. Would it be possible to include in the anmnesis of redemption a summary account of Christian martyrs, missionaries, theologians, mystics, social reformers, preachers, pastors—or, indeed, a summary mention of the varied and gifted people of God? At any rate, it would be a valuable and chastening exercise to try it.

The story of salvation tends to be told as the triumph of God—for, in the long run that is what it is. But its historical working-out is complex. What God did and now does for human redemption was and is done against incomprehension and resistance. If we want to identify with the redemptive outcome, should we not also identify with the stubborn refusal of grace? At times the biblical literature tells the story with that dual emphasis. Psalm 105, which is unmistakably liturgical in character, tells the saga of divine wonders in Israel's behalf. But Psalm 106, which is paired with it, tells much the same story from the point of view of human resistance and disobedience. Is it possible for the church's *anamnesis* in the eucharistic prayer to keep its tone as thanksgiving while at the same time counterpointing the reality of human failure? Some liturgists have felt that, in our tragic times, the Good News is facile and cheap unless it is held against the bad news of human refusal. Can a prayer of consecration weave these two threads together so that our liturgy of glory stands alongside a liturgy of the cross?

When the Great Thanksgiving presents its summary account of salvation history, the story is not told dispassionately. It is *our* story, told from within the believing interpretation of its meaning. In telling it, we orient ourselves freshly to determinative inaugural events. But in the eschatological categories native to the Bible and the liturgy, the past is not *then;* in being remembered it is *now.* Further, the Christ who stands in our past and in our present stands in our future as well. The Eucharist has a forward reference; it is "a victory banquet celebrated in advance." Paradoxically, in the peculiar Hebrew handling of time, we "remember" the future. The anamnesis of redemption, in the eucharistic prayer, when it touches definitive moments of origin, touches pledges of completion as well. The wording of the prayer should include this factor, for it is the role of faith to give substance to hope.

4. *Narrative of institution:* The directions for this Order require that the eucharistic prayer include the narrative of Jesus' words and actions at the Last Supper. The tradition of what Jesus said and did "on the night in which he was betrayed" was apparently formalized and handed on very early. The earliest account we have, in point of writing, is in 1 Corinthians 11:23ff. (c. 55 CE), where Paul describes his narrative as something he had himself "received" and then "delivered" when, some years prior to the letter, he had come to Corinth with the Christian message. He had acted then as transmitter of a well-formed tradition older than his own experience as a Christian. He uses this traditional material, moreover, to regulate conduct among the Christians at Corinth. Through all subsequent generations, the story has occupied a central place in the eucharistic action in all parts of the Christian church. Using these words, Christians at the eucharistic assembly say, in effect, that we do now what we do because he did then what he did.

Although this narrative is a constant part of the Eucharist, there have been different understandings of its function. It may have been missing in the very early—possibly in part as early as 200 CE—liturgy of Addai and Mari. If that was the case, its absence from one of the earliest liturgical sources at least raises a question as to whether it should be considered absolutely essential to the eucharistic prayer. The widely held opinion that this narrative and Jesus' words in it are the operative "moment of consecration" is certainly mistaken. Jesus' words "this is my body . . . my blood" are not, in the narrative, words of blessing, but words of interpretation attached to the act of distributing or giving: "Take, eat; this is my body . . . Drink of it . . .; for this is my blood." Some liturgies in the Reformed traditions have set this New Testament narrative prior to and outside of the central prayer, reading it as a historical warrant for the Holy Communion. That may well be its function even when it stands within the consecration prayer.

Liturgical texts tend to conflate the four New Testament accounts of the institution. (That is to say, they combine features of the Paul-Luke accounts with features of the Mark-Matthew accounts.) And the texts in the Roman tradition have inserted wordings such as "and lifting up his eyes to thee, his heavenly Father, he blessed . . ."—wordings that hold the story in its context of prayer. But Anglican texts have been restrained and close to the New Testament, as those of An Order for Celebrating the Holy Eucharist are. The requirement in the Prayer Book Order that this element be included, and the printing of its text, with rubrics directing manual actions, clearly emphasizes the integral place of the institution in the consecration. The Prayer Book seems to say at this point: "Whatever else is done or not done in this quite free form, do this, and do it in this way."

5. *Epiclesis, invocation of the Holy Spirit:* Along with the use of the narrative of institution, the Order requires the use of a prayer for the Holy Spirit, often called by the Greek term "epiclesis." A brief text for this prayer is provided in both Form 1 and Form 2.

This element of the consecration action has not always held such a place of importance, neither in the long Western liturgical tradition nor in the Prayer Books of Anglicanism. In this matter the liturgical tradition demonstrates two emphases: The Latin liturgy in the West, for a millenium and a half, stressed the words of Jesus' institution and made no mention of the Holy Spirit in the canon. These characteristics were followed by the Prayer Books of the 1552/1662 model. By contrast, the Eastern liturgies have contained, together with the institution account, a prayer for the Holy Spirit, and theologians have underlined its importance. The Prayer Books of the 1549/1789 type have incorporated this feature in their consecration prayers.

Of course, the Holy Spirit is present and active in the Eucharist, whether mentioned in the central prayer or not. When God acts, it is by the Spirit. But as long as the Spirit is present and active, should not the central prayer say so? For reasons that trace to the historical foundation of the Episcopal Church in the United States, its Prayer Books, unlike those of the Church of England, have contained an explicit invocation of the Holy Spirit in the eucharistic prayer. The 1965 report on "The Structure and Contents of the Eucharistic Liturgy" (which was cited in Chapter Four) seemed to commend such a feature to provinces of the Anglican Communion that previously had not known it.

This emphasis on the Holy Spirit complements the emphasis on remembering which was spoken of in item 3, above. To use two technical but handy liturgical terms, *anamnesis* and *epiclesis* need one another. A recent ecumenical document put it: *"anamnesis leads to epiclesis."* The story of redemption in Christ *(anamnesis)* culminates in the Holy Spirit and the church. It is by the Spirit that the decisive events of that one moment are linked with every moment. The Spirit *(epiclesis)* is present divine action, present in the sacraments because present in life. The God who has acted still acts—on and in persons, "us," but through the world of things, "these gifts." The explicit prayer for the Spirit, within the eucharistic prayer, voices the openness of the faith community to a fresh, revelatory, uniting, freeing act of God, actualized in the sacrament.

The prescribed material of both Form 1 and Form 2 contains a text of the invocation of the Spirit, but in Form 1 it is located prior to the narrative of institution, while in Form 2, it comes after it. This placement reflects two different historical traditions of structure. The sequence found in Form 1 is also in the 1549 Prayer Book and in Prayer C of the present book. But the epiclesis followed the institution narrative in the American Prayer Books from 1789 to 1928, and it holds that position in Prayers 1,2,A,B and D of the present book. Preference for one sequence or the other is a matter of judgment.

The wording provided for this invocation in both Form 1 and Form 2 is quite terse. Clearly anyone using the "Order for Eucharist" will want to say, at this moment in the eucharistic action, at least as much as the Prayer Book says. But is one forbidden to say more? This free structure is not meant to be confining. The classic liturgies, if they speak of the Holy Spirit at all (as many do not), do not develop the theme in an extended way. This might be a place for reverent creativity. (Note C, appended to this chapter, gives an epiclesis based on biblical texts, from a seventeenth-century Puritan liturgy; it could be a source of suggestion.)

6. *Offering:* The inclusion in the consecration of an act of offering has been a divisive point, both between churches and within Anglicanism. From the start of its independent liturgical tradition the consecration prayer of the Episcopal Church has contained such a moment. In the 1928 Prayer Book it was in a paragraph with the interior title "the oblation"—a designation that must have mystified at least some worshipers, if they noticed it. The Scottish source from which this liturgical trait came into the American book printed the effecting words in capitals, WHICH WE HERE OFFER UNTO THEE—lest the point be missed. (Note D, at the end of this chapter, speaks more fully of this history.)

American Episcopalians using "An Order for Celebrating the Holy Eucharist" will be heirs of this liturgical tradition and, one presumes, will have no hesitation, in principle, about thinking of consecration as being, among other things, an act of offering. Two different approaches to this action are represented in this Order. Form 1 speaks of the elements: "Father, we now celebrate the memorial of your Son. By means of this holy bread and cup, we show forth the sacrifice of his death, and proclaim his resurrection, until he comes again." Although nothing is expressly *offered*, these words clearly identify the bread and wine as means for *showing forth* "the mystery of faith." Form 2, however, asks God to "accept our sacrifice of praise, this memorial of our redemption." The act of offering (a memorial offering of praise) does not expressly mention the bread and wine, even though "this memorial" is an act that involves bread and wine centrally and necessarily. The sequence in Form 1 places the action in a climactic location after the epiclesis and the institution account.

[7. *Intercession:* Intercession entered the eucharistic prayer at an early period. Perhaps it did so as the prayers of the people began to drop out, or perhaps there was simply a wish to bring names of persons known and remembered into this prominent location. In the Latin Mass that was in use in the Medieval West and in the Roman church until the reforms of Vatican II, names of the living and of the departed could be inserted silently by the celebrant at two places in the canon.

The first Prayer Book of 1549 retained intercessions in the consecration, placing them at the start of the prayer, immediately after the *Sanctus*. (These intercessions had a somewhat intrusive introduction: "Let us pray for the whole state of Christ's church." They ended with a tone of finality, after which the lengthy prayer addressed the consecratory acts. One wonders whether this was the original and only intended location for them.) The prayers for the living and for the departed were combined. Some later Anglican rites (including the 1786 Communion Office of Samuel Seabury) kept these prayers as the opening section of the consecration. Beginning with the Prayer Book of 1552, all of the official English and American Prayer Books have placed the intercessions as a unit prior to consecration and have had none within the consecration action itself.

In the 1979 Prayer Book, however, eucharistic Prayer D (an ecumenically prepared text) brings this feature into the consecration. The brackets in Prayer D indicate that intercessions are not necessary. Wordings are not prescribed, but are left to the leaders and planners. Whatever is done here is not to displace the Prayer of the Faithful, which occupies its accustomed place and is meant to be quite inclusive. The wording of this feature in Prayer D may be taken as saying that while intercession within the consecration is not essential, neither is it theologically or liturgically objectionable.

In using the Order for Eucharist, intercessions might well find a place in the Great Thanksgiving. They could be woven into the early prayers that arise from the occasion of the celebration, as both Form 1 and Form 2 allow. Or they could be part of the late passage on the purpose of the Eucharist. But they should be used judiciously, if they are included at all, for there is great power in this location. The matter should be thought out in advance so that these prayers do not duplicate things already prayed for. Matters that lie close to the liturgical occasion may well be voiced here, but in such a way as to maintain the proportion and tone of the consecration action as a whole. There are no real models in the Prayer Book tradition for wording intercession for this place, only the openings in the text of Prayer D. It is up to liturgical leaders to do competently what these incomplete pointers make possible.]

8. *The benefits of communion:* A part of prayer in the Prayer Book tradition is the expression in the prayer itself of why the community seeks what it does. Even units as short as the collects customarily pass from petition to an "in order that" clause. (A text for young people of a few years back called it the "hoped-for-result" clause.) The idea that a complete prayer should include a statement of the intention in asking expresses our acceptance of responsibility. We seek graces from God to be used for purposes of God's determining. The consecration prayers in the Prayer Book speak of the eternal destiny of the church and of each Christian, a destiny that is touched and pledged in the sacrament. Prayer C, picking up a note that is more common in postcommunion prayers than in consecration prayers, speaks of close-at-hand service in the world. It asks, quite memorably: "Open our eyes to see your hand at work in the world about us. . . . Let the grace of this Holy Communion make us one body, one spirit in Christ, that we may worthily serve the world in his name."

In the "Order for Eucharist," Form 1 has a very brief passage on the intention of the communion, located just before the closing doxology. But Form 2, by rubric, invites a fresh wording of the matter. Thus anyone using Form 2 must ask what is sought in the Eucharist and for what purposes. The answers to such questions are fairly exacting. The New Testament encourages the community of faith to ask freely and confidently: "Ask what you will," (Jn.15:7; also 14:13f; 16:23; Mt. 7:7ff). At the same time, believing prayer must be under constraints; we seek for ourselves what God seeks for us; our prayer, when it is true, is Christ's prayer in us. The right and responsibility of wording this portion of the Great Thanksgiving can be an invitation to explain or exhort under guise of prayer—and in doing so to lose the catholic note that is so well maintained in the fully worded consecration prayers.

We often do not know what we intend until we try to put our intentions into words. The Eucharist renews the church in the complex and subtle bonds between it and God, and renews it for its appointed tasks in today's bewildering world. When one tries to gather this rich purpose into appropriate, representative, economical words, it becomes clear that "we do not know how to pray as we ought" (Rom.8:26). Since we cannot describe the purpose of the Eucharist exhaustively, our words for this purpose must often suggest more than they state. So we use the best words we can, falling back gratefully when we must on the general, familiar words of the tradition. Often a leader concludes, trusting that the people (who always intend more than the liturgical president says), the occasion and its varied associations, and the Spirit will make more of her or his words than, literally construed, they say.

9. *Closing doxology and Amen:* At its conclusion, the prayer returns to the praiseful note on which it began. It is occupied with God, with glory, and with the eternal. This ending is a place for formal structured phrases speaking of the One from whom and through whom and to whom are all things. Form 1 contains a brief triadic doxology, while Form 2 provides a text but allows for free wording.

The final Amen of the prayer deserves notice. The rubric on p. 401 emphasizes it: "The people respond—Amen!" (How many exclamation marks are there in the Prayer Book rubrics?) And both Form 1 and Form 2 conclude with the word in large-point italic capital letters. This word stands as the people's ratification of the Great Thanksgiving. It was spoken of by early Christian writers as though it were cherished by the laity and said heartily. Jerome said that the Amens of the Christian congregations resounded in the basilicas of Rome like peals of heavenly thunder. It was the people's way of saying that the central eucharistic prayer was participatory even though it had been spoken by a single person; the faith to which it gave expression was the common faith. In time, the canon came to be said secretly, in Latin; and the people's Amen was lost. Its recovery was one of the earliest marks of the modern-day liturgical stir in the Roman church. The consecration prayer in the Prayer Books of Anglicanism has been in the vernacular, and the Amen has been said by the congregation. On occasion one has heard "peals of heavenly thunder."

Note: On Congregational Acclamations: Another textual feature that has given the people a vocal part in the Great Thanksgiving is the use of congregational acclamations. No such acclamations appeared in Anglican eucharistic prayers until the modern revisions—although Jeremy Taylor pioneered this device in the late seventeenth century. Now they are introduced widely (sometimes they are sung, even when the prayer as a whole is said, see Hymnal 1982, S 132–S141) to bring the congregation into this central body of words. If this dialogic feature is used, the congregation's parts must be *written* and put in the hands of the worshipers, or else *memorized*. Perhaps most groups of Episcopalians can fall back on the formulaic material from Rite II. The acclamations from Prayers A and B, with their characteristic cue lines by the leader, are probably well enough known to be used within other prayers. But not everyone in every group will be familiar with them, and easy participation is what is sought. If the designers of a celebration following the Order for Eucharist seek to use original wordings, it will have to be made clear to the people what they are to say and how they will know when to say it.

If several acclamations are used (as in Prayer C), it is important to consider where, in the structure of the prayer, they should come. (In prayers A,B and D, a single acclamation is provided, coming immediately after the narrative of institution—a practice that has been criticized on the grounds that only one acclamation, in that location, tends to designate the institution as the operative "moment" in consecration.) These brief congregational interjections punctuate the Great Thanksgiving. Anyone who is drafting a consecration prayer and who would like to use such congregational interjections must ask: What part(s) of the Thanksgiving should they follow? What part(s) might they bracket? And what should they say?

Note: On the Lord's Prayer: It is a Prayer Book tradition that the Lord's Prayer follow immediately after the eucharistic prayer, as it comes after central moments in some other ritual actions. Other liturgical traditions have placed the Lord's Prayer after the fraction—a location that tends to unite the "blessing" and the "breaking" quite closely. In the rubrics of this Order, the Lord's Prayer is neither required nor forbidden; it simply goes unmentioned. The persons planning a rite using this Prayer Book outline must decide whether to use it. If it is used, where will it come? Which rhetoric will be used? How will it be introduced?

The Great Thanksgiving has been discussed here in terms of a series of separate components. This approach could suggest a prayer that is a choppy sequence of short units. Each of the elements that have been discussed has some importance, and each requires thought. But they all take their place in a prayer that, as a whole, must have unity, proportion and flow. Perhaps a prayer will come to mind pretty much as an organic unit, whose parts then require separate attention. Other prayers may begin as discrete ingredients that are separately developed, and only later will care be given to transitions, the elimination of repetitions and unnecessary words, and the drawing of the parts into a consistent shaped whole: the creative process must look at the whole prayer as well as its parts.

Since this chapter assumes a congregation is using An Order for Celebrating the Holy Eucharist rather than a completely experimental text, it may be well to set Forms 1 and 2 in tabular outline:

> The elements noted with an asterisk are required.
> The italicized elements are required and have a full text given.

Form 1   Form 2

Introductory dialogue   *Introductory dialogue*
        (required; a text is printed in both Forms,
            but in partially different wordings)
*Thanks for creation and   *Thanks for creation and
    revelation   revelation
        (required; but the wording is free)
Recalling of the occasion   Recalling of the occasion
    being celebrated   being celebrated
            (optional; wording free)

Proper Preface, or
    adaptation of it
	Proper Preface, or
	    adaptation of it

(optional; wording free)

Sanctus, Benedictus qui
    venit
	Sanctus, Benedictus qui
	    venit

(optional; but the text is printed for the times it is used)

*Praise for salvation in
    Christ
	*Praise for salvation in
	    Christ

(required; but wording is free)

*Epiclesis
(required; text given)

*Institution, with manual
    actions
	*Institution, with manual
	    actions

(required; text printed, with directions for actions)

*Anamnesis of passion,
    resurrection and ascension
(required; text given)

*Oblation (mentions gifts)	*Oblation (sacrifice of praise)

(required; texts printed)

*Epiclesis
(required; text given)

*Prayer for benefits (required; text given)	*Prayer for benefits (required; wording free)
*Doxology, Amen. (required; text given)	*Doxology, Amen. (required; text given, but free wording allowed)

Summary:	Form 1	Form 2
Items [based on the BCP lines that begin at the left margin]	11	12
Required	8	9
Required, with wordings given	6	5

It is apparent that in using either of these outlines, one will pass between Prayer Book wording and one's own independent wording. Part of the challenge of using this Prayer Book provision is to weave one's own prose and the prose of the given text into a well-crafted unit.

Perhaps a few rather Strunk-and-White remarks here on matters of technique will be to the point:

Selectivity: Since no eucharistic prayer can say everything, choices must be made. If the whole is not long, each part must exhibit some economy. One wants to include the important things of course, and firm structure can give a sense of completeness to a unit that may be fairly brief. But one must often speak concretely of selected things that stand for a large category of unspoken things. Drafters of eucharistic prayers must identify and delete items on a list that has grown too long—the distractions, the wasted words, the adjectives.

Restraint: Christian liturgy in the Prayer Book tradition is modest. It does not strain for rhetorical effect. Its emotion-filled words are effective because of the general sobriety of the prose. It would not be hard to gather some memorable expressions from recent Anglican liturgies:

"He stretched out his arms on the cross. . . ."
(Prayer A)
". . . for solace only, and not for strength . . ."
(Prayer C)
"The tree of defeat became the tree of glory; and where life was lost, there life has been restored."
(Church of England, *Alternative Services Book,* Holy Communion B, Preface for Passiontide)

The first of these uses a pictorial image based on Hippolytus's text (c. 215 CE). The second points a contrast while keeping the same consonant in its key words. The third plays poetically, but seriously on the symbol "tree," and speaks of life lost and restored. In this central prayer, one wants to speak graphically, interestingly and forcefully, without sounding catchy or affected. Liturgical language does not fail when it is clear, exact and straightforward. When one seeks verbal dash and color, falseness easily creeps in. Perhaps something that a Scottish theologian once said about preaching could apply here: It is impossible for a writer of eucharistic prayers at the same time to convince us that God is great and that the writer is clever.

Orality: The Great Thanksgiving, if it is written, is meant to be spoken. It needs to be sayable, breathable. The clauses should move ahead without intricacy. There should be no doubt as to where relative units and pronouns attach. There is a knack to writing in such a way as to listen to one's clauses and phrases for clarity, rhythm and sound, and for the verbal flow from one unit to the next. There can be no neat rules for doing this sort of thing, but when a passage is read aloud a listener usually knows at once when the author has attended to the matter and when not.

The practice in the 1979 Prayer Book of printing some of the major spoken units for officiants and for congregations in short lines, with subordinate elements indented, is a useful technique for one's own composition. It is possible to lay out the sentences on a page in such a way that the words are virtually heard as well as seen. When such a device is tried, inevitably it becomes clear that a phrase should be relocated or a concrete word substituted for one that is abstract. The preparation of the Great Thanksgiving for the "Order for Eucharist" is an exercise in oral communication, even if pencil and eraser (or "enter" and "delete" keys) are used.

Objectivity: The prayers of the tradition are centrally occupied with God—who God is, what God has done, is doing, and will do. They are not dispassionate, but celebrational. The leader and the congregation are involved in the things being said. In celebrational speech, attention is on the One being celebrated. The eucharistic prayer is flawed if we become expansive about our unworthiness or our fallings, or even about our joy and our renewed dedication. Prayer should not seem to compel our emotions; its task is not to exhort, inspire, or improve while seeming to pray. Liturgical prayer speaks from the classic Christian experience, about God; not from our present experience, about experience.

These comments are largely cautionary—do not err on this side or that; do not go to excess. Perhaps it is easier to identify possible faults than it is to say what makes a good eucharistic prayer good. Clearly the parts and the whole are held together and given energy and conviction by the central theological vision by which they are informed. The prayer is a creative act of imagination and critical thought.

The Prayer Book asks the users of this Order for Eucharist some profound questions: What is your understanding of God and of the relation of human life to the divine? What is your theology of creation? of revelation? of Israel? of Christ? of redemption? of the Holy Spirit? of the work of God in the world? of the church, its task in the world, its destiny? of the eucharistic action? of the life of faith? Can you state your convictions on these matters, not as linear explanation addressed to others, but as prayer? Can your "voice" in this prayer be simultaneously your own voice, the representative voice of a eucharistic community, and the voice of the catholic church? It is not a matter of working out and then assembling separate components. These things cohere in the depth of vital existence in faith. Whether one writes at greater length or more briefly, whether one has a special intention in mind or not, the imagined whole can be brought to expression with a sense of sustained vitality and satisfying completeness. Although the task may be exacting, the Prayer Book includes this provision expecting that the gifts for using it may be quite widely present in the church. The liturgy, at this point, says, "Look in thy heart, and write."

• Break the Bread •

In the acts cited in the Order for Eucharist (as in many outlines of the structure of the eucharist), the breaking of the bread follows the Great Thanksgiving. In the New Testament, "the breaking of bread" became perhaps the first name for the church's ritual meal (Acts 2:42,46; 20:7,-11; 27:35;1 Cor.10:16; Lk.24:35). The place of the breaking (or "fraction") as a transition from consecration to administration (from "blessing" to "giving") had largely been obscured until Dix identified it as the third of the "four actions." (For centuries in Anglican liturgies it had, by rubric, been performed within the narrative of institution as a mimetic action. Celebrants "broke" the host as they read about Jesus "breaking" the bread.)

The fraction seems, in early Christian generations, not to have been formal so much as functional. It should be so again. The bread and the wine are consecrated each in one unit (see the rubric on p. 409, which speaks of consecrating the wine in a single vessel; and see the comments in Chapter Five about the desirability of having the bread in a single loaf). But they are intended for many persons, for many mouths. The fraction is the time at which the one loaf and the one cup are reduced, as that may be necessary, to a readiness for distribution to the many. The point was lost in the adoption, in the Middle Ages, of individual hosts, and in the custom of consecrating in many cups (and, of course, in the use, in parts of Protestantism, of individual cups). Sadly, but understandably, the breaking of the bread and the pouring of the wine came, throughout Western sacramental piety, Catholic and Protestant, to be understood as emblematic of Jesus' passion—his body broken and his blood shed. Rather, the appropriate imagery would seem to be the oneness and manyness of the people of Christ.

There is no deep tradition of exactly what is done or said at the fraction. To some extent, the action will be determined by what the amounts of bread and wine and the number of vessels and ministers of communion make necessary. The action is public and for the people, so it might well begin with a gesture of breaking, carried out with some flair, but most of the work here needs to be smooth, economical and businesslike. It should not seem to stop the flow of the liturgy from "blessing" to "giving."

Any words that may be used (which rubrics on pp. 339 and 366 suggest might best come after the action is concluded and a silence has been observed) should be appropriate and brief. (Some suggestions for wordings are given in Note E at the end of this chapter.)

• Share in the Gifts of God •

The Eucharist comes to its ritual climax in the act of eating and drinking, a gesture of sharing in the life of the living Christ. Nothing is said in the rubrics of this Order as to how this action should be carried out, nor as to what should be said. The whole must be done "reverently," and the remaining elements should be consumed. The ways of administering are no different in this rite than in any other: the people can be served by ministers who move down rows at a rail or around a group; or the people can come to ministers at set stations. The rubrics for this Order do not direct (as they do in Rites I and II) that the ministers shall receive communion first, and then serve others. Thus they open the possibility for the people to serve one another as the bread and wine are passed through the group. The practical problems, such as the movement of ministers and people, the space, and resupplying, are the same as in any other rite. So, important though this action is, it can pass with little discussion here.

Rather surprisingly, nothing is said in the Prayer Book outline of the Order for Eucharist concerning postcommunion devotions. Since nothing is said, such devotions are neither required nor discouraged. But the logic of the 1965 Inter-Anglican report (cited in Chapter Four) would seem to make them desirable virtually without fail. In receiving the bread and wine, the communal form in which the worshiping group was shaped for the early part of the Eucharist has fallen apart. People move in awareness of one another, governed by many quiet courtesies. They fill the rail and leave, or else they pass by stations; they eat and drink in sequence, sometimes over a lengthy period of time. Each person's eating and drinking apparatus is unshared. This is an act that, in some sense, people cannot do unitedly. Thus it seems fitting that, having received communion, the people reassemble in a unified formation and together make some act of response and receive a dismissal.

There is risk in doing too much in the postcommunion location, creating anticlimax, but silence, a prayer of thanks, and a hymn leading to a sending out would not be excessive. The rubrics concerning the close of Rites I and II should carry over here, because they are eminently sensible. That is to say, if there is to be a spoken dismissal, all the singing and praying should be completed first. There is something false when a word of dismissal: "Go in peace . . .," is followed by further busy actions. Generally, the last things done and said require thought and care, just as the first things do.

It has required a lengthy, somewhat complicated discussion to explain a rite that takes up only six pages of the Prayer Book, only two of them for the basic outline. While it is fairly simple to name the actions whose sequence carries forward the eucharistic rite, it is another thing to give some account of what these names signify. Like many other things that become habituated and internalized—tying one's shoes, catching a ball, or driving a car—a liturgy using this free form is easier to do than it is to explain. Once the knack is acquired (which may not take long for some persons), such a liturgy can have a spontaneous, free and joyful flow. When the liturgical provision is carried out well, there is certainly some serious reflection, perhaps largely at an implicit level, behind the enactment.

The simple outline in the Prayer Book distills a context of learning and reflection. The outline can be carried into effect best by individuals and groups that understand and have internalized some of that context. The aim of these many pages has been to raise to explicitness some of the understandings that make this lean sketch of ritual actions among the most eloquent and valuable pages in the Prayer Book.

• Note A: At the Preparation of the Table •

At this point in the liturgy (which is likely to go on being referred to as "the offertory," despite the ambiguities of that name), it is difficult for a celebrant to speak at any length and with definiteness without duplicating themes that are native to the consecration prayer—such as thanksgiving, acknowledgment of creation and providence, and offering. The wording of this small part of the eucharistic liturgy is a theological challenge. Clearly, bread and wine must be brought to the table. But how is this act interpreted in words? What and where is the "offertory" of the eucharist? What is one doing and what is one not doing at this "preparation of the table?"

The contemporary "Lima" liturgy, an ecumenical text drafted principally by Max Thurian of the Taize community, makes good use of traditional material at the "preparation." The text is:

> *Minister* [not necessarily the celebrant]:
>   Blessed are you, Lord God of the universe,
>   you are the giver of this bread,
>   fruit of the earth and of human labor,
>   let it become the bread of Life.
> *Congregation:*
>   *Blessed be God, now and for ever!*
> *M:* Blessed are you, Lord God of the universe,
>   you are the giver of this wine,
>   fruit of the vine and of human labor,
>   let it become the wine of the eternal Kingdom.
> *C: Blessed be God, now and forever!*

M: As the grain once scattered in the fields
and the grapes once dispersed on the hillside
are now reunited on this table
in bread and wine,
so, Lord, may your whole Church
soon be gathered together
from the corners of the earth into your Kingdom.
  C: Maranatha! Come Lord Jesus!

This text is clearly about the bread and wine, in anticipation of the consecration. The first two parts are Jewish blessings, which are now used also in this place in the Roman Catholic *Sacramentary.* The third part uses an image from the early Christian document, the *Didache,* 9:4.

• Note B: Sanctus Settings for Voices Unaccompanied •

The text of this chapter spoke of the desirability of having musical settings for the Sanctus that congregations can sing without printed texts and without accompaniment. Melodies seem to win acceptance in the church through processes that no one controls. But note might be taken of some simple Sanctus settings for unaccompanied voices that are now in hand.

Mention was made earlier of numbers S 121 through S 125 in the Hymnal 1982. Of these, S 121 and S 122 are adaptations of plainsong; their melodic idiom will often be familiar through exposure to plainsong elsewhere; and if the idiom is unfamiliar, it is easy to learn. The matching of notes to the syllables of the text only needs to be heard a time or two to be learned: S 123 is taken from Mozarabic Chant and uses elemental melodic material; S 124, by David Hurd, is a fresh melody in the plainsong style. A keyboard accompaniment is printed in the Accompaniment Edition, Volume 1, but the setting is quite singable without it. The setting S 125 is not derived from older modal idioms, but it is well suited to the voice. It falls within a range of seven notes; it moves, for the most part, by one- or two-step intervals; when intervals of a fourth or fifth occur, they bring the melody to easily expected notes. Although a harmonization is printed in the Accompaniment Edition, Volume 1, the melody can stand alone.

Another setting might be suggested which uses a well-known folk tune. In the Music Commission's publication *Congregational Music for*

Eucharist, number E-46 sets the words of the Sanctus to a melody found in both the 1982 and the 1940 Hymnals. The final "Hosanna in the highest" is repeated in order to meet the demands of the melodic line. The melody is printed with guitar chords, and a harmonized version appears in the Hymnal [304, 620] (the music played through twice, with slight alterations in the rhythm), but voices could manage it alone very well:

E-46   American Folk Hymn
        arr. by Marcia Pruner

• Note C: An Expanded Invocation of the Spirit •

The words of the epiclesis, in the liturgies that have an epiclesis at all, tend to be minimal. If one wanted to be more expansive at this point, what might one say?

A seventeenth-century Puritan liturgy could provide some suggestion. The theology of the Puritans was, to use a word of the time and tradition, "experimental." It emphasized the inward testimony of the Holy Spirit and the validation in experience of the word of God.

For a century, the Puritans had not been very creative liturgically. They repeated a bill of complaints against the Prayer Book, and their own liturgies were long, prosy and nonparticipatory. When in seventeenth-century England the Puritan Commonwealth came to an end and both the monarchy and the Church of England were to be restored, the Savoy Conference met in 1661 to determine ecclesiastical and liturgical issues. No reconciliation with the Puritans took place, and the 1661/62 Prayer Book was drawn up. During the conference, one of the ablest of the Puritans, Richard Baxter, was, in effect, asked what he might seek if he could have what he wanted in liturgy. He retired from the Conference for a time, taking with him the Church of England's *Book of Common Prayer,* the Puritan *Westminster Directory of Worship,* and a Bible. His "Savoy Liturgy" was never adopted by any church, and there would be problems in making it widely usable. Among its other interesting liturgical features, is the expression it gives to the emphasis in Puritan spirituality on the interior work of the Spirit.

Baxter's lengthy consecration prayer is expressly trinitarian. The opening part is addressed to the Father. A second part, which contains a recalling of Christ's work and the narrative of institution, is addressed, "Most merciful Saviour." The final part is concerned with the Holy Spirit and is spoken to the Holy Spirit. Baxter's liturgy is notable for the way in which it weaves its text from phrases of Scripture without sounding choppy or scissors-and-paste. His passage on the Holy Spirit is heavily based on the New Testament. It says nothing that would connect the Holy Spirit with the eucharistic bread and wine. Rather, it is concerned with the inward working of the Spirit, and on that subject it is eloquent:

> Most Holy Spirit, proceeding from the Father and the
> Son: by whom Christ was conceived; by whom the
> prophets and apostles were inspired, and the ministers of

Christ are qualified and called: that dwellest and workest in all the members of Christ, whom thou sanctifiest to the image and for the service of their Head, and comfortest that by faith we may show forth his praise: illuminate us, that by faith we may see him that is here represented to us. Soften and quicken us, that we may relish the spiritual food, and feed on it to our nourishment and growth in grace. Shed abroad the love of God upon our hearts, and draw us out in love to him. Fill us with thankfulness and holy joy, and with love to one another. Comfort us by witnessing that we are the children of God. Confirm us for new obedience. Be the earnest of our inheritance, and seal us up to everlasting life. *Amen.*

Perhaps no one would want to use this text just as it stands (although a version of it in modern rhetoric was interpolated at a Pentecost Vigil a few years ago) because it would throw off the proportion of most eucharistic prayers. But it seems a mine of ideas.

● Note D: Eucharistic Offering, Prayer Book History ●

The theological and liturgical differences over sacramental offering—like much else that has been contentious about the eucharist—trace to the medieval inheritance. The Latin canon was overloaded with expressions of the mass as a sacrifice of gifts, or indeed of Christ, to God to secure the remission of sins. Such terms seemed to the Reformers to make the mass into a *work,* a human attempt to do again or to add to what had been done in Christ finally and alone. There may have been more subtlety in the late medieval theology of the eucharistic sacrifice than the Reformers granted. At least F.J. Clark, in his careful and respected study, *Eucharistic Sacrifice and the Reformation* (1967, 1st ed, 1960), has argued that theologians of the period guarded the finality and completeness of Christ's sacrifice. But the Reformers, who had themselves been brought up in the old learning, and who thought they knew what its words said and meant, rejected the Latin canon. The Lutheran and Reformed liturgies excised anything that seemed to speak of the Eucharist as an action moving from the church to God to secure divine favor.

When the Prayer Books of the Church of England entered in the sixteenth century, the 1549 Book spoke often *in the consecration itself* of offering, but with essential changes. When the central prayer used terms of sacrifice and offering, it spoke of offering several things: a memorial of Christ's sacrifice, our sacrifice of prayer and thanks, and our offering of "ourselves, our souls and bodies." The 1552 Book, which followed before its predecessor had time to become familiar, truncated the Prayer of Consecration, removing all terms of offering. But a rich expression of self-offering was placed *after the communion.* It was clearly a response-sacrifice, an act rising from the faithful to God based on a prior act of divine favor and self-imparting in the communion.

There is something to be said for this 1552 sequence. By holding all expressions of our sacrifice until after consecration and communion, the rite reproduces in liturgy the pattern of divine initiative and human response. It is a ritual reminder that we have nothing to offer until we have received; but having received, we offer all that we are and have. Even though the English Prayer Books, from 1552 until the twentieth-century Authorized Services, have held to this pattern, to Anglicans accustomed to another pattern, it can seem too schematic. In the Eucharist one cannot draw a line and say, "Up to this point, God is speaking, acting and giving; from there on, it is we who, having heard and received, speak and act in response." In liturgy, divine initiative and human response mingle. In worship, as in life, sacrifice is a pervasive factor. God approaches us sacrificially in Christ, and the responding sacrifice of Christians is in the sacrifice of Christ. It is on such grounds that parts of the Anglican Communion, including the Episcopal Church, have celebrated with substantially the 1549 pattern.

But not exactly the 1549 pattern. With respect to the bread and wine, the 1549 text prayed: ". . . we thy humble servants do celebrate, and make here before thy divine Majesty, with these thy holy gifts, the memorial which thy son hath willed us to make"—words that involve the elements ("thy holy gifts") in the sacramental act, but that fall short of expressly offering them. Although the subsequent English rites omitted this idea, many theologians thought of the Eucharist in sacrificial terms. But it was a spiritual sacrifice, which they often urged was the highest form of sacrifice. In the seventeenth and early eighteenth centuries, the Scottish and Nonjuring tradition mounted a high-church critique of the

Church of England's Prayer Book. One of the marks of the liturgies from these sources is the express offering of the bread and wine in the consecration prayer. This act of offering usually took the form of adding to the 1549 wording along such lines as ". . . these thy holy gifts, which we offer unto thee, . . ." All of this action was understood to be a participation in Christ. He was the redemptive sacrifice, made, as it were, from God's side. But he is also the model of the human sacrifice of response. The offering of the church, in the self-offering of Christ, involves also the offering of the material elements of the sacrament.

Passions have run high on the point. Some writers have been persuaded, on the basis of early liturgies, that the act of offering is necessary to true consecration. Through Bishop Seabury, whose episcopal orders came by way of Scottish Nonjuring bishops, and whose own convictions were similar to theirs, "the oblatory words" (as William White called them) were restored to the consecration prayer. In the formative events of the American Prayer Book, Seabury and others held strong convictions in favor of this feature, and evidently few persons felt strongly against it.

• Note E: At the Fraction •

Some Anglican liturgies have turned 1 Corinthians 10:16f into a versicle and response along such lines as:

V. The cup of blessing which we bless,
R. *is it not a participation in the blood of Christ?*
V. The bread which we break,
R. *is it not a participation in the body of Christ?*
V. Because there is one loaf, we who are many are one
　 body,
R. *for we all partake of the same loaf.*

The 1979 Prayer Book, lacking recent models, reached back to Cranmer's 1549 rite for his "Christ our Passover has been sacrificed for us; *Therefore let us keep the feast,*" (1 Cor.5:7b–8a), which came at this place in that liturgy. Cranmer actually extended the Pauline words into something like a short canticle, working in a line from the Agnus Dei. Has his text been tried? It is:

Christ our Paschal Lamb is offered up for us,
    once for all, when he bare our sins on his body
        upon the cross,
for he is the very lamb of God,
    that taketh away the sins of the world;
wherefore let us keep a joyful and holy feast with
        the Lord.

• Note F: A Full Anaphora, Using Form II •

This prayer is a skillful weaving of prescribed and free elements from the "Order for Eucharist." The text was prepared by Professor Lloyd G. Patterson for use at St. John's Chapel of the Episcopal Divinity School, Cambridge, Massachusetts.

[following the Sursum Corda:]

We give you thanks and praise, Holy One of Israel, whom we address as "Abba" through Jesus Christ, in whom we have been made your children.

We give you thanks for your whole creation, made through your Word; for its mirroring of your grandeur and glory; and for human life made in your image.

We bless you for holding with us through our waywardness and sin; for calling a people to bear witness to your Name; and for all those in every age who have heard your call and followed in your truth.

Above all, we praise you for your Word made flesh, Jesus Christ, your only offspring and child; for your re-creation of human life in Christ; for Christ's self-giving and vindication at your hands.

And so we set before you Christ's death and resurrection, your own promise and gift of new life in him.

On the night he was handed over to suffering and death, our Lord Jesus Christ took bread; and when he had given thanks to you, he broke it, and gave it to his disciples, and

said: Take, eat. This is my body which is given for you.
Do this for the remembrance of me.

After supper he took the cup of wine; and when he had
given thanks, he gave it to them and said: Drink this all of
you. This is my blood of the New Covenant, which is shed
for you and for many for the forgiveness of sins.
Whenever you drink it, do this for the remembrance of
me.

Recalling now his suffering and death, and celebrating his
resurrection and ascension, we await his coming in glory.

Accept, O Lord, our sacrifice of Praise, this memorial of
our redemption.

Send your Holy Spirit upon these gifts. Let them be for us
the body and blood of your Son, and grant that we who
eat this bread and drink this cup may be filled with your
life and goodness.

May we bring to light our new life as your children, the
foretaste of your remaking of all humanity as one family
with you.

Make our life together in this place a witness to your
purpose for the renewal and reconciliation of your whole
creation in peace and justice.

Join our praises with the blessed Virgin Mary, Blessed
John the Evangelist, patron of our community, and all
those who have gone before us as your witnesses.

Bring us and all humanity under your gracious rule and
into your eternal presence.

> All this we ask through your Son Jesus Christ,
> by him, and with him, and in him,
> in the unity of the Holy Spirit,
> all honor and glory is your
> Almighty God, now and forever.
> *AMEN.*

For Further Reading

1. On Worship and the Present Liturgical Situation
2. On the Sacramental System
3. The Prayer Book and Anglican Worship
4. On Liturgical Preparation
5. Community and Ministries
6. Time, the Year, Seasons, Sunday
   - On the Year
   - On Holy Week and Easter
   - On Sunday
   - On Saints' Days, Commemorations
7. Language and Symbol
   - Liturgical speech and imagery
   - "Sexist" language and liturgy
8. On the Eucharist
   - On the eucharistic order as a whole
   - On eucharistic theology
   - The service of the word; (1) Lectionary and lectors
     - Guides to pronunciation of biblical terms
   - The service of the word; (2) Preaching
     - Homiletic helps based on the lectionary
   - Intercessions
   - The peace
   - The offertory

1. On Worship and the Present Liturgical Situation

Avila, Rafael, *Worship and Politics,* Maryknoll, NY: Orbis Books, 1981.

Burkhart, John E., *Worship,* Philadelphia: Westminster Press, 1982. (A theologian on the role of worship.)

Clark, Neville, *Call to Worship,* London: SCM, 1960. (A brief incisive consideration of worship by an ecumenically minded English Baptist, informed by biblical theology.)

Davies, J.G., *Worship and Mission,* New York: Association Press, 1967. (A splendid brief statement.)

Frederick, John, *The Future of Liturgical Reform,* Wilton, CT: Morehouse-Barlow, 1987. (Short for the scope of the ideas introduced, but on some issues quite fine.)

Gelineau, Joseph, *The Liturgy Today and Tomorrow,* London: Darton, Longman and Todd, 1978. (A brief book by a French liturgical leader, full of wisdom.)

Hatchett, Marion J., *Sanctifying Life, Space and Time,* New York: Seabury, 1976. (A widely read, reliable general introduction to the history and the major components of liturgy; original periodization by the media of the spoken text.)

Jennings, Theodore W., *Life as Worship:* Prayer and Praise in Jesus' Name, Grand Rapids, MI: Wm. B. Eerdmans, 1982. (A theological statement that cuts through much superficiality concerning prayer and praise.)

Jones, Cheslyn; Wainwright, Geoffrey; and Yarnold, Edward, eds., *The Study of Liturgy,* OUP: 1978. (The fullest and most authoritative introductory volume on liturgy, despite just complaints about its omissions and the inadequacy of its topical chapters; a wide range of information is well presented.)

Kavanagh, Aidan, *On Liturgical Theology,* New York: Pueblo Publishing Co., 1984. (A richly articulated book that stands against the cliches of the age.)

Marshall, Michael, *Renewal in Worship,* Wilton, CT: Morehouse-Barlow, 1985. (Brief; interestingly written.)

Micks, Marianne, *The Future Present:* The Phenomenon of Christian Worship, New York: Seabury Press, 1970. (Thematic reflections on worship; a respected work since its publication.)

Pieper, Josef, *In Tune with the World:* A Theory of Festivity, New York: Harcourt, Brace and World, 1965. (A small, elegant study of a theme that is often treated in a "pop" way, but not here.)

Senn, Frank C., *Christian Worship:* and Its Cultural Setting, Philadelphia: Fortress Press, 1983.

Stevenson, Kenneth, ed., *Liturgy Reshaped,* London: SPCK, 1982. (A symposium, generally Anglican, of high quality.)

Taft, Robert, "Liturgy as Theology," in *Worship* 56(1982), pp. 113–17.

Thurian, Max and Wainwright, Geoffrey, eds., *Baptism and Eucharist:* Ecumenical Convergence in Celebration, Geneva: World Council of Churches, and Grand Rapids, MI: Eerdmans, 1983. (A significant collection of liturgical texts, historical, modern and ecumenical; with introductions pointing out today's remarkable sacramental "convergence.")

von Allmen, J.J., *Worship: Its Theology and Practice,* Oxford University Press, 1965. (A profound, intellectually forceful work by an author from the European Reformed tradition.)

Wainwright, Geoffrey, *Doxology: The Praise of God in Worship, Doctrine and Life,* Oxford University Press, 1982. (An important study that looks at theology from the vantage of worship.)

White, James F., *Introduction to Christian Worship,* Nashville, TN: Abingdon Press, 1980. (An informative, well-organized introductory work in which technical terms are explained.)

Willimon, William H., *The Service of God: How Worship and Ethics are Related,* Nashville, TN: Abingdon Press, 1983. (A well-written book with theological and pastoral wisdom.)

2. On the Sacramental System

Bouyer, Louis, *Liturgical Piety,* Notre Dame, IN: University of Notre Dame Press, 1954. (A generation ago this book demonstrated to many readers the intrinsic coherence of the liturgical life of the Christian community. Much has taken place since it was published, and parts may seem dated. But perhaps a reader can still capture from its pages the excitement this author communicated about the church's ordered life of prayer.)

Clark, Neville, *An Approach to the Theology of the Sacraments,* London: SCM, 1956. (A concise work, rooted in biblical inquiry.)

Ganoczy, Alexandre, *An Introduction To Catholic Sacramental Theology,* New York: Paulist Press: ET 1984. (A fresh, brief theological statement.)

Guzie, Tad, *A Book of Sacramental Basics,* Ramsey, NJ: Paulist Press, 1981. (A good brief study of sacramentality.)

Lawler, Michael G., *Symbol and Sacrament:* A Contemporary Sacramental Theology, New York: Paulist Press, 1987. (A recent Roman work, drawing insight from many fields of study.)

Martos, Joseph, *Doors to the Sacred,* New York: Doubleday, 1981. (Another recent, quite fine Roman study of the sacramental system.)

Schmemann, Alexander, *Sacraments and Orthodoxy,* Boston: St. Vladimir's Press, 1965 [also published as *For the Life of the World*]. (The churches of the East have been less inclined than those of the West to allow the sacramental system to fall into a cluster of isolated events, attached to separable definitions of meaning. This beautifully written book has shown many Western readers the organic unity of liturgical life. Perhaps—if readers can make allowances for what seems to be a gratuitous antifeminine streak—it can still weave its spell.)

Schwarz, Hans, *Divine Communication:* Word and Sacrament in Biblical, Historical and Contemporary Perspective, Philadelphia: Fortress Press, 1985.

Book's directions require, what they suggest, and what they make possible; combines technical and historical knowledge with pastoral wisdom and practicality; good comments on ceremonial and music. Indispensable for persons preparing liturgy for the Episcopal Church.)

Weil, Louis, *Gathered to Pray: Understanding Liturgical Prayer*, Cambridge, MA: Cowley Publications, 1986. (Not about the Prayer Book, but about liturgical prayer; contains an especially good account of the collects.)

Wright, J. Robert, *Prayer Book Spirituality*, New York: Church Hymnal Corporation, 1989. (A splendid gathering of appreciative devotional comment on the Prayer Book since 1552; rich material, expertly edited.)

4. On Liturgical Preparation

Baker, Thomas and Ferrone, Frank, *Liturgy Committee Basics:* A No-Nonsense Guide, Washington, DC: The Pastoral Press, 1985. (Brightly written and practical; assumes the Roman parish and its specific problems, but generally adaptable to other churches; particularly good on the dynamics of planning groups.)

Fleming, Austin, *Preparing for Liturgy:* A Theology and Spirituality, Washington, DC: The Pastoral Press, 1985. (Written for Roman parishes but usable by others; theological without being heavy-handed; fine comments on style and on liturgy as an art.)

Huck, Gabe, *Liturgy With Style and Grace,* Chicago: Liturgy Training Publications, 1984. (Attractively written; serious but simple; although it is full of practical guidelines, it helps readers come to their own judgments.)

Ostdiek, Gilbert, *Catechesis for Liturgy,* New York: The Pastoral Press, 1986. (Rather analytic; investigates the various media of liturgy; pastoral and educational concern for the spiritual growth of the congregation through worship. Roman Catholic, but eminently usable by others.)

Pregnall, William S. *Laity and Liturgy:* A Handbook for Parish Worship, New York: Seabury Press, 1975. (One of the few books on liturgical planning that has been written with the Episcopal Church specifically in mind; contains many good insights on liturgy and preparing it;

FURTHER READ 22

3. The Prayer Book and Anglican Worship

Dunlop, Colin, *Anglican Public Worship,* London: SCM, 1953
book, now old, and written from a distinctly English viewpoi
ing the 1662 Prayer Book. Yet it goes beneath the surface
and speaks of enduring characteristics of the Anglican
Where this book is out of date, few readers will be misled b
where it is still applicable, it has much to say.)

Guilbert, Charles Mortimer, *Words of Our Worship,* New York:
Hymnal Corporation, 1989. (This valuable short work explain
of the technical and somewhat esoteric terms that have con
liturgy from its history and from several languages.)

Hatchett, Marion J., *Commentary on the American Prayer Book,* New
Seabury Press, 1981. (A large commentary on the 1979 Prayer I
emphasizing sources and structures; a basic reference, now an
years to come.)

Mitchell, Leonel L., *Liturgical Change:* How Much Do We Need?,
York: Seabury Press, 1975. (A small book, written while Prayer B
revision was under discussion; still valuable as a study of permaner
and change in liturgy.)

————, *Praying Shapes Believing:* A Theological Commentary on tl
Book of Common Prayer, Minneapolis: Winston Press, 1985. (A
informative, readable book that follows the Prayer Book sequence
underlining interpretive ideas and themes but generally letting the
Prayer Book speak for itself.)

Perham, Michael, *Liturgy Pastoral and Parochial,* London: SPCK, 1984.
(A wise book, English in orientation; not readily found in the US.)

Price, Charles P. and Weil, Louis, *Liturgy for Living,* New York: Seabury
Press, 1979. (A fine account of the liturgical system of the Episcopal
Church, prepared for "The Church's Teaching Series"; good for read-
ing through or for adult study groups.)

Stevick, Daniel B., "The Spirituality of the Book of Common Prayer,"
in Wolf, Wm., ed., *Anglican Spirituality,* Wilton, CT: Morehouse-
Barlow, 1982, pp. 105–120. (An essay on the relation between worshipers and a written liturgical text.)

Stuhlman, Byron D., *Prayer Book Rubrics Expanded,* New York: Church
Hymnal Corporation, 1987. (An explanation of what the Prayer

engagingly written; perhaps overuses the "dramatistic" model; too brief and sketchy to provide the help that would usually be needed.)

Sloyan, Virginia, ed., *A Liturgy Committee Handbook,* Washington, DC: The Liturgical Conference, 1965. (One of the first practical aids for planners of worship, and still useful.)

5. Community and Ministries

Allen, Horace T., ed., *The Reader as Minister,* Washington, DC: The Liturgical Conference, 1980. (An attractive presentation of the serious liturgical role of the lector.)

Buchanan, Colin, ed., *The Bishop in Liturgy:* An Anglican Symposium on the role and task of the Bishop in the field of Liturgy, Bramcote, Notts.: The Grove Press, 1988. (A valuable brief English symposium.)

Erickson, Craig Douglas, *Participating in Worship:* History, Theory and Practice, Louisville: Westminster/John Knox, 1989. (A substantial work, written from a somewhat ecclectic point of view but containing much insight.)

Gusmer, Charles W., *Wholesome Worship,* Washington, DC: The Pastoral Press, 1989. (Combines theological wisdom and practical counsel; valuable on criteria for liturgy; Roman in orientation, but many sections are widely useful.)

Hovda, Robert, *Strong, Loving and Wise: Presiding in Liturgy,* Collegeville, MN: The Liturgical Press, 1980. (A deeply personal, wise and helpful book on liturgical presidency; full of practical counsel; but more basically it presents the profound spiritual task and joy that liturgical leadership involves).

Largo, Gerald A., *Community and Liturgy:* An Historical Overview, Lanham, MD.: University Press of America, 1980. (A brief review of history, Roman in focus; informative.)

Llewellyn, R., "The Congregation Shares in the Prayers of the President," in L. Sheppard (ed.), *The New Liturgy,* pp. 103–112. (A good essay; worshipers participate, even when they are not themselves speaking or singing.)

Power, David N., *Gifts that Differ:* Lay Ministries Established and Unestablished, New York: Pueblo, 1980. (An important Roman Catholic theological and historical consideration of corporate life and individual gifts and callings.)

Roles in the Liturgical Assembly [Papers of the 23rd Liturgical Conference Saint Serge], New York: Pueblo, 1981. (Papers from an ecumenical conference that speak learnedly, and often historically of the ministries that contribute to the liturgical event.)

Schmidt, Herman, ed., *Prayer and Community* [Concilium, vol. 52], New York: Herder and Herder, 1970. (A good symposium; outstanding essays include: Cyrille Vogel, "An Alienated Liturgy," David Power, "Sacramental Celebration and Liturgical Ministry," and Aidan Kavanagh, "Ministries in the Community and in the Liturgy.")

Searle, Mark, ed., *Parish: A Place for Worship,* Collegeville, MN: The Liturgical Press, 1981. (A diversified symposium containing some first-rate essays.)

Sloyan, Virginia, ed., *Touchstones for Liturgical Ministers,* Washington, DC: The Liturgical Conference, 1978. (A slender, popularly written book containing wise counsel for musicians, lectors, presiders, ushers and others.)

Talley, Thomas J., ed., *A Kingdom of Priests:* Liturgical Formation of the People of God, Bramcote, Notts: Grove Books, 1988. (A small book containing valuable Anglican essays on liturgy and the shaping of a community of faith and witness.)

6. Time, the Year, Seasons, Sunday

On the Year

Adam, A., *The Liturgical Year:* Its History and Its Meaning after the Reform of the Liturgy, New York: Pueblo, ET 1981. (A large, informative, recent Roman work.)

Dix, G., *The Shape of the Liturgy,* ch. XI, "The Sanctification of Time." (On Dix and this book, see sec. 8. Dix's thesis in this chapter is overstated (see T. Talley's article and book listed below), but this chapter has stood so long as a scholarly reference point that an inquirer still needs to be acquainted with it.)

The Episcopal Church Lesson Calendar, Wilton, CT: Morehouse-Barlow Company, published yearly. (One of the truly indispensable tools for liturgical planners in the Episcopal Church. Each year's edition begins with Advent; the format has one week to each page. This calendar lists the propers for each Sunday and Feast Day, the daily lections, suggested hymns, and much more. There are instances of judgment in any calendar such as this, and no user is required to follow all of them. But the material here is always a place to start, and often the editors' careful judgments will seem quite inspired when one has weighed the alternatives for oneself.)

L'Engle, Madeline, *The Irrational Season,* New York: Seabury Press, 1977. (Imaginative reflections on the church's time and human experience.)

McArthur, A., *The Evolution of the Christian Year,* London: SCM Press, 1953. (A small, reliable study by a Scottish Presbyterian that has introduced the study of the Christian year to many students.)

Maertens, Th., *A Feast in Honor of Yahweh,* Notre Dame, IN: Fides Publishers, ET 1965. (Emphasizes the derivation of Christian ritual time from Jewish sources.)

Martimort, A.G., ed., *The Church at Prayer, Vol. IV: The Liturgy and Time,* Collegeville, MN: The Liturgical Press, 1986. (Comments, historical and interpretive, representing the best recent Continental Roman scholarship.)

Nocent, A., *The Liturgical Year,* Collegeville, MN: The Liturgical Press, 1977. (An interpretation of the year and its seasons.)

Porter, H.B., *Keeping the Church Year,* New York: Seabury Press, 1977. (A pastoral and practical book, with good scholarship behind it.)

Talley, T.J., *The Origins of the Liturgical Year,* New York: Pueblo, 1986. (The most recent and authoritative study of the early history; quite technical in character and perhaps difficult reading.)

Westerhoff, John H., *A Pilgrim People:* Learning through the Church Year, New York: Harper & Row, 1984. (A short, brightly written correlation between the liturgical year and growing into faith.)

On Holy Week and Easter

Davies, J.G., *Holy Week:* A Short History, Richmond, VA: John Knox Press, 1963. (A small book that presents the essential history interestingly and reliably.)

Hamman, A., ed., *The Paschal Mystery:* Ancient Liturgies and Patristic Texts, Staten Island, NY: Alba House, ET 1969. (An anthology of sources from the early church.)

Stevenson, Kenneth, *Jerusalem Revisited:* The Liturgical Meaning of Holy Week, Washington, DC: The Pastoral Press, 1988. (A readable, informative work by a Church of England scholar, combining historical information with practical counsel.)

Talley, T., "History and Eschatology in the Primitive Pascha," in *Worship* 47(1973), pp. 212–221.

On Sunday

Heschel, A.J., *The Sabbath,* Its Meaning for Modern Man, New York: Farrar, Straus & Giroux, 1951 [and later publishings]. (A small poetically written book by a great interpreter of Judaism.)

Porter, H.B., *The Day of Light:* The Biblical and Liturgical Meaning of Sunday, Washington, DC: The Pastoral Press, 1988. (A small book with rich content.)

Rordorff, W., *Sunday,* Philadelphia: Westminster Press, ET 1968. (A very large, deeply informed book.)

On Saints' Days, Commemorations

Brown, Peter, *The Cult of the Saints:* Its Rise and Function in Latin Christianity, Chicago: University of Chicago Press, 1981.

Castle, Tony, *Lives of Famous Christians:* A Biographical Dictionary, Ann Arbor, MI: Servant Books, 1988. (A general biographical reference, containing more than 1500 entries; brief as these articles are, they often supplement *Lesser Feasts and Fasts,* as does the material in the widely used *Oxford Dictionary of the Christian Church.*)

Commission Report, 1957, "The Commemoration of Saints and Heroes of the Faith in the Anglican Communion."

Farmer, David Hugh, *The Oxford Dictionary of Saints,* Oxford University Press, 1987. (Deals exclusively with saints who have a history of being honored in Britain; with that limitation, a fine reference.)

Holeton, D.R., "Eight Modern Anglican Calendars," in *Ephemerides Liturgicae* 95(1981), pp. 252–274.

Lesser Feasts and Fasts, New York: Church Hymnal Corporation, fourth edition, 1989. (This book, issued by the Standing Liturgical Commission, contains the collects and scripture readings for each of the commemoration days on the Prayer Book calendar, including those added between 1979 and 1988. For each person there is a biography— sometimes half a page or so that contains virtually all that is known about a person from the church's past, and sometimes a page about someone who has been the subject of many volumes. Anyone who is following the Prayer Book calendar will need this work. It also contains eucharistic readings for the weekdays of the Lenten and Easter seasons.)

Perham, M., *The Communion of Saints:* An Examination of the Place of the Christian Dead in the Belief, Worship and Calendars of the Church, London: SPCK, 1980. (The best modern Anglican study of the subject.)

7. Language and Symbol

Liturgical Speech and Imagery

Dillistone, F.W., *The Power of Symbols in Religion and Culture.* New York: Crossroad, 1986. (Not specifically on liturgical language, but a recent study of symbol by a theologian who has written on the subject effectively for many years.)

Frost, D.L., "Liturgical Language from Cranmer to Series 3," in Jasper, R.C.D., ed, *The Eucharist Today,* London: SPCK, 1974, pp. 142–167. (An essay by an able English philologist who recognizes the need for a new liturgical rhetoric.)

Power, David N., *Unsearchable Riches:* The Symbolic Nature of Liturgy, New York: Pueblo, 1984. (The finest recent book on this subject; closely written but rewarding.)

Ramshaw, Gail, *Worship: Searching for Language,* Washington, DC: The Pastoral Press, 1988. (A gathering of essays by a writer grounded in theology and sensitive to literary nuance.)

Schmidt, H. and Power, D., eds., *Liturgical Experience of Faith* [Concilium #82], New York: Herder and Herder, 1973. (A symposium containing several essays on language.)

230 ■ FURTHER READING

Stevick, Daniel B., *Language in Worship:* Reflections on a Crisis, New York: Seabury Press, 1970. (The first book-length treatment of the adoption of contemporary rhetoric. Written when the amount of authorized material in modern speech was small, it concludes that the old rhetoric is to a great extent unusable and the new is unexciting; and it regards this option as unattractive. If the same sort of study were being done today, there would be more printed material and more experience of it to take into account.)

————, "The Language of Prayer," in *Worship* 52 (1978), pp. 542–560. (An exploratory study of what makes vital speech vital.)

"Sexist" Language and Liturgy

Bennett, Robert A., "The Power and the Promise of Language in Worship: Inclusive Language Guidelines for the Church, [Occasional Paper Number 5], in *The Occasional Papers of the Standing Liturgical Commission,* New York: The Church Hymnal Corporation, 1987, pp. 38–50. (In a few pages this paper explains the issue and suggests principles and wordings for editing.)

Hardesty, Nancy A., *Inclusive Language in the Church,* Atlanta: John Knox Press, 1987.

Lutheran Church in America, Office of Communications, 231 Madison Avenue, New York 10016, "Guidelines for Inclusive Language." (A booklet of suggestions about terms that are best avoided and substitutes that work well. Useful for persons who are editing old texts or writing new.)

Mollenkott, Virginia R., *The Divine Feminine: The Biblical Imagery of God as Female,* New York: Crossroad, 1987. (Not about liturgical language, but about biblical imagery, and hence with implications for liturgical language.)

Ramshaw-Schmidt, Gail, *Christ in Sacred Speech:* The Meaning of Liturgical Language, Philadelphia: Fortress Press, 1986. (A particularly fine work; theologically informed, and aware of the subtlety of language in religious speech.)

————, "Naming the Trinity: Orthodoxy and Inclusivity," in *Worship* 60/6 (1986), pp. 491–498. (Included in *Worship: Searching for Language,* noted above.)

Russell, Letty, *The Liberating Word:* A Guide to Nonsexist Interpretation of the Bible, Philadelphia: Westminster Press, 1976. (A pioneering book that still makes basic points convincingly.)

Supplemental Liturgical Texts: Prayer Book Studies 30, New York: The Church Hymnal Corporation, 1989. (Published for the Standing Liturgical Commission of the Episcopal Church, this booklet represents a considered attempt to produce, at a representative official level, texts that are inclusive in language. Musical settings for some texts are included and a commentary volume is also published. These texts are not thought of as the last word, but as subject to further "refinement.")

Swidler, Leonard, *Biblical Affirmations of Woman,* Philadelphia: Westminster Press, 1979. (A handy summary study of the biblical material that is the basis for liturgical speech.)

Terrien, Samuel, *Till the Heart Sings:* A Biblical Theology of Manhood and Womanhood, Philadelphia: Fortress Press, 1985. (An informed study of the language and thought forms of the biblical literature; it qualifies or questions many ideas of what the texts are taken to say about the relation of the sexes.)

Trible, Phyllis, *God and the Rhetoric of Sexuality,* Philadelphia: Fortress Press, 1978. (A basic study of biblical God-language; one of the earliest, and still one of the best books in the field.)

8. On the Eucharist

On the Eucharistic Order as a Whole

Deiss, L., *It's the Lord's Supper:* The Eucharist of Christians, New York: Paulist Press, ET 1976. (A popular work which imparts the style and sense of well-grounded contemporary liturgy.)

————, ed., *The Springtime of the Liturgy,* Collegeville, MN: Liturgical Press, 1979. (Eucharistic texts from the early centuries, attractively presented; the primary sources given here provide the best possible introduction to the vital liturgical spirituality of the early period.)

Dix, Gregory, *The Shape of the Liturgy,* Westminster: Dacre Press, 1945. New edition with additional notes by Paul V. Marshall, New York: The Seabury Press, 1982. (A classic work, originally published in 1945, it deserves to be read with gratitude. This richly woven book depicts the central role of liturgy in the life of the early Christian community more convincingly than anything else that one can read. But a reader should be aware that some of the things that Dix presents persuasively have not stood up under later scholarly investigation. If a reader can use the Seabury/Harper edition, 1982, which contains notes by Paul V. Marshall, or can read Kenneth Stevenson's booklet in the Grove series, *Dom Gregory, 25 Years After,* this deservedly influential book may be put in perspective.)

Every, George, *The Mass,* Dublin: Gill and Macmillan, 1978. (An attractive, serious but popular study, historically organized.)

Jasper, R.C.D., ed., *The Eucharist Today:* Studies on Series 3, London: SPCK, 1974. (A symposium treating aspects of the Eucharist, and illustrating the thought that lies behind the current revisions in the Church of England.)

Kay, Melissa, ed., *It Is Your Own Mystery:* A Guide to the Communion Rite, Washington, DC: The Liturgical Conference, 1977. (A simple, effectively written symposium on many matters of eucharistic ministry and celebration.)

Kiefer, Ralph, *Blessed and Broken:* An Explanation of the Contemporary Experience of God in Eucharistic Celebration, Wilmington, DE: Michael Glazier, Inc., 1982. (Popularly written, with insights on the Eucharist and the involvement of worshipers in its action.)

Martimort, A.G., ed., *The Church at Prayer, Vol. II: The Eucharist,* Collegeville, MN: Liturgical Press, 1985. (Detailed explanatory material on the general history of the Eucharist and on the history and meaning of each part; learned but readable chapters that represent the best of Continental Roman Catholic scholarship.)

Seasoltz, K., ed., *Living Bread, Saving Cup:* Readings on the Eucharist, Collegeville, MN: Liturgical Press, 1982. (Essays that appeared over a number of years in *Worship;* several are classics.)

Stuhlman, Byron D., *Eucharistic Celebration 1789–1979,* New York: The Church Hymnal Corporation, 1988. (The focus is on the eucharistic rite, but this book tells a great deal about the Prayer Books of the Episcopal Church, and in particular about the making of the 1979 Book; informative on such matters as the ceremonial tradition and liturgical space.)

Wilkinson, John, *The Supper and the Eucharist:* A Layman's Guide to Anglican Revision, New York: St. Martin's Press, 1965.

On Eucharistic Theology

Balasuriya, Tissa, *The Eucharist and Human Liberation,* Maryknoll, NY: Orbis Books, 1979. (An examination of the Eucharist from the viewpoint of liberation theology.)

Church of England Doctrine Commission, *Thinking About the Eucharist,* London: SCM, 1972. (Reflections on the meaning of the Eucharist by theologians of the C of E; several chapters are outstandingly good.)

Clements, R.E., et al., *Eucharistic Theology Then and Now,* London: SPCK, 1968. (An English symposium containing good essays, some historical and some constructive.)

Gore, Charles, *The Body of Christ,* New York: Charles Scribner's Sons, 1901. (A doughty Anglican classic giving a sense of the tradition and of the past issues through which the present can be understood.)

Guzie, T., *Jesus and the Eucharist,* New York: Paulist Press, 1974. (A short well-written book, full of fresh ideas and biblical insights.)

Lee, B., "Towards a Process Theology of the Eucharist," in *Worship* 48 (1974), pp. 194–205. (Eucharistic theology informed by process categories.)

Martelet, G., *The Risen Christ and the Eucharistic World,* New York: Seabury Press, ET 1976. (An original and impressive book using insights informed by Teilhard.)

Moule, C.F.D., *The Sacrifice of Christ,* London: Hodder and Stoughton, 1956. (By a respected Anglican evangelical; the chapter on "The Eucharistic Sacrifice," coming at the end of the author's careful argument, is very effective.)

Oulton, J.E.L., *Holy Communion and Holy Spirit:* A Study in Doctrinal Relationship, London: SPCK, 1951. (An original theological work that deserves to be better remembered.)

Powers, J., *Eucharistic Theology,* New York: Herder and Herder, 1967.

———, *Spirit and Sacrament:* The Humanizing Experience, New York: The Seabury Press, 1973. (Two books by one of the best contemporary Roman Catholic sacramental theologians.)

234 ■ FURTHER READING

234 ■ FURTHER READING

Rahner, K., "The Presence of Christ in the Sacrament of the Lord's Supper," in *Theological Investigations,* IV., pp. 287–311. (A closely written, profound essay.)

Reumann, J., *The Supper of the Lord:* The New Testament, Ecumenical Dialogues, and Faith and Order on the Eucharist, Philadelphia: Fortress Press, 1985. (A good clear book that gathers exegetical insight, summarizes contemporary ecumenical discussions, and points up consensus.)

Schillebeeckx, E., *Christ the Sacrament of the Encounter with God,* New York: Sheed and Ward, 1963. (An epochal Roman Catholic study by a gifted theologian who uses the idea of "encounter"; now old, but not really dated.)

————, "Transubstantiation, Transfinalization, Transignification," in *Worship* 40 (1966), pp. 324–338. (An important theoretical essay, reprinted in Seasoltz, ed., *Living Bread, Saving Cup.*)

Stevenson, Kenneth, *Accept This Offering:* The Eucharist as Sacrifice Today, Collegeville, MN: The Liturgical Press, 1989. (A brief book that makes valuable clarifications.)

Thurian, M., *The Eucharistic Memorial,* 2 vol., London: The Lutterworth Press, ET 1961. (An irenic study by a distinguished ecumenical figure; it may make some points by a certain vagueness.)

von Allmen, J.J., *The Lord's Supper,* London: The Lutterworth Press, ET 1969. (A short but intellectually forceful study by a Reformed scholar.)

Wainwright, G., *Eucharist and Eschatology,* London: Epworth Press, 1971. (An original and important book.)

"The Windsor Statement on Eucharistic Doctrine," in *Worship* 46 (1972), pp. 2–5. (An important ecumenical paper by the Anglican/Roman Catholic consultation; significant both for the agreement it represents and as a record of the divisive issues that seem to have disappeared. It has been printed in a number of places.)

The Service of the Word; (1) Lectionary and Lectors

Achtemeier, Elizabeth, "Aids and Resources for the Interpretation of Lectionary Texts"

Bailey, L., "The Lectionary in Critical Perspective"

Reumann, J., "A History of Lectionaries: From the Synagogue at Nazareth to Post-Vatican II"

Sloyan, G., "The Lectionary as a Context for Interpretation" (Important articles that appeared in the journal *Interpretation* XXXI/2[1977])

Allen, Horace T., ed., *The Reader as Minister,* see sec. 7 of this list.

Atkinson, Clifford W., *A Lay-Reader's Guide to the Proposed Book of Common Prayer,* Wilton, CT: Morehouse-Barlow, 1977.

Borsch, Frederick H., *Introducing the Lessons of the Church Year,* New York: Seabury Press, 1978. (An introduction to the ministry of the lector; brief paragraphs suitable for reading aloud prior to the actual lessons appointed.)

Lathrop, Gordon and Ramshaw-Schmidt, Gail, eds., *Lectionary for the Christian People,* New York: Pueblo, 1977 *et.seq.* (A good lector's text of the eucharistic readings, using the Roman, Lutheran and Episcopalian lectionaries, and issued in separate volumes for the A, B and C years. It is based on the RSV, but it takes account of the endemic "sexism" of biblical patterns of speech. It is aware of poetic overtones in biblical language and imagery. The attractively printed and sturdily bound books are suitable for use in the liturgy.)

Sydnor, William, *Sunday Scriptures: An Interpretation,* Wilton, CT: Morehouse-Barlow, 1976. (Brief comments on the biblical passages appointed in the BCP; suitable for public use in connection with the readings.)

Most congregations are using the Prayer Book lectionary gratefully and would be surprised to know that it has come under serious friendly criticism. The criticisms are based largely on its reduction of the Jewish Scriptures to illustrative material for Christian themes. Such use of the Bible has deep roots; the "matter of Israel," used typologically, was the first material the Christian community had for interpreting its own message. But proposals have been made for other ways of using the two testaments in liturgical reading. Two items that would introduce the issues are:

Allen, Horace, ed., *Common Lectionary:* The Lectionary Proposed by the Consultation on Common Texts, New York: Church Hymnal Corporation, 1981. (Brief rationale, followed by an ecumenically prepared proposed order of readings.)

Sloyan, Gerard S., "Some Suggestions for a Biblical Three-Year Lectionary," in *Worship* 63/6(1989), pp. 521–535. (A recent informed discussion of the issues.)

Guides to Pronunciation of Biblical Terms

Scott-Craig, T.S.K., *A Guide to Pronouncing Biblical Names,* Wilton, CT: Morehouse-Barlow, 1982.

Staudacher, Joseph M., *Lector's Guide to Biblical Pronunciations,* Huntington, IN: Our Sunday Visitor, 1979.

Walker, William O., *Harper's Bible Pronunciation Guide,* Hagerstown, MD: Torch Publishing Group, 1989. (A substantial work with much information; the pronunciation key is carried at the bottom of each page.)

The Service of the Word; (2) Preaching

Bowles, C.W.J., "The Ministry of the Word," in Jasper, R.C.D., ed., *The Eucharist Today,* ch.4, pp. 46–53.

Browne, R.E.C., *The Ministry of the Word,* Philadelphia: Fortress Press, 1976 [originally published, London: SCM Press, 1958]. (A splendid brief account of the mystery of preaching.)

Buechner, Frederick, *Telling the Truth:* The Gospel as Tragedy, Comedy and Fairy Tale, New York: Harper & Row, 1977. (An attractive small book that makes profound points about preaching subtly and by suggestion.)

Buttrick, David, *Homiletic:* Moves and Structures, Philadelphia: Fortress Press, 1987. (Perhaps the most important theoretical study of preaching in a generation; the author virtually reconceives the subject and the terms in which it should be discussed; original, based on wide study.)

Craddock, Fred, *Overhearing the Gospel,* Nashville, TN: Abingdon, 1978. (Help on the problem of telling the Gospel to those who have often heard it before.)

————, *Preaching,* Nashville, TN: Abingdon, 1985. (One the best recent books on homiletics, by a biblical interpreter.)

Crum, Milton, *Manual on Preaching,* Wilton, CT: Morehouse-Barlow, 1977. (A stimulating but perhaps somewhat schematic approach to sermon preparation and homiletic strategy.)

Edwards, O.C., *Elements of Homiletic:* A Method for Preparing to Preach, New York: Pueblo Publishing Company, 1982. (A simple, useful guide.)

————, *The Living and Active Word:* One Way to Preach from the Bible Today, New York: Seabury Press, 1975.

Eslinger, R., *A New Hearing: Living Options in Homiletic Method,* Nashville, TN: Abingdon, 1987. (A review of several present-day theoretical approaches to preaching.)

Fuller, Reginald, *The Use of the Bible in Preaching,* Philadelphia: Fortress Press, 1981. (By an eminent New Testament scholar who cares that preachers use the Bible with integrity.)

————, *What Is Liturgical Preaching?,* London: SCM Press, 1957. (A fundamental statement of the place of preaching in the act that comprises word and sacrament.)

Jensen, Richard A., *Telling the Story:* Variety and Imagination in Preaching, Minneapolis: Augsburg Pub. House, 1980. (A theologian's account of the basic role of narrative in preaching.)

Muehl, William, *Why Preach? Why Listen?,* Philadelphia: Fortress Press, 1986.

Skudlarek, William, *The Word in Worship:* Preaching in a Liturgical Context, Nashville, TN: Abington, 1981. (A brief account of liturgy and lectionary as the context for preaching; informative on the structure of the lectionary.)

Sloyan, Gerard, *Worshipful Preaching,* Philadelphia: Fortress Press, 1984. (A good short book by an author who is interested in Scripture, liturgy and preaching.)

Wardlaw, D.M., ed., *Preaching Biblically:* Creating Sermons in the Shape of Scripture, Philadelphia: Fortress Press, 1983. (Counsel on not forcing biblical material into alien forms.)

Waznak, P.W., *Sunday after Sunday:* Preaching the Homily as Story, New York: Paulist Press, 1983.

Homiletic Helps Based on the Lectionary

Craddock, Fred; Hayes, John H.; Holladay, Carl R.; and Tucker, Gene M., *Preaching the New Common Lectionary,* Nashville, TN: Abingdon Press. (This guide is being issued three volumes a year, for each of the

238 ■ FURTHER READING

three years of the ecumenical lectionary. It is keyed to the Prayer Book readings satisfactorily. The comments on the lections and the Psalms are excellent.)

Fuller, Reginald, *Preaching the New Lectionary,* Collegeville, MN: The Liturgical Press, 1974. (A large volume by an Episcopalian exegete and based on the Roman lectionary; clear analytic comments that point to preaching ideas helpfully; a deservedly admired work.)

Homily Service: An Ecumenical Resource for Sharing the Word, Washington DC: The Liturgical Conference. (A periodical with much suggestion on the weekly readings; the work of many writers, but under the general editorship of Virginia Sloyan; widely used and appreciated.)

Johnson, Sherman E., *The Year of the Lord's Favor:* Preaching the Three-year Lectionary, New York: Seabury Press, 1983. (Concise, but the brief comments carry much suggestion.)

Proclamation, Philadelphia: The Fortress Press. (A multivolume set. Each small volume gives exegetical and homiletical comment on the readings for several Sundays or special days. The series, which began in 1973, has by now gone through the three-year cycle several times, with new booklets constantly being issued. Its level remains consistently high.)

Sloyan, Gerard, *A Commentary on the New Lectionary,* Ramsey, NJ: The Paulist Press, 1975. (Clarifies the biblical text while leaving the preacher's mind free to do its own work; Roman, but with indices that make it usable with the BCP.)

Synthesis: A Weekly Resource for Preaching and Worship in the Episcopal Tradition, Chattanooga, TN. (Issued in a series of four-page leaflets, one for each week, it contains comment on the scriptures, plus material from other sources old and new. Full of suggestion.)

Intercessions

Hovda, Robert, "The Amen Corner: Real and Worshipful General Intercessions," in *Worship* 60 (1986), pp. 527–534.

———, "The Prayer of General Intercession," in *Worship* 44/8 (1970), pp. 497–502. (A short, wise article.)

Johnson, David E., *The Prayers of the People:* Ways to Make Them Your Own, Cincinnati: Forward Movement Publications, 1988. (A good brief guide to using and adapting the printed Intercessions of the Prayer Book.)

Melloh, John, "The General Intercession Revisited," in *Worship* 61 (1987), pp. 152–162.

Ramshaw, Gail, ed., *Intercessions for the Christian People:* Prayers of the People for Cycles A, B, and C of the Roman, Episcopal, and Lutheran Lectionaries, New York: Pueblo, 1988. (Texts that may well act somewhat as notes toward prayers that a congregation might develop on its own—written by an ecumenical group of authors, turns material from the lectionary into intercessory prayer.)

Stevenson, Kenneth, " 'Ye shall pray for . . .': The Intercessions," in Stevenson, ed., *Liturgy Reshaped* (see sec. 1), pp. 32–47.

Vasey, Michael, *Intercessions in Worship,* [Grove Worship Series No.77], Bramcote, Notts.: Grove Books, 1981. (A booklet that contains a great deal of information and points some practical directions.)

Whitaker, E.C., "The Intercessions," in Jasper, R.C.D. ed., *The Eucharist Today,* ch. 5, pp. 54–65.

The Peace

Buchanan, Colin, *The Kiss of Peace* [Grove Worship Series, No.80], Bramcote, Notts.: Grove Books, 1982. (The author thinks, with cause, that this booklet gathers more information on this subject than can be found in any other single source.)

Halliburton, R.J., "The Peace and the Taking," in Jasper, R.C.D., ed., *The Eucharist Today,* ch.7, pp. 88–94.

The Offertory:

Buchanan, Colin, *The End of the Offertory—An Anglican Study* [Grove Liturgical Study No. 14], Bramcote, Notts.: Grove Books, 1978.

Hanson, R.P.C., *Eucharistic Offering in the Early Church,* [Grove Liturgical Study, No.19], Bramcote, Notts.: Grove Books, 1979.

The Consecration

Allchin, A.M., "The Eucharistic Offering," in *Studia Liturgica* 1 (1962), pp. 101–114. (Not on "the offertory," but on the Eucharist as offering.)

Audet, J.P., "Literary Forms and Contents of a Normal *Eucharistia* in the First Century," in *Studia Evangelica,* 1959, pp. 643–662. (An influential paper.)

Bouley, A., *From Freedom to Formula,* Washington, DC: Catholic University of America Press, 1981. (A scholarly analysis of the consecration action in our earliest sources and the effect of the change from oral to written form).

Bouyer, Louis, *Eucharist:* Theology and Spirituality of the Eucharistic Prayer, Notre Dame, IN: University of Notre Dame Press, 1968. (A major work on the consecration prayer; particularly rich on the continuities of form and thought between Jewish prayers and the prayers of the early church.)

Buxton, R.F., *Eucharist and Institution Narrative,* [Alcuin Club, #58], Great Wakering, Essex: Mayhew-McCrimmon, 1976.

Cuming, Geoffrey, *He Gave Thanks: An Introduction to the Eucharistic Prayer* [Grove Liturgical Study, No.28], Bramcote, Notts.: Grove Books, 1981. (A short study that introduces much information and many thought issues.)

Dallen, James, "The Congregation's Share in the Eucharistic Prayer," in *Worship* 52/4 (1978), pp. 329–341. Reprinted in Seasoltz, ed., *Living Bread, Saving Cup.*

Every, G., *Basic Liturgy,* London: Faith Press, 1966. (A short elegant work examining the structure and content of some of the classic prayers.)

Gelineau, Joseph, *The Eucharistic Prayer:* Praise of the Whole Assembly, Washington, DC: The Pastoral Press, 1985. (Brief; what the eucharistic prayer is and what it might be.)

Halliburton, R.J., "The Canon of Series 3," in Jasper, R.C.D. ed., *The Eucharist Today,* ch.8, pp. 95–129.

Jasper, R.C.D. and Cuming, G.J., eds., *Prayers of the Eucharist:* Early and Reformed, Oxford University Press, 3rd edition, 1988. (An anthology of consecration prayers that includes so many items in a small space that it cannot say much about any of them; but it gives a reader access to basic sources.)

Leon-Dufour, X., *Sharing the Eucharistic Bread:* The Witness of the New Testament, Mahwah, NJ: Paulist Press, 1987. (Original ideas with implications for liturgy, by a French New Testament scholar.)

McKenna, J., *Eucharist and Holy Spirit:* The Eucharistic Epiclesis in 20th Century Theology, [Alcuin Club, #57], Great Wakering, Essex: Mayhew-McCrimmon, 1975. (A good recent scholarly survey that examines an important topic somewhat neglected in the literature.)

Ryan, J.B., *The Eucharistic Prayer:* A Study in Contemporary Liturgy, New York: Paulist Press, 1974. (A valuable comparative study of several modern consecration prayers.)

Senn, Frank C., ed., *New Eucharistic Prayers:* An Ecumenical Study of their Development and Structure, New York: Paulist Press, 1987. (A splendid symposium with chapters by first-rate writers, full of information and comparative analyses.)

Stevenson, Kenneth, *Eucharist and Offering,* New York: Pueblo, 1986. (A large, yet readable work on this central but elusive subject of eucharistic liturgy and doctrine.)

Talley, T., "Eucharistic Prayer: Tradition and Development," in K. Stevenson (ed.), *The Liturgy Reshaped,* pp. 48–64.

————, "From *Berakah* to *Eucharistia:* A Reopening Question," in *Worship* 52/2 (1976), pp. 115–137. Reprinted in Seasoltz, ed., *Living Bread, Saving Cup.*

Children and Communion

Brand, Eugene, "Baptism and Communion of Infants: A Lutheran View," in *Worship* 59 (1976), pp. 29–42.

Holeton, David, *Infant Communion—Then and Now* [Grove Liturgical Study No.27], Bramcote, Notts.: Grove Books, 1981.

Holmes, Urban T., *Young Children and the Eucharist,* New York: The Seabury Press, 1972.

Jenson, Robert, "The Eucharist: For Infants?" in *Living Worship* 15/6 (1979), pp. 1–4.

Mitchell, Leonel L., "The Communion of Infants and Little Children," in *ATR* LXXI/1 (Winter 1989), pp. 63–78.

Mueller-Fahrenholz, Geiko, ed.,... *and do not hinder them:* An Ecumenical Plea for the Admission of Children to the Eucharist [Faith and Order Paper No.109], Geneva: The World Council of Churches, 1982.

Nurturing Young Children at Communion [Grove Liturgical Study, No.44], Bramcote, Notts.: Grove Books, 1985. (A portion of this work, by a group of Anglican liturgical scholars, also appeared as "Nurturing Children in Communion," in *ATR* LXVIII (1986), pp. 185–97.)

Stevick, Daniel B., *Baptismal Moments; Baptismal Meanings,* New York: The Church Hymnal Corporation, 1987. (Chapter 6, "Persistent Issues: First Communion," discusses this subject.)

9. Architecture, Liturgical Space, and Visual Environment

Addleshaw, G.W.O. and Etchells, Frederick, *The Architectural Setting of Anglican Worship,* London: Faber and Faber, 1948. (A splendid survey of the architecture of the Church of England; historically organized; full of detailed information; old, but not superseded.)

Anson, Peter F., *Fashions in Church Furnishings 1840–1940,* London: The Faith Press, 1960. (An interesting and informative account of a busy period, with many illustrations. But quite maddening inasmuch as the author shows no interest whatever in the theology of liturgy or its outward array.)

Bishops' Committee on the Liturgy, *Environment and Art in Catholic Worship,* Washington, DC: National Conference of Catholic Bishops, 1978. (A short, illustrated, well-presented directive for buildings that serve the modern Roman liturgy.)

Bouyer, Louis, *Liturgy and Architecture,* Notre Dame, IN: University of Notre Dame Press, 1967. (A brief authoritative study at its best in the very early periods.)

Davies, J.G., *Temples, Churches and Mosques:* A Guide to the Appreciation of Religious Architecture, Oxford: Blackwell, 1982. (The best historical overview; interprets sympathetically Greek, Islamic, Jewish and Christian structures.)

Debuyst, Frederic, *Modern Architecture and Christian Celebration,* Richmond, VA: John Knox Press, 1968. (Although this book is small, it is a superb statement of criteria for liturgical space for today. It goes beyond a minimalist functionalism.)

Hammond, Peter, *Liturgy and Architecture,* London: Barrie and Rockliff, 1960. (A fine study both of historical material, showing the varieties of church design for worship, and of principles as to what is desirable and why.)

———, ed., *Towards a Church Architecture,* London: The Architectural Press, 1962. (Despite the events since it was written, still a good topical study of space for liturgy.)

Hatchett, M.J., "Architectural Implications of the Book of Common Prayer 1979," Occasional Papers Number 7, New York: Standing Liturgical Commission, 1984. (A concise, helpful account of the spatial requirements of the Prayer Book.)

Maldonado, Luis and Power, David, eds., *Symbol and Art in Worship* [Concilium series], New York: Seabury Press, 1980. (Contains several outstanding essays.)

Mauck, Marchita, *Shaping a House for the Church,* Chicago: Liturgy Training Publications, 1990. (A short, illustrated guide to building and renovation; sensitive to liturgy and history, but eminently practical; thinks of the church as sign.)

Miles, Margaret R., *Image as Insight:* Visual Understanding in Western Christianity and Secular Culture, Boston: Beacon Press, 1985. (Informative; historically organized, but with clear implications for the importance of art in any period.)

Nichols, Aidan, *The Art of God Incarnate:* Theology and Image in Christian Tradition, London: Darton, Longman and Todd, 1980. (A fine work, theologically informed.)

Rasmussen, Steen Eiler, *Experiencing Architecture,* Cambridge, MA: MIT Press, 1959. (A brief readable book, not about buildings nor about churches but about the encounter between an observer and a work of architecture.)

Regamy, Pie-Raymond, *Religious Art in the Twentieth Century,* New York: Herder and Herder, 1963. (A basic, influential modern statement.)

Reinhold, H.A., *Liturgy and Art* [Religious Perspectives, Vol. 16], New York: Harper & Row, 1966. (A good short work by an author who wrote passionately on the subject for many years.)

White, James F. and Susan J., *Church Architecture:* Building and Renovating for Christian Worship, Nashville, TN: Abingdon Press, 1988. (Recent and very fine; practical counsel, historically and liturgically informed.)

10. Ceremonial, Ritual

Bouyer, Louis, *Rite and Man: Natural Sacredness and Christian Liturgy,* Notre Dame, IN: University of Notre Dame Press, 1963. (A basic theoretical attempt to identify the commonly human and the specifically Christian in the ritual inheritance.)

Galley, Howard, *The Ceremonies of the Eucharist:* A Guide to Celebration, Cambridge, MA: Cowley Publications, 1989. (A fine guide to ceremonial, keyed to the Prayer Book; although it concentrates on the Eucharist, it takes account of other ministers beside the celebrant; theologically and historically informed.)

Kavanagh, Aidan, *Elements of Rite:* A Handbook of Liturgical Style, New York: Pueblo, 1982. (A splendid little book containing deep principles and practical wisdom about liturgy; serious learning and fierce warnings are all presented with a light touch.)

Michno, Dennis G., *A Priest's Handbook:* The Ceremonies of the Church, Wilton, CN: Morehouse-Barlow, 1983. (This was the first detailed guide to ceremonial since the 1979 Prayer Book made all previous such guides out of date. It is attractively done, undogmatic and sensible.)

Mitchell, Leonel, *The Meaning of Ritual,* Wilton, CT: Morehouse-Barlow, 2nd ed, rev., 1988. (Not a guide to ceremonial but a good introduction to ritual.)

Pottebaum, Gerard A., *The Rites of People:* Exploring the Ritual Character of Human Experience, Washington, DC: The Liturgical Conference, 1975. (A popular provocative inquiry into ritual in everyday life, always with liturgy in mind.)

Shaughnessy, James, ed., *The Roots of Ritual,* Grand Rapids, MI: Eerdmans, 1973. (A symposium volume containing important theoretical papers.)

Stuhlman, Byron D., *Prayer Book Rubrics Expanded,* and *Eucharistic Celebration 1789–1979.* (These books, both of them mentioned earlier, are noted again here for their sound guidance on matters of ceremony.)

11. Music

Bauman, William A., *The Ministry of Music:* A Guide for the Practising Church Musician, Washington, DC: The Liturgical Conference, 2nd ed., rev., 1979. (A clear practical work, written for the Roman communion but generally usable.)

Dakers, Lionel, *Choosing—and Using—Hymns,* Wilton, CT: Morehouse-Barlow, 1985.

Deiss, Lucien, *Spirit and Song of the New Liturgy,* Cincinnati: World Library Publications, 1970. (A guide to music and liturgy by a leader of liturgical renewal in France.)

Douglas, Winfred, *Church Music in History and Practice,* New York: Scribners, 1952; rev. ed., with additional material by Leonard Ellinwood, 1962. (This book, originally published in 1937, gives an authoritative survey of history and offers some principles for church music. The material added for the 1962 edition helps, but there is much in contemporary church music that Canon Douglas could not have anticipated. Despite its age, this book has not really been replaced in the literature. Used copies, which are fairly abundant, should be snapped up.)

Funk, Virgil and Huck, Gabe, eds., *Pastoral Music in Practice,* Chicago: Liturgy Training Publications, 1981.

Gelineau, Joseph, *Learning to Celebrate:* The Mass and Its Music, Washington, D.C.: The Pastoral Press, tr. 1985.

Hatchett, Marion J., *A Guide to the Practice of Church Music,* New York: Church Hymnal Corporation, 1989. (A practical guide for musicians; prepared for the Episcopal Church, drawing on detailed knowledge of the Bible, the Prayer Book, and the Hymnal. Published in 1980 as *Manual for Clergy and Church Musicians,* now thoroughly revised.)

Hymnal Studies, New York: Church Hymnal Corporation. (There are now six books in this series of "studies" introducing and explaining the contents of *The Hymnal 1982.* Some are on specialized topics such as planning for a new organ or for major organ repairs [No.4], or for "Teaching Music in Small Churches," [No.3]. The "Liturgical Index to *The Hymnal 1982*" [No.5] is particularly useful for planners. It suggests hymns that correspond to the readings of all three years of the Lectionary. "A Commentary on New Hymns," [No. 6] contains brief essays on 77 hymns new to the Episcopal Church.)

Long, Kenneth R., *The Music of the English Church,* London: Hodder and Stoughton, 1972. (A full, authoritative historical survey, perhaps rather technical for some readers.)

Routley, Erik, *Church Music and Theology,* London: SCM Press, 1959. (One of several theoretical studies on church music by this able writer.)

————, *A Short History of English Church Music,* London: Mowbrays, 1977.

Weil, Louis, "The Musical Implications of the Book of Common Prayer," in *The Occasional Papers of the Standing Liturgical Commission,* New York: The Church Hymnal Corporation, pp. 51–56.

Westermeyer, Paul, *The Church Musician,* New York: Harper & Row, 1988.

12. Some Books of Prayers

The literature is large and this list is select. All of these books are good, but not all are good for every purpose, and not all will suit every taste. Prayers that one cannot use as they stand can start ideas of one's own.

Collections that Use the Old Rhetoric:

Books that were compiled when all prayers used sixteenth-century rhetoric, or that use whatever rhetoric their sources use:

Appleton, George, ed., *The Oxford Book of Prayers,* New York: Oxford University Press, 1985. (A large anthology containing material from many traditions, including some that are non-Christian; prepared with both theological and literary sensitivity.)

Castle, Tony, ed., *The New Book of Christian Prayers,* New York: Crossroad, 1987. (A large collection drawn from many ages and traditions and arranged topically. The rhetoric of each prayer is left as it was when the prayer was written or translated; thus this book is, with respect to language, a mixture.)

Heuss, John, ed., *A Book of Prayers,* New York: Morehouse-Gorham, 1957. (A small collection of high quality, drawn from parish use.)

Hunt, Cecil, *Uncommon Prayers* (American edition, arranged and edited by J.W. Suter), Greenwich, CT: Seabury Press, 1955. (Almost every prayer in this short collection has something unusual and attractive about it.)

The Kingdom, The Power and the Glory, An American Edition of the Grey Book, New York: Oxford University Press, 1933. (An edition of the most widely used of the small books of prayers that were issued in England to supplement the Prayer Book revision that was proposed in 1928/29.)

Rodenmayer, R., ed., *The Pastor's Prayer Book,* New York: Oxford University Press, 1960. (A small book, packed with material gathered and organized with pastoral needs in mind; when published this book sold well, but it is long out of print and hard to locate secondhand— probably because most copies were given hard use, and if they are still intact are treasured.)

Suter, J.W., ed., *The Book of English Collects,* New York: Harper and Brothers, 1940. (A rich, elegant collection demonstrating the variety, interest and depth in this one classic prayer form.)

Original Prayers in the Old Rhetoric

Baillie, J., *A Diary of Private Prayer,* New York: Charles Scribner's, 1949. (Morning and evening prayers for a month; intended for private rather than for congregational use, but full of usable ideas and careful wordings.)

Ferris, Theodore Parker, *Book of Prayer for Everyman,* New York: Seabury Press, 1962. (A small book of pointed, well-worded prayers for the church year and for personal and pastoral occasions, written by Dr. Ferris during his years of preaching and parish ministry at Trinity Church, Boston.)

Milner-White, Eric, *My God My Glory,* London: SPCK, 1954. (One of the finest works of this sort; the prayers are beautifully worded and expressively shaped; many of them might serve for public, corporate prayer, either as they stand or with a little adapting. For one's own use, this book is a treasure.)

Offices for Days, Weeks, Occasions

Appleton, George, ed., *Acts of Devotion,* Richmond, VA: John Knox Press, 1963. (Still a fine vital work; the first English edition was published in 1928.)

Coughlan, P.; Jasper, R., and Rodrigues, T., eds., *A Christian's Prayer Book:* Psalms, Poems and Prayers for the Church's Year, Chicago: Franciscan Herald Press, 1972. (A small manual of prayers intended for individual use.)

Melloh, J., Storey, W., et al., *Praise God in Song:* Ecumenical Daily Prayer, Chicago: GIA Publications, 1979. (For corporate use.)

Milner-White, E. and Briggs, G.W., eds., *Daily Prayer,* Oxford University Press, 1941. (A good book, meant for private use.)

Storey, W., ed., *Praise Him!* A Prayer Book for Today's Christian, Notre Dame, IN: Fides, 1973. (A short, handy book that holds to a high level of content.)

Storey, W.G.; Quinn, F.C.; and Wright, D.F., eds., *Morning Praise and Evensong:* A liturgy of the Hours in Musical Setting, Notre Dame, IN: Fides, 1973. (An expertly edited book containing a week of sung offices for morning and evening for congregational use.)

Collections of Prayers in New Prayer Rhetoric

Prior to the late 1960s, virtually all prayers that were spoken or printed in the English-speaking world used the rhetoric of the King James Bible and the Book of Common Prayer. It was an accepted convention of English speech that, whatever had happened to the language that was used for other functions, prayer should retain this classic idiom. People in all traditions of faith and worship who talked that way for no other purpose shifted easily into Tudor-period English when they prayed. And few persons proposed that it should be otherwise. The RSV New Testament, when it was issued in 1946, used "you" when people talked to one another, but it kept "thee" and "thou" and the related verb forms—"art," "wast," "hast" and the like—for address to God. Prayer required a special rhetoric.

But change, when it came, was rapid and general. Since the early 1970s, hardly any new published prayers have been issued that are not in contemporary speech. And one gathers that most, certainly not all, extempore prayer has made the same change.

This shift should not cut off today's Christians from the richness that remains lodged in the old speech forms, forms that probably ought not, in most cases, to be methodically updated. Old prayers, when they are altered, often sound neither old nor new. Rhetoric represents a systemic grasp of reality, and it cannot be changed gracefully by patchwork. The material that has been written in the new rhetoric represents a remarkable watershed in the language of faith and prayer.

Morley, Janet, *All Desires Known,* Wilton, CT: Morehouse-Barlow, 1989. (A short collection with a feminist perspective.)

Rowthorn, Jeffery W., ed., *The Wideness of God's Mercy:* Litanies to Enlarge Our Prayer, Minneapolis, MN: Winston Press, 1985. (A splendid collection of prayers from many sources; all have been adapted into litany form and made suitable for congregational use. The collection is in two volumes: "Prayers for the Church" and "Prayers for the World." They suit many liturgical functions and many themes for prayer.)

Original Prayers, New in Language, Style and Themes

The publication dates of these books indicate the interest there was in new speech and manner for prayer in the 1960s. Some of these works are more dated than others, but together they had a freeing effect on the understanding and practice of prayer.

Boyd, Malcolm, *Are You Running with Me, Jesus? A Spiritual Companion for the 1990s,* Boston: Beacon Press, updated 1990. (When this highly personal book was initially published in 1965, it shocked many people. Nevertheless, the direct honesty (a bit heart-on-the-sleeve, to be sure), and use of common experience gave many grateful readers a new sense of what prayer might be. Boyd's landmark work, reissued for the twenty-fifth anniversary, features substantial additions directed toward current concerns.

Evely, Louis, *That Man Is You,* New York: Paulist Press, 1964. (The special gift of this book is to put one inside biblical events so that one prays as a participant in them. That characteristic is carried out with real skill; the drama of the events meets one with searching depth. These prayers were not drafted with congregational intercession in mind, but they may suggest ideas to anyone who uses them sympathetically.)

Karay, Diane, *All the Seasons of Mercy,* Philadelphia: Westminster Press, 1987. (This unusually good recent work contains calls to worship, prayers of praise, of confession or affirmation, and pastoral prayers for the seasons of the church year: All were prepared and used in a Presbyterian congregation and maintain a balance between reserve and freshness of phrase.)

Oosterhuis, Huub, *Your Word Is Near:* Contemporary Christian Prayers, Westminster, MD: Newman Press, tr. 1968, and later editions. (This Dutch Roman Catholic writer is widely considered the most successful stylist among the modern writers of prayers. Even in translation, his writing has a fresh conversational sound, yet its dignity and restraint make it suitable for public as well as for private use. This was the first of his books to be translated into English. The material here is extensive and varied. The book merits careful reading to see how it might be used or adapted.)

————, *Prayers, Poems and Songs,* New York: Herder and Herder, tr. 1970. (A shorter collection, containing some of this author's most attractive work.)

————, *Open Your Hearts,* New York: Herder and Herder, tr. 1971. (Contains a section of "ten table prayers.")

————, *At Times I See:* Reflections, Prayers, Poems and Songs, New York: Seabury Press, tr. 1974. (Bright thought-provoking items.)

————, *Times of Life:* Prayers and Poems, New York: Paulist Press, tr. 1979. (A brief collection of work in this writer's most psychological manner.)

Quoist, Michel, *Prayers,* New York: Sheed and Ward, 1963. (This book by a French Roman Catholic remains quite convincing more than twenty-five years after its initial impact. It turns bits of everyday experience into prayer or meditation shared with God. In using it, one feels, "I could do that too, now that Quoist has shown me how." These prayers are so specific and individual that their use, in their printed form, for public gatherings would probably be quite limited. But they represent a sort of devotion that many persons find fresh and accessible.)